this glorious cause . . .

by HERBERT T. WADE *and* ROBERT A. LIVELY

PRINCETON UNIVERSITY PRESS · 1958

PRINCETON, NEW JERSEY

this glorious

cause...

The *Adventures of Two Company Officers*

in Washington's Army

6672

THE adventures of two company officers in Washington's army are recorded here as an extended footnote to general accounts of the American Revolution. The personal experiences of these minor figures seem worth recalling because, for all our knowledge of the conflict, we still wonder about the land where our fathers died; we seek the place and date and time, the slope of the field, and most of all the idea that armed our kin for sacrifice. We can generalize about these particulars for a mass of men, but the motives of individual officers in the middle ranks grow more elusive as wars recede in memory. While it is true that social histories of the "private soldier" provide clear descriptions of the camps and fields, composite images of Brother Jonathan, Johnny Reb, Billy Yank, or GI Joe, the common denominator stereotypes drawn from contemporary diaries and reminiscences, lack the clarity that more orthodox biographical study may afford.

The following pages contain fragments from the service records of a cobbler, Joseph Hodgkins, and a carpenter, Nathaniel Wade, both of Ipswich, Massachusetts. The two turned out for the Lexington Alarm, fought at Bunker Hill, retreated from Long Island past White Plains, attacked at Trenton and Princeton, and enjoyed triumph at Saratoga. One of them wintered at Valley Forge, and the other was promoted to the command of the garrison at West Point on the night that Benedict Arnold was revealed as a traitor. When the fighting in the north was done they returned to Ipswich, earned dignified places in the town, and won the respect of their sons and grandsons, to the fifth generation. Just as they themselves outlived most of their fellows, putting off death until they attended the fiftieth centennial of the Battle of Bunker Hill, so their story, constantly retold by a proud family, has survived longer than most personal memories of the Revolution. Their grandsons collected and assembled their papers, and contributed genealogical sketches to antiquarian quarterlies and state historical magazines, so that memory of their experiences was preserved until changing historical custom invested with new meaning the contribution of "plain people" to American achievements. Heroes, usually tiresome and increasingly unfashionable, have given way to the common man who is rising this century, even from the dead. The documents of his resurrection occupy a growing shelf in our public libraries.

This book is another volume for the shelf. It offers no new truths about the causes or conduct of the Revolution, nor does it question accepted views of the conflict. It is rather an effort to give personal dimension to truths that Americans have always believed, to recover the old soldiers' tales that so often die with the passing of each generation of veterans. The story of two patriots who fought for "this glorious cause" may inform our understanding of all patriots, and of patriotism itself.

Since this writer joined the project after the death of the senior author, a description of our collaboration seems appropriate here. I was employed in June 1956 by the estate of the late Herbert T. Wade to assemble a book from the voluminous notes and manuscripts prepared by Mr. Wade during the last decade of his life. Before his death at eighty-two, in 1955, he had completed the research on which I depended and had written some twenty-five hundred typed pages describing the fortunes of his ancestors from the September day in 1632 on which Jonathan Wade was landed at Charlestown, Massachusetts, off the *Lion* out of Bristol. His account of the Wades at Ipswich, roughly chronological in outline, marched across the centuries without a single chapter division, and was proceeding into the nineteenth century when his labors were cut short. He had anticipated this contingency in his will, which provided a substantial sum for the completion of his work. The executors of his estate, free by the terms of the bequest to interpret "completion" according to their best judgment, delivered the contents of the Wade study to me and left to my discretion the structure of the book. Research for the project, therefore, was Mr. Wade's; selection, interpretation, and writing have been my responsibility.

My initial view of the task as a chore was quickly dissolved in the mounting respect with which I retraced the senior author's steps through the collections and documents on which the book is based. Mr. Wade was, to be sure, an "amateur" historian; he pursued his ancestors out of pride of family and fascination with genealogical detail in a mood that was uncritically patriotic. On the other hand his whole career had sharpened his expert professional judgment, had prepared him for the infinite patience that search for obscure facts requires, and had confirmed the integrity with which he recorded conclusions that he would have preferred not to reach.

Herbert T. Wade was a professional editor and an occasional author in technical and scientific fields. Born on September 2, 1872, son of Daniel T. Wade, a flour merchant doing business on the New York Produce Exchange, he was the great great grandson of both Joseph Hodgkins and Nathaniel Wade. He was educated at Columbia College, where he graduated with honors in Chemistry and English in 1893. He worked for a brief period as an assistant in the Physics Department at Columbia before his occasional contributions as science reporter for the *New York Evening Post* brought him appointment in 1900 as editor of technical materials for F. M. Colby's *New International Encyclopedia*. Subsequently, he was editor of the *Engineering Index Annual* (1909), literary editor of the *Review of Reviews' Photographic History of the Civil War* (1911), and finally general editor, from the mid-1920's, of *The New International Encyclopedia* and the *New International Year Book*. He was a frequent contributor to such popular magazines as *Scientific American* and to more technical journals as well. His books include *Evolution of Weights and Measures and the Metric System* (with William Halleck, 1906), *Astronomy* (with Waldemar Kaempffert, in the "Science in the History of the Universe" series, 1911), and *Everyday Electricity* (1924).

Like his forebears Wade was a militiaman, and after brief service during the First World War as a captain assigned to the preparation of digests of technical data for lay use in the Ordnance section, he remained an enthusiastic participant in reserve activities. He inherited the research project that filled his years of retirement. Daniel Treadwell, who grew up in Nathaniel Wade's home, and Daniel Treadwell Wade, Herbert Wade's father, began the biographical sketches which the senior author extended. Many of the documents on which he relied were copied by his father in the 1880's and 1890's, and a few of the original manuscripts were passed down to him through his branch of the family.

As historian, Herbert Wade took his lessons from the nineteenth century, imitating such figures as Richard Frothingham, Henry P. Johnston, and William S. Stryker. He incorporated great slices from the documents into his work, paused for twenty-page asides about a bridge that his heroes might have crossed, and examined military detail at interminable lengths. When I went to Ipswich to check the accuracy of his notes from manuscript material, I found that he had completely ignored the bulk of Sarah Hodgkins' letters to her husband, except for their occasional references to battles. He examined the Wade Orderly Books in much the same way, passing over evidence of how men lived in the camps to seek the order of march for battle. In checking his use of the records, I encountered very few items that he had not seen, but I usually found that his exclusive concern with military history had robbed his ancestors of their considerable human appeal.

This book, therefore, is different from the one that he would have completed. I have cut out hundreds of pages of general military history and have attempted to hold the work to the personal stories of Nathaniel Wade and Joseph Hodgkins. Somewhere along the way these two exchanged roles in my version of their service; for Herbert Wade, Nathaniel was the hero and Hodgkins was of minor interest. The documents led me to different conclusions. I like to think that Mr. Wade would have approved my reading of his story, just as I am enormously respectful of the care with which he assembled the materials for it. I have checked every citation in the following pages, except those referring to Massachusetts archives, back to the indicated sources, and I have found my predecessor painstakingly accurate in his transcriptions. His view of history was narrower than that of contemporary fashion, but his scholarly standards were those that we hope our students will attain.

My pleasure in working with Mr. Wade's notes was heightened by my introduction to present representatives of his family. The current holders of the Hodgkins letters, Mr. and Mrs. Francis C. Wade, of Ipswich, went beyond courtesy in opening their home and documents to me; and Mr. Alfred M. Wade, of Princeton, New Jersey, was my first and most enthusiastic reader as well as my generous employer. I am also deeply grateful to my colleague, Professor Wesley Frank Craven, who nerved me to encroach on his field and who saved me from many errors.

Six months with "this glorious cause" have been more rewarding to me than these hurriedly written pages can possibly reveal. I had never walked a Revolutionary battleground before, though I live within a mile of the slope at Princeton of which some record is given here. My own people, in 1775, were lately arrived Georgians who adhered to the King's cause, and their only brush with the armies came when the battle at Briar Creek was fought on a corner of their land. I am grateful, therefore, for my experience with fathers I had not known before, and for my new sense of the cost of freedom.

ROBERT A. LIVELY

4 January 1958
Menlo Park, California

CONTENTS

this glorious cause . . .

". . . I am willing to sarve my Contery in the Best way & mannar that I am Capeble of and as our Enemy are gone from us I Expect we must follow them. . . . I would not Be understood that I should Chuse to March But as I am ingaged in this glories Cause I am will to go whare I am Called."—*Joseph to Sarah Hodgkins, Boston, March 20, 1776*

The Ipswich Minute Men

THE VILLAGE of Ipswich, Massachusetts, lay twenty-five miles
north of the march of the British regulars on the 19th of April
in 1775. Ipswich was halfway from Salem to Newburyport, on
the far side of Cape Ann from Boston. The town which contributed the patriots of this narrative to the American Revolution is not much noticed in the nation's history—only the fact
that the Reverend John Wise spoke for freedom there made a
place for it in the index to the American colonial record.

The night of the Lexington Alarm left Ipswich sleeping
undisturbed, and the morning of the nineteenth was well along
before the company of minute men commanded by Captain
Nathaniel Wade and Lieutenant Joseph Hodgkins was called
to arms. Wade's men marched by Danvers and Salem to Medford, returned to Salem the following day, and probably were
safe at home again on the third day of their excursion. Of the
twenty thousand men named on the Lexington Alarm Lists,
fewer than four thousand were actually engaged on April
19th; the others marched and counter-marched, extending the
shock of the day leagues beyond the bloody path from Concord
back to Charlestown.

Coastal towns like Ipswich, waked by the news from the
south, looked across their harbors for danger. The British
navy, protector for generations, now loomed as an agent of
destruction, and the alarmed coast watched for enemies by sea.
Ipswich found a poet to give lasting notoriety to the attack of
nerves under which its citizens adjusted to war. The legend of
the "great Ipswich fright" can be documented in part from
contemporary records, but the story as told by John Greenleaf
Whittier is preferred by local historians. On the second day after
the Lexington Alarm, according to this account, a rumor spread
through the village to the effect that the regulars had landed on

Plum Island and would soon march on the town. The minute men were still away, and terror in the village was heightened by exaggerated tales of British brutality at the engagement of April 19th. The Ipswich fright spread like a brush fire to Beverly, at the south, and to Newburyport at the north:

"Flight was resolved upon. All the horses and vehicles in the town were put in requisition; men, women, and children hurried as for life toward the north. Large numbers crossed the Merrimac, and spent the night in the deserted houses of Salisbury, whose inhabitants, stricken by the strange terror, had fled into New Hampshire to take up their lodgings in dwellings also abandoned by their owners. . . . One man got his family into a boat to go to Ram Island for safety. He imagined he was pursued by the enemy through the dusk of the evening, and was annoyed by the crying of an infant in the after part of the boat. 'Do throw that squalling brat overboard,' he called to his wife, 'or we shall all be discovered and killed.' A poor woman ran four or five miles up the river and stopped to take breath and nurse her child, when she found to her great horror that she had brought off the cat instead of the baby!"[1]

Sanity returned with investigation by a young man of Exeter, New Hampshire, who, having determined that no redcoats were in the vicinity, galloped after the fugitives with his reassuring news. By the following day the terror had subsided and the townsmen were back in their homes. They recovered the mood of April 20, when the pastor of Chebacco Parish, the Reverend John Cleaveland, had been quoted by the *Essex Gazette* in vigorous renunciation of King, country, and General Gage.[2] The same Cleaveland was to respond with remarkable vituperation to General Thomas Gage's peace offer of the following June: "Thou profane, wicked monster of falsehood and perfidy . . . your late infamous proclamation is as full of notorious lies, as a toad or rattlesnake of deadly poison. . . . Without

[1] John Greenleaf Whittier, *Prose Works*, II (Boston, 1866), pp. 116-117. Although Whittier exercised his right to considerable poetic license in this account, his facts are reasonably close to the truth. Various early reporters left a record of the Ipswich fright and the exodus.

[2] *Essex Gazette*, April 20, 1775, quoted in Peter Force, ed., *American Archives*, Series 4, II, p. 369.

speedy repentence, you will have an aggravated damnation in hell. . . ."[3]

Both fright and impudence must have been alien to Ipswich. The town was "one of those steady, conservative villages," as Whittier put it, "wherein a contemporary of Cotton Mather and Governor Endicott, were he permitted to revisit the scenes of his painful probation, would scarcely find himself a stranger."[4] Steadfast in its support of the seaboard resistance to British "usurpations,"[5] the town had moved nonetheless with caution into the year of crisis. The same town meeting that authorized "Encouragement of Military Discipline" in November 1774 also resolved against the "Enemies among ourselves," "wicked Persons" who "insinuate . . . that This Province is seeking after Independency & want to break off from their allegiance to the Crown of Great Britain, which is a thing that has not the Least Foundation in Truth. . . ."[6]

Preparing for the worst, however, was in the best New England tradition; delegates from the town had been with the men of Worcester, Essex, and Middlesex Counties who met at Faneuil Hall, Boston, in August 1774 to resolve "That the military art . . . ought attentively to be practiced by the people of this province, as a necessary means to secure their liberties against the designs of enemies whether foreign or domestic."[7] The colonial militia system came under close scrutiny as the towns moved to eliminate officers loyal to the Crown and as new units were created for emergency service. As early as 1645, thirty men from each company of militiamen were required to be ready "at halfe an howers warning" for any service; and in 1756 men in the Crown Point expedition commanded by Captain Obadiah

---

[3] *Essex Gazette*, July 13, 1775, quoted by John Richard Alden, *The American Revolution, 1775-1783* (New York, 1954), p. 36. The same Cleaveland soon followed the Ipswich men to the wars. In a return for Colonel Moses Little's Regiment, dated March 16, 1776, he was reported as chaplain, enlisted on July 1, 1775.

[4] Whittier, *op.cit.*, p. 113.

[5] Thomas Franklin Waters, *Ipswich in the Massachusetts Bay Colony*, II (Salem, 1917), pp. 293-311.

[6] *Ibid.*, p. 314.

[7] Richard Frothingham, *History of the Siege of Boston, and of the Battles of Lexington, Concord, and Bunker Hill. Also, An Account of the Bunker Hill Monument* (second edition, Boston, 1851), p. 363.

Cooley described themselves as "minnit men," a term that spread rapidly in the developing crisis of 1774.[8]

The Provincial Congress of Massachusetts was seeking a colonial force in which a quarter of the men enrolled would be ready to assemble at the slightest notice and be known as "minute men." General officers were appointed and the Committee of Safety was empowered to assemble the militia when circumstances invited action. The Committee on the State of the Province reported to the Congress on December 10, 1774, an address to the "Freeholders and other Inhabitants of the Towns and Districts of Massachusetts Bay" which defined precisely the required preparations:

"We now think that particular care should be taken by the Towns and Districts in this Colony, that each of the minute men not already provided therewith, should be immediately equipped with an effective Fire arm, Bayonet, Pouch, Knapsack, Thirty rounds of Cartridges and Ball, and that they be disciplined three times a week and oftener as opportunity may offer. To encourage their own worthy Countrymen to obtain the skill of complete soldiers. We recommend it to the Towns and Districts forthwith to pay their own minute men a reasonable consideration for their services. And in case of a general Muster, their further services must be recompensed by the province."[9]

At Ipswich, on November 21, 1774, permission had been voted a number of subscribers to erect a building fifty feet long and twenty-five feet wide on land east of the Town House, where townsmen might meet "for the encouragement of military discipline." It was there during the cold winter of 1774-1775 that five companies of minute men were formed and drilled. An entry of December 26, 1774, in the Town Records promised "A Committee contract with minute men who may enlist agreably to the proposal of the Provincial Congress."[10]

[8] Allen French, *The First Year of the American Revolution* (Boston, 1934), pp. 32-33.
[9] Massachusetts Archives, *Soldiers and Sailors of the Revolutionary War*, I (Boston, 1896), p. xi.
[10] Joseph B. Felt, *History of Ipswich, Essex, and Hamilton* (Cambridge, 1834), p. 148.

With such a contract the town engaged the services of the cobbler and the carpenter whose adventures are described in the following pages. Except for genealogical detail,[11] little is known of the two before they set out for the weary siege at Boston; they share the anonymity that armies have always conferred on men in the ranks. The classic image of the minute man is one of the most familiar symbols of the Republic, yet search for two individuals among the twenty thousand whose names adorn the Lexington Alarm Rolls reveals the degree to which the shadows of time have closed around the men who created the symbol. Nathaniel Wade and Joseph Hodgkins enter history as names on muster lists and pay records, but only as names. Of personal appearance, dress, experience, or hope they had left little record; and they were to come but gradually into focus through their letters and orderly books of the war years.

Wade was born of substantial people in a house built in 1727 by his grandfather, the handsome brown homestead that still stands facing the South Common at Ipswich. He attended the village grammar school, and wandered the area in his young manhood as a carpenter. In 1772, shortly after he came of age, his mother gave him six acres of land in the town.[12] In 1774, according to uncertain evidence, he was working as a carpenter in Boston.[13] A young, unmarried artisan would logically have hurried to the center of affairs only twenty-five miles from his home, where the city taverns were gaining their reputation as the "nurseries of revolution."[14] Whether as the "Indians" who

[11] Nathaniel Wade was born at Ipswich on February 27, 1750, the son of Timothy Wade and Ruth Woodbury, daughter of Captain Robert Woodbury of Beverly. Timothy Wade (1712-1763) was the son of Captain Thomas Wade (1673-1737) and Elizabeth Thornton of Boston, while Thomas was the second son of an older Thomas (1651), who in turn was the third son of Jonathan, landed from the *Lion* out of Bristol at Charlestown, September 16, 1632. In 1636 Jonathan Wade had settled at Ipswich, where he became a large landowner.

Joseph Hodgkins was born at Ipswich in 1743, son of Thomas (1692-1788) and Hannah Hodgkins, grandson of Sergeant Thomas Hodgkins, and great grandson of William Hodgkins, who settled at Ipswich in 1665.

[12] Ipswich Deeds, Vol. 134, p. 52.

[13] The authority for his location is an obituary sketch in the *Boston Palladium*, reprinted in the *Salem Gazette* of November 7, 1826. The assertion is made quite positively, however, and is probably correct.

[14] John Chester Miller, *Sam Adams, Pioneer in Propaganda* (Boston, 1936), p. 40.

dumped the tea in Boston Harbor, or as the passive resisters who refused to build barracks for the growing British garrison,[15] the workmen of Boston were necessary recruits to the bands of agitators who helped to translate northern colonial unrest into riot and bloodshed.

Joseph Hodgkins was an older, steadier man than Wade. The town records of Ipswich document his trade in an entry of 1770, noting that his shoemaker's shop was ordered removed from town land, to make way for a new jail. Married in 1764, he had fathered five children by his first wife, Joanna Webber of Methuen, before her death in 1772. Of the children, only the eldest, ten-year-old Joanna, survived at the eve of the war. Hodgkins had lost his wife in a chain of personal disasters; two daughters were born and died young, and his wife succumbed shortly after her fifth child, the second named Hannah, fell victim to the terrible infant mortality of the century. There survives in Hodgkins' own hand a record of the stark facts of this marriage; the loose page, which looks as though it may have been torn from a small Bible, reads:[16]

Ipswich, New Engelland

August ye 16: 1764 Joseph Hodgkins & Joanna his wife whas
Married

July ye 8: 1765   Joanna whas Born it whas monday

June ye 10 1767   Joseph whas Born it whas wensday

Augst ye 2 1767   Joseph Departed this Life it whas Sunday

July ye 1: 1768   Mary whas Born it was friday

March ye 21: 1770   Hannah whas Born

Decemr ye 15: 1771   Hannah departed this Life it whas Sunday

ye 29 Decem 1771   our Other Hanna whas Born it whas Sunday

January ye 3 1772   Hannah Departed this Life it whas Friday

Jan ye 21 1772   My wife Departed this Life in ye 31 years
of her Eage on Tusday

---

[15] Richard Frothingham, *op.cit.*, p. 363.

[16] The Wade Papers, including the Hodgkins material, are now in the possession of Francis C. Wade, of Ipswich. The "Mary" born according to the above list on July 1, 1768, did not survive her first year, according to genealogies held by the family.

[8]

Within the year he married again, on December 3, 1772, taking twenty-two-year-old Sarah Perkins as wife and mother to his suriving child. A daughter born to this marriage the following year was named Sarah, the "Salle" of his letters home from the wars. A second Joseph was born on March 2, 1775.

Wade was twenty-four years old, and Hodgkins thirty-one, when the two signed articles of enlistment in the Provincial Service on January 24, 1775. The obligation they assumed is set forth in the document to which they put their names, preserved in the Wade Papers:

"We whose Names are hereunto subscribed, do voluntarily Inlist our selves, as Minute Men, to be ready for military operation, upon the shortest notice. And we hereby Promise & engage, that we will immediately, each of us, provide for & equip himself, with an effective fire arm, Bayonet, Pouch, Knapsack, & Thirty rounds of Cartridges ready made. And that we may obtain the skill of compleat Soldiers, We promise to Convene for exercise in the Art Military, at least twice every week; and oftener if our officers shall think necessary. And as soon as Such a Number shall be Inlisted, as the present Captain, Lieutenant, & Ensign, of ye Company of Militia shall think necessary, we will proceed to choose such Officers as shall appear to them, & to ye Company to be necessary. The Officers to be chose by a majority of ye votes of the Inlisted Company, and when ye Officers are duly chosen, We hereby promise & engage, that we will punctually render all that obedience to them respectively, as is required by the Laws of this Province, or practiced by any well regulated Troops, And if any Officer or Soldier shall neglect to attend the time & place of exercise, he shall forefeit & pay the sum of two shillings Lawfull money for the use of 'ye Company, unles he can offer such an excuse to the Officers of ye Company as to them shall appear sufficient.

"N.B. It is to be understood that when nine Company's of fifty Men Each are Inlisted, that then the said Officers of the Minute Company's Proceed to Choose their Field Officers, agreable to the proposal of the Provincial Congress, Ipswich, Jan'y 24th, 1775."

This company of minute men was one of five such units raised at Ipswich. In accordance with its articles of enlistment, and by ancient custom of the militia, the company elected its officers, choosing Nathaniel Wade as Captain and Joseph Hodgkins as Lieutenant. The choice of Wade as leader was reported on April 17, when he was returned as captain of a company in Colonel John Baker's Third Essex Regiment.[17] Men chosen to head such units tended to be those who could raise a company, and it seems probable that Wade, with his fresh budget of news from Boston, was one of the key spirits in the town's organization for defense. The fact that he came from a family of substance would have done him no harm, and his freedom from family cares left him time for the canvass by which a company was assembled. The choice of Hodgkins, a man eight years his senior, as second in command gives some testimony to the impression young Wade must have made on his fellows.

The men obligated to muster twice a week on the village common were very private soldiers. They not only elected sergeant, captain, and colonel; they furnished the guns and packs that armed the unit for action. Social standing was on occasion established by the age of their muskets—a piece that had been to Louisburg in 1745 took precedence over one fired on the Plains of Abraham in 1759. Confusion prevailed from the top down, as well as from the bottom up, during the spring months when the minute men were assembling. An elected captain or his subalterns could be turned out for more popular choices; and the record reveals a fine democratic rotation in leadership at the company level. The Provincial Congress took notice of such military improbabilities when it moved on April 14 to scrap the whole system. Only five days before the engagement at Concord, it provided for a new volunteer army, in which officers were to be appointed by superior authority, and the men enlisted. Preference in selection of officers was to be given to

---

[17] Massachusetts Archives, *Soldiers Orders*, LV, p. 53. Colonel Baker had been commissioned as colonel of the Third Essex County Regiment on June 1, 1764. Apparently he was too old for active service or was one of the officers replaced in the "purge" of the militia, for Wade's company marched under other commanders to service around Boston.

leaders chosen earlier by the minute men.[18] Before the minute men disappeared into the new organization, however, General Thomas Gage decided to confiscate the stores at Concord.

Unlike the farmers in Middlesex County, the men of Essex were not among those aroused by the midnight rides of Revere and Dawes, bringing news of the British march to Lexington and Concord. The alarm reached the southern part of Essex County between eight and nine o'clock on April 19. Colonel Timothy Pickering, commander of a regiment of minute men at Salem, was seated in his office at the Salem Registry of Deeds when one Captain Epes, of a Danvers Company, galloped up with news of bloodshed at Lexington. Epes was ordered to muster his company and march south without waiting assembly of the regiment—a chore he undertook with such dispatch that the Danvers company suffered casualties near Menotomy (the modern Arlington) before the day was done. Colonel Pickering also ordered Captain David Mason, with an artillery unit, into action in time for the fight.[19]

To the north, Captain Wade's company at Ipswich was alerted somewhat later in the morning and marched out the day without sight of the enemy. Neither orderly books nor diaries reveal the authority by which the unit proceeded by Danvers and Salem to the Mystic River on the British line of retreat. In all probability such bands as Wade's sought their fights independently that day; it was no secret that Boston was the only source of British activity against the colonials, and that the road to Lexington was a sensible route to the stores at Concord. The rapid spread of the alarm by couriers suggests that some mobilization plans were in effect, but no record remains of any chain of command coordinating the patriot movements. In any event, the Ipswich men camped on the night of April 19 near Medford, returned to Salem on the 20th, and were back in Ipswich on the 21st. The company remained on active duty, returning to the vicinity of Cambridge within a short time. In a claim for travel and subsistence filed on December 30, 1775, and allowed by the Colony on March 23, 1776, Wade reported eighty-eight miles of travel

[18] Allen French, *op.cit.*, pp. 41-42.
[19] *Essex Institute Historical Collections*, XLVIII (1912), p. 208.

and three weeks' service for his men.[20] A penny a mile was allowed for travel, which, added to other allowances, brought a captain £4.17.4, a lieutenant £3.7.4, a sergeant £2.3.4, a corporal £2.0.4, and a private £1.17.4. Fifty-one officers and men marched with Wade on April 19, at a total cost to the Colony of £101 15s 2d.

Massachusetts authorities had a formidable task in converting these irregular forces into an army; many a company like Wade's arrived at Cambridge for a look at the British in Boston, only to melt away again for late spring duties at the plow. Scarcely a day passed, after the engagement of April 19, without some new communiqué from the Provincial Congress to the towns urging the dangers and pleading the needs of the Colony. A letter from the Congress, dated at Watertown on April 20, is representative:

"Gentlemen,—The barbarous Murders on our innocent Brethren on Wednesday the 19th Instant, has made it absolutely necessary that we immediately raise an army to defend our Wives and our Children from the butchering Hands of an inhuman Soldiery, who, incensed at the Obstacles they meet with in their bloody progress, and enraged at being repulsed from the Field of Slaughter, will, without the least doubt, take the first Opportunity in their Power to ravage this devoted Country with Fire and Sword. We conjure you, therefore, that you give all Assistance possible in forming an Army. Our all is at Stake. Death and Devastation are the certain Consequences of Delay; every Moment is infinitely precious; an Hour lost may deluge your Country in Blood, and entail perpetual Slavery upon the few of your Posterity who may survive the Carnage. We beg and entreat you, as you will answer it to your Country, to your own Consciences, and above all, as you will answer to God himself, that you will hasten and encourage, by all possible Means, the Enlistment of Men to form the Army, and send

---

[20] Massachusetts Archives, *Lexington Alarm Roll*, XIII, p. 157. In this claim, Wade swore that "my Company of Minute men raised agreeable to the advice of the provincial Congress, marched from Ipswich the 19th day of April to Mistick—on the 20th ordered to Salem, on the 21st to Ipswich from thence to head quarters at Cambridge remained in service as minute men till the 10th May."

them forward to Headquarters at Cambridge, with that expedition which the vast Importance and instant Urgency of the affair demands."[21]

The Ipswich minute men were probably enlisted in the provincial service about May 10, as the above subsistence claims indicate, though officers of the company were not formally commissioned until June 26, 1775, several days after their participation in the Battle of Bunker Hill. The unit was near Cambridge by the end of April, for Lieutenant Hodgkins, in a letter to his wife dated at Cambridge on May 7, thanked her for a package he had received that morning at Watertown and declared, in the manner of a man out of touch with affairs at home, "I whant to know wether you have got a paster for the Cows for I cannot tell when I shall com home."[22] The first official report of the company's presence near headquarters was made in a return by Christian Febiger, Adjutant of Colonel Samuel Gerrish's Second Essex County Regiment, on May 19.[23] The unit shifted its bivouac to the Common at Cambridge on June 6.[24]

Incorporation of Wade's company into the army did not teach it respect for discipline nor free it from a democratic approach to the military hierarchy. For reasons that seemed sufficient to Captain Wade and several other captains of the Second Essex County Regiment, there was a strong disinclination to serve under Colonel Samuel Gerrish of Newbury. The way in which Gerrish had offended his subordinates is unknown, but their wisdom in rejecting his leadership is indicated by the fact that the Colonel was cashiered for cowardice after Bunker Hill. The custom of the times, despite efforts of the Committee of Safety to impose regular authority on the army, was for any captain who could win the allegiance of his fellows to move forward to the role of colonel over them. The preference of Wade and his co-captains was for service under Captain Moses Little, who,

[21] William Lincoln, ed., *Journals of Each Provincial Congress of Massachusetts* (Boston, 1838), p. 518.
[22] Joseph to Sarah Hodgkins, Cambridge, May 7, 1775. The Hodgkins letters quoted in the following pages are among the papers held by Francis C. Wade.
[23] Frank A. Gardner, "Colonel Samuel Gerrish's Regiment," *The Massachusetts Magazine*, IV (1911), p. 222.
[24] Joseph to Sarah Hodgkins, Cambridge, June 8, 1775.

on the Lexington Alarm, had marched in command of a company from Newbury. Little, fifty-one years old, had been Surveyor of the King's Woods and had a wide acquaintance in northern New England. In 1753 he had commanded a company of soldiers from Newbury in an expedition against Louisburg. Respecting his years and experience, the several captains addressed the following petition "To the Honorable Committee of Safety for the Colony of Massachusetts Bay":

"Gentleman

We the Subscribers, being Captains of the Companies now enlisted in the Service of the Government have made Choice of Captain Moses Little to be our Chief Colonel, and Major Isaac Smith to be our Lieutenant Colonel, & have agreed that . . . shall be our Major. We beg that your Honors will be pleased to direct or recommend that the aforesed Persons may be commissioned as officers over us & your Petitioners as in Duty bound shall ever pray.

Cambridge, May 25, 1775.

	No. of men
Joseph Gerish	59
Ezra Lunt	61
Nathl Warner	59
Abraham Dodge	70
Nathl Wade	59
Benjn Perkins	75
John Baker	59
	422

N.B. Capt Collins, Chairman of this meeting of choice has now a company of 59 men

422 in the whole 481"[25]

Since six of these petitioners had been returned by Colonel Gerrish as his captains, the Provincial Congress under date of June 2, 1775, appointed a committee to consider the matter[26]

[25] Frank A. Gardner, "Colonel Moses Little's Regiment," *Massachusetts Magazine*, IX (1916), p. 18.

[26] William Lincoln, ed., *Journals of Each Provincial Congress of Massachusetts* (Boston, 1838), p. 292.

[14]

and ordered Colonel Gerrish to attend a meeting on the following day. It was decided that the petitioners should apply to the
Committee of Safety for commissioning of Captain Moses Little
as a colonel in the Massachusetts army. The uncertainty as to the
regimental command continued for two weeks more. After the
officers went to the Committee of Safety, which in the recess of the
Provincial Congress was empowered to grant commissions,
that body on June 13 ordered Colonel Little and seven other
colonels: "to make a true return to the Committee of the claims
and pretensions of the several gentlemen claiming to be commissioned as Colonels; of the number of Captains with their
respective companies, who choose to serve under the above
named gentlemen as Colonels; and of the number of efficient
firearms in each company, and of the place or places where said
companies are; at pain of forfeiting all pretensions to a commission as Colonel, in case of making a false return."[27]

Within two more days Little's claims were granted, the Committee having found that "the said Little has raised eight companies . . . amounting inclusive of officers to the number of 509
men, who choose to serve under him as their chief Colonel;
and all the said men are armed with good effective firelocks,
and 382 of them with good bayonets, fitted to their firelocks. . . ."[28] On the same day, June 15, Colonel Little reported
that Captain Wade's company was in Cambridge, its strength
"1 Captain, 1 lieutenant, 1 ensign, 4 sergeants, 4 corporals, 1
drummer, 1 fifer, 51 privates."[29]

Settlement of the command issue came at the eleventh hour:
two days later Captain Wade and his men marched under Colo-
nel Little to the bloodiest engagement of the war, at Bunker
Hill. It was at some hour on the afternoon of June 17, 1775,
that the American rebellion became the Revolutionary War.
Perhaps the casualty-laden British retreat down the Concord
Road on April 19 or the bloodless capture of Ticonderoga on
May 10 had made it one; but the character of the conflict was
established without doubt in the engagement at Bunker Hill.
The battle there is a minor classic in military annals—a story

[27] *Ibid.*, p. 327.   [28] *Ibid.*, p. 339.
[29] Massachusetts Archives, *Returns of Officers*, CXLVI, p. 207.

of strategic blunders retrieved by valor, and of luck as a substitute for leadership. In their exhausting victory the British inflicted on the colonials what proved to be a providential defeat.

The Massachusetts Committee of Safety had urged the fortification of Bunker Hill, on the Charlestown peninsula, as early as May 12, but caution prevailed; General Ward and Dr. Joseph Warren feared that such a movement might bring a general engagement for which the Americans were not prepared. The delay disappointed General Israel Putnam, who urged that from entrenchments the colonial forces would give a good account of themselves. "Americans," he argued, were "not afraid of their heads, though very much afraid of their legs; if you cover these, they will fight forever."[30] The decision to fortify the hill came a month later, when the American headquarters received reliable intelligence of plans by General Gage to fortify Dorchester Heights on June 18. Dorchester Heights threatened the peninsula and harbor of Boston from the south, as the hills of Charlestown threatened them from the north. Accordingly, on June 15, decision was taken to forestall the Dorchester move by occupation of the heights at Charlestown.

Eighteenth-century Charlestown, like Boston, lay on a pear-shaped peninsula, almost an island, connected to the mainland by a very narrow stem, a neck so low that it was sometimes swept by water at high tides. Just across the neck from the mainland lay Bunker Hill, standing 110 feet high. South of Bunker was Breed's Hill, 75 feet high, looking down on the village of Charlestown at the right and Morton's Point, scene of the British landing, at the left. Facing Morton's Point, but separated from it by a considerable distance, was a rail and stone fence, stretching from the rear of Breed's Hill to the bank of the Mystic River, which bounded the peninsula on the north. The water approaches to Charlestown Neck were protected by a dam and millpond at the south, but from the north boats on the Mystic River could sweep the neck with close fire.

On the evening of June 16, American forces moved under

[30] Quoted in Willard M. Wallace, *Appeal to Arms, A Military History of the American Revolution* (New York, 1951), p. 33.

orders to fortify Bunker Hill. Plans for the march have not survived; from the record one learns that at sundown 1,000 Massachusetts men joined the President of Harvard College in a prayer for God's grace and set out for Charlestown Neck. With Colonel William Prescott commanding, they were soon joined by Colonel Richard Gridley, engineer of the enterprise; Captain Thomas Knowlton, with 200 Connecticut men; and General Israel Putnam. They marched up Bunker Hill and down again, having chosen, after discussion, to fortify Breed's Hill at the center of the peninsula.[31] At midnight the digging commenced and by morning light a redoubt some forty yards square, with parapets six feet high, was nearly finished. Dawn revealed the vulnerability of the hill to a flanking attack on either side, and Prescott ordered a breastwork constructed running off for a hundred yards from the left of the redoubt. The American position on Breed's Hill thus resembled the inscription for a musical note, with its staff pointed up toward the Mystic River.

The story of the day that followed was known, until recent years, by every American schoolboy. Dawn brought cannon fire from British ships in the harbor, encouraging more frenzied effort by the diggers on the hilltop. Across the Charles River at Boston, General Gage was heavily armed with military talent. Majors General William Howe, Henry Clinton, and John Burgoyne had joined him on May 25, and command of the assault on the American position was given to Howe. Courageous, able, and dilatory, Howe loitered out the morning as he waited for the high tide that would permit an easy landing on Morton's Point. Rejected, meanwhile, was advice in favor of an action against the Neck from the Mystic River; Breed's Hill was easily approached, and the redoubt was not yet picketed or ditched. It was early afternoon before Howe's 2,200 men were

---

[31] A century of investigation appears to have established the fact that Gridley, the engineer, wanted to fortify Bunker Hill, a defensible point that commanded the Mystic River approaches to Medford, protected Cambridge from any march out of Charlestown, and dominated the Neck. Tradition has it that General Putnam, thirsting for a fight, overruled him, and chose Breed's Hill, approached by gentle slopes, which by the fact that it had Boston within cannon range would surely excite immediate British counter measures. Allen French, *op.cit.*, p. 215.

assembled on Morton's Point and near Charlestown; probably the armies were not engaged before three o'clock.

The passing hours were vital for the patriot forces—a whole morning was required to convince General Ward of the wisdom of reinforcement; and Howe's evident intentions invited detachment of Knowlton's Connecticut men for service along the rail fence at the left flank of the American fortification. By this time the New Hampshiremen of John Stark and James Reed were moving across the Neck, and units of several Massachusetts regiments were coming up. Stark joined Knowlton at the rail fence, and other companies took posts on the right flank, supporting the skirmishers who had been in Charlestown since before daylight. Between 1,400 and 1,700 Americans were on the ground when the British troops formed perfect lines for their magnificent march into disaster.

Howe chose to concentrate on the American left flank, leading in person picked troops against the rail fence. Success in this maneuver would have permitted encirclement of the redoubt on Breed's, engaged simultaneously by a direct frontal attack. The effect of his decision was murderous. Displaying raw courage that defies comparison, the British marched twice, according to this plan, into slaughter unmatched again on American battlefields until the Battle of New Orleans in 1815. The homespun American militia, guarded by fences and earthworks, held its fire until the enemy was within effective musket range—some fifty yards; the whites of their eyes may not have been visible, but white shoulder straps on redcoated breasts made perfect targets. Only on the third assault, undertaken two or three hours after the action commenced, did Howe, this time with the bulk of his force concentrated on the redoubt, carry the field. The American troops, out of powder, were driven from the hill, but the men on the rail fence held long enough to cover their retreat. The day cost the British 1,054 men killed or wounded; American casualties totaled 100 killed, 271 wounded, and 31 taken prisoner. The colonials might have held the hill if the supplies and troops ordered up by General Ward had reached them, but had they survived the third assault, they would surely have been pinched off by British resort to the only sensible plan of action, an amphibious assault at their rear on Charlestown Neck.

The battle thus briefly described had pattern and form; but a narrative carried from the mainland side, rather than from Morton's Point, is disordered to the point of unintelligibility. General Artemas Ward probably gave sufficient orders to hold the peninsula, but between headquarters and the company level incompetence in staff and supply organization clogged the roads from Cambridge to Charlestown with monumental confusion. An effort to follow the course of Little's regiment and Wade's company illustrates the courage, cowardice, obedience, and independence that supported the redoubt on Breed's Hill.

There is no doubt but that the Ipswich men were in the action of June 17th. Lieutenant Hodgkins hurried to inform his wife, in a letter of the 18th, "I would Just inform you that we had a verry hot ingagement yester Day but God Preserved all of us for whitch mercey I desire Ever to be thankful. . . ." Nearly a week later, at greater leisure, Hodgkins added a few more words: "I have not time to write Perticklers of ye Engagement But we whare Exposed to a very hot fire of Cannon and small armes about two ours But we whare Presarved I had one Ball went under my arme and cut a large hole in my Coate & a Buck shot went throue my coate & Jacket But neither of them Did me any harme. . . ."[32]

Were it not for the fact that "two ours," by the time sense of a soldier under fire, might be anywhere from five minutes to half a day by the sun's movement, the above letters could be accepted as proof that Wade's company was present throughout the engagement. Captain Wade himself, in a deposition given in 1825 at the centennial of the battle, said "I was at the rail fence. . . ."[33] Other documents, however, confuse the issue. Colonel Little's regiment, according to one surviving orderly book, was assigned to a four o'clock march from Cambridge, well after the armies were joined. Nathan Stow, a sergeant in a company of Colonel John Nixon's regiment, copied orders for

[32] Joseph to Sarah Hodgkins, Cambridge, June 18 and June 23, 1775.
[33] Samuel Swett, *Notes to his Sketch of Bunker-Hill Battle* (Boston, 1825), p. 14.

[19]

"Col Nixon Col Little Col Mansfield with their Reg'ts 200 Connecticut Troops with two days provision & ammunition march to relieve Col Prescot Col Fry & Col Bridge's Reg'ts Charlestown that they be well dressed before they march from camp and that they be on the parade at 4 o'clock ready to march. . . ."[34]

General Ward's biographer concluded that the Massachusetts reinforcements were ordered out from Cambridge between twelve and one o'clock[35]—the orders of the day might well have been altered with evidence that the British were preparing an attack. Colonel Little, according to some accounts, led Wade's, Warner's, and Perkins' companies into the line just before the action began, and received orders from General Putnam to take up posts where his men were most needed, some in the redoubt, some on the right flank, and some at the rail fence.[36] But Putnam was everywhere that day—in the redoubt, at the rail fence, on Bunker Hill, galloping to Cambridge with pleas for reinforcement—performing singlehanded the functions of the staff that he did not have. Few regiments, or companies, for that matter, kept their order once they started across the Neck; and the units that nerved themselves for descent from Bunker Hill were separated as they approached the front. As General Charles Lee put it in a review of the battle, "The Americans were composed in part of raw lads and old men half armed, with no practice of discipline, commanded without order, and God knows by whom."[37]

Two eyewitness accounts, one from a man in Wade's company, suggest that Little's men were engaged in covering the retreat rather than in the whole action. Francis Merrifield, a corporal in the Ipswich company, was quoted many years after the battle as saying, "When we got so near we could fairly see them they looked too handsome to be fired at; but we

---

[34] Entry of June 17, 1775, Nathan Stow Orderly Book, Concord Public Library.

[35] Charles Martyn, *Life of Artemas Ward* (New York, 1921), p. 131.

[36] Richard Frothingham, *op.cit.*, pp. 136, 177. See also Samuel Swett, *Who Was the Commander at Bunker Hill? With Remarks on Frothingham's History of the Battle* (Boston, 1850), p. 28.

[37] *The Lee Papers*, III, p. 262, in *New York Historical Society Collections* (1873).

had to do it."[38] The phrasing of the remark indicates that Americans were moving toward British, rather than waiting their charge at the rail fence. The number of casualties suffered by Captain Nathaniel Warner's company strengthens this impression: of 23 men on the field, 17 were killed or wounded, a far greater casualty rate than was suffered by the men behind cover.[39] Further evidence for the assumption that Little arrived during the retreat lies in a paragraph of a letter written by an unnamed neighbor from Newbury on June 21, in which a generally accurate account of the battle was given: "Mr. Little, of Turky Hill (who I have heard is lately made a colo.) show'd great courage, & march'd with those under his command, thro' two regiments of our men who were looking on at a distance, but were affraid to advance, he set them an example, it seems, which they did not chuse to follow—he proceeded till he found our people retreating from the Hill, being overpower'd by numbers. He cover'd their retreat & got off without much loss. He narrowly escap'd with his life, as two men were kill'd one on each side of him, & he came to the camp all bespattered with blood."[40]

Whether for five minutes or two hours, approach to the action was a terrifying experience for most citizen-soldiers. A lieutenant in a Connecticut regiment, which marched down from Bunker Hill to cover the retiring American force, described his sensations vividly: "Good God, how the balls flew,—I freely acknowledge I never had such a tremor. I confess, when I was descending into the Valley from off Bunker's Hill side by side of Capt. Chester at the head of our Company, I had no more thot of ever rising the Hill again than I had of ascending to Heaven as Elijah did, Soul and Body together."[41] The lieutenant's unit was in action for six minutes, before the men in the redoubt dropped back to safety, but time lost its meaning in the close combat of the disengagement.

[38] Uriah G. Spofford, "Reminiscences of Ipswich." See note 44, p. 163.
[39] Richard Frothingham, *op.cit.*, p. 177.
[40] Massachusetts Historical Society, *Proceedings*, XI (1869-1870), pp. 226-227.
[41] Massachusetts Historical Society, *Proceedings*, XIV (1875-1876), pp. 82-83.

It was here that Colonel Samuel Gerrish left his honor and lost his command. Colonel Little's Newbury neighbor, quoted above, left a graphic account of the moment: ". . . Gerrish was ordered also to Charlestown with a reinforcement, but he no sooner came in sight of the enemy than a tremor seiz'd him & he began to bellow, 'Retreat! retreat! or you'l all be cutt off!' which so confus'd & scar'd our men, that they retreated most precipitately, & our soldiery now sware vengeance against him & determine not to be under his comm'd."[42] Gerrish was not the only colonel cashiered for cowardice that afternoon,[43] nor was Little the only colonel who had to force a path for his men through the timid and uncertain regiments that lingered out of range.[44]

The final word on the conduct of the Ipswich men can be given to Captain Wade. After fifty years he reported his memories of the action in the following words: "The British field-pieces fired a great deal before small arms. I was at the rail fence. I saw Putnam, while we were engaged with the enemy, riding down Bunker Hill toward the rail fence. He was the only officer I saw on horseback. He seemed busily engaged bringing on troops. One of our cannon, deserted by Callender, was fired a number of times at the rail fence very near me; two men in our Regt. Halliday and Dutton, of Newburyport, fired one of the cannon 3 or 4 times and hurraed very loud. On the retreat, I saw Putnam on Bunker Hill; there were intrenching tools there, and he tried to stop our troops to throw up works there. He said, 'make a halt here, my lads, and we can stop them yet.' "[45]

[42] Massachusetts Historical Society, *Proceedings*, XI (1869-1870), p. 227.

[43] Gerrish might have survived the dishonor of June 17, had he not repeated his performance at Sewall's Point during a skirmish several weeks later. For his conduct on the two occasions, he was found guilty of "conduct unworthy of an officer," and cashiered. The judge-advocate of the court-martial thought his sentence much too severe. Richard Frothingham, *The Centennial: Battle of Bunker Hill* (Boston, 1875), pp. 85-86. See also entry of August 19, 1775, Orderly Book of Colonel Moses Little, June 26 to October 20, 1775, transcribed from photostats of the original in the Library of the Massachusetts Historical Society.

[44] Allen French, *op.cit.*, pp. 244-247.

[45] Quoted in Samuel Swett, *Notes to his Sketch of Bunker-Hill Battle* (Boston, 1825), p. 14.

Massachusetts was satisfied with Wade's record on the day; by order in Council on June 13, 1776, payments were made to him and his men for losses suffered in the battle.[46]

Of the battle in general, the conclusions of Charles Francis Adams seem justified: "a more singular exhibition of apparently unconscious temerity on one side, and professional military incapacity on the other, it would be difficult to imagine."[47] For the colonial cause, though, the action was decisive. The British held Bunker Hill, but they did not again venture from Boston, and the siege about them slowly tightened. The colonial troops, once they recovered from the shock of the retreat, gained pride and confidence from their performance against the regulars. Further, the story of Bunker Hill provided generations with faith in the notion that any God-fearing American citizen could grab up his musket and march into battle as the equal of a professional soldier. The subsequent service of Nathaniel Wade and Joseph Hodgkins helps to indicate whether this faith should be put among credits or debits for the day.

[46] Massachusetts Archives, *Massachusetts Soldiers and Sailors of Revolutionary War*, XVI p. 373.

[47] Charles Francis Adams, *Studies Military and Diplomatic, 1775-1865* (New York, 1911), p. 5.

CHAPTER II

Making an Army

No MAN who lived to give a firsthand account of Bunker Hill was ever quite the same again. Lieutenant Joseph Hodgkins, in letters to his wife, revealed in almost every sentence the changed mood with which the colonial forces settled to the siege of Boston. The letters of early June had been written in a "wish-you-were-here" mood, and suggested a summer excursion rather than a serious campaign. The British army had not been very frightening: "they say that General gagees Reinforcement is got in to Boston But what Number we know not nor Dont Care much. . . ."[1] The tents at Cambridge were comfortable in early June—"the officers have a Verry Plesant Chamber for there quarters so we have our Choice wether to lodg in the Chamber or tents Capt Wade & I Lodged in the tents last knight and we where much Pleased with our Lodgen." On the whole, the company lived "Verry well" and complained only that it was "obliged to Expend Considerable of Cash." Clean linen posed a problem that Hodgkins solved by sending home bundles for his wife to launder and return. Military duties were not taken too seriously; four days before Bunker Hill Hodgkins wrote that Captain Wade and Ensign Perkins "are gone to take a walk this after noon with there friends & I am obliged to Perrade the Cumpany. . . ." On the fifteenth of June, he said that he would be home for a visit as soon as possible.[2]

On June 18th, however, in his first report of the battle, Hodgkins recorded his thanks that "God Preserved all of us for whitch mercey I Desire Ever to be thankful . . . I hope that we shall be Carred thrue all our Deffittes and have abundant occasion to Prase the Lord to gether. . . ."[3] For a week after the

---

[1] Joseph to Sarah Hodgkins, Cambridge, June 13, 1775.
[2] *Ibid.*, Cambridge, June 8, 13, 15, 1775.
[3] *Ibid.*, Cambridge, June 18, 1775.

battle, his letters were numerous and short. Providence was summoned urgently, constant alarms reported, and the task of digging entrenchments taken very seriously. On June 18: "we have Bin alarmed to Day But Came to no Engagement it is all most Knight now and we are going to Entrenching to night."[4] On June 20: "I am well but Verry Much Worred with our Last Satterday Curmege & yesterdays moving Down to Winter Hill where we now are & Live in Expectation of further Engagements with the Enemy But I desire to be content with the alotments of gods Providence and hope in his mercy for Salvation & Deliverance from all these Eavels witch we feel & fear . . . ."[5]

By the third of July, some measure of composure had returned to the author of the letters; he spoke of dosing a stomach ache with "drops" and described the arrival of the commanders assigned by the Continental Congress: "geaneral Washington & Leas got into Cambridge yesterday and to Day thay are to take a vew of ye Army & that will be atended with a grate deal of grandor there is at this time one and twenty Drummers & as many feffors a Beting and Playing Round the Prayde. . . ."[6] It is unlikely that George Washington and Charles Lee, despite the fifing and beating, saw in the camp the grandeur that Hodgkins found. The Reverend William Emerson, grandfather of Ralph Waldo, described accurately the scene presented to the new commanders:

"It is very diverting to walk among the camps. They are as different in their form as the owners are in their dress; and every tent is a portraiture of the temper and taste of the persons who encamp in it. Some are made of boards, and some of sailcloth. Some partly of one and partly of the other. Again, others are made of stone and turf, brick or brush. Some are thrown up in a hurry; others curiously wrought with doors and windows,

---

[4] *Ibid.*   [5] *Ibid.*, Cambridge, June 20, 1775.
[6] *Ibid.*, Prospect Hill, July 3, 1775. Hodgkins did not describe his medicine, but a soldier with a similar complaint, described as "gravels in the Kitteney," found relief by drinking every morning a glass from a brew concocted from a "quart of ginn and a tea dish of muster seed, and a hand full of horseradish roots . . . ." Charles Knowles Bolton, *The Private Soldier Under Washington* (New York, 1902), p. 181.

[25]

N

Winter Hill

Prospect Hill

Plow'd Hill

Mystic River

Cobble Hill

Bunker's Hill
(rail fence)

CAMBRIDGE

Breed's Hill

CHARLES TOWN

Noddle Island

Charles River

BOSTON

ROXBURY

Dorchester Heights

Boston
on the road to Dorchester

done with wreaths and withes, in the manner of a basket. .... I think this great variety is rather a beauty than a blemish in the army."[7]

Nondescript huts and men without uniform were to be expected; it was the men themselves who gave greatest pause to the generals. Lee, a professional soldier, observed that the privates were "admirable—young, stout, healthy, zealous, and good humor'd and sober." The officers, though, were something else: "These N. England men are so defective in materials for officers, that it must require time to make a real good army out of 'em."[8] Washington, too, complained that the New England officers were "*nearly* of the same kidney with the privates"; the Virginia landowner was not happy with an army in which the spirit of democracy was valued over military discipline. Within a few weeks Washington's misgivings had grown to a sense of outrage: "The People of this government have obtained a Character which they by no means deserved; their officers generally speaking are the most indifferent kind of People I ever saw ... I dare say the Men would fight very well (if properly Officered) although they are an exceeding dirty and nasty people. ...."[9]

The effect of professional command was soon felt, however, and to those slow to appreciate the change the lash brought the lesson home. "New lords, new laws," wrote Emerson. "The Generals Washington and Lee are upon the lines every day .... The strictest government is taking place, and great distinction is made between officers and soldiers. Every one is made to know his place, and keep in it, or be tied up and receive thirty or forty lashes, according to his crime."[10] The season in which a captain was observed shaving his men or a colonel carrying meat to his cooks was soon past.[11] One of the most frequent

[7] Quoted in Jared Sparks, ed., *The Writings of George Washington*, III (Boston, 1834), p. 492.

[8] Quoted in Charles Knowles Bolton, *The Private Soldier Under Washington* (New York, 1902), pp. 133-134.

[9] John C. Fitzpatrick, ed., *The Writings of George Washington, from the Original Manuscript Sources, 1745-1799*, III (Washington, 1932), pp. 433, 450.

[10] Quoted in Sparks, *op.cit.*, III, p. 491.

[11] Bolton, *op.cit.*, pp. 128-129.

duties to which Captain Wade and Lieutenant Hodgkins were assigned was service on regimental courts martial; the Wade and Little Orderly Books are filled with accounts of disciplinary action against both officers and men. The entries in Little's Orderly Book for a single day suggest the size of the problem:

Colonel John Mansfield, of the 19th Foot Regiment, was cashiered "For remisness and Backwardness in the execution of his duty at the late Ingagement on Bunker Hill." "Moses Piquet . . . For disobedience of Orders and damning his Officer, is Found Guilty and Sentenc'd to receive thirty lashes on his Bare Back, and afterwards Drum'd out of the Reg't. the Gen'l orders the Punishment to be Inflicted at the head of the Reg't to Morrow Morning at Troop Beating." An uncaught thief was given a chance to return without punishment money that he might have taken "Through Simplicity." James Fendly, "For Expressing himself disrespectfully of the Continental Association and Drinking Gen'l Gages Health," was sentenced to be stripped of his arms, "Put in a horse Cart with a Rope round his Neck and drum'd out of the army." Two sentries accused of violating general orders by idle fire at British troops out of range were acquitted; and Sgt. John Cotton, convicted of defrauding his unit of rations due them, was required to make restitution of fourteen pounds and was disqualified from further quartermaster service. Thomas Giles, absent without leave from Saturday to Monday, and Shadrick Ireland, disobedient and insolent, were given fifteen days of double fatigue duty on the latrine digging detail.[12]

On another day, a captain in Little's regiment was court martialed for rescuing one of his men from the quarter guard; neighborly obligations were being forcibly dissolved under the new regime.[13] New problems followed from the fact that the army was not only unmilitary; it grew daily more sinful as the siege wore on. In a letter urging his wife to hurry his rum to him, Lieutenant Hodgkins said that "Wickedness Prevales Verry much to the astonishment of any that Behold them I

[12] Entry of September 15, 1775, Little Orderly Book.
[13] William Henshaw Orderly Book, Massachusetts Historical Society, *Proceedings*, XV (Boston, 1876), p. 126.

have not Time to be Pertickler now about maters. . . ."[14] Some diarists found time for particulars; Private David How, during a single week of the siege, included in his diary the following notes:

". . . This Day two men in Cambridge got a bantering Who wodd Drink the most and they Drinkd So much that one of them Died in About one hour or two after.

". . . There was two women Drumd out of Camp this fore noon. That man was Buried that killed himself Drinking.

". . . There was a man found Dead in a room with a Woman this morning. It is not known what killed him."[15]

Custom gradually reinforced discipline as men adjusted to the privileges of rank or the status of inferiors. The three officers of the Ipswich company, Wade, Hodgkins, and Ensign Aaron Perkins, soon established a separate mess and accepted as their right the service of privates as waiters. They never quite fit the stereotype of "officers and gentlemen"; Hodgkins, as a matter of fact, went back to his shoemaker's last and by winter had developed a thriving trade in boots and shoes among his fellow officers.[16]

The irregular status of the Ipswich men was cleared up by action of the Provincial Congress on June 26th, when it was "Ordered That Commissions be delivered to the officers of Col. Little's regiment agreeably to a list recommended by the committee of safety."[17] By this action the colonel, lieutenant colonel, major, ten captains, and twenty lieutenants were duly commissioned, and the command established as the 17th Provincial Regiment until on January 1, 1776 it became in the new army the 12th Continental Foot. On June 26, Colonel Moses Little marked the change by making the first of daily entries in his Orderly Book, and Captain Wade began his record of general and regimental orders on June 28. In the absence of uniforms,

[14] Joseph to Sarah Hodgkins, Prospect Hill, September 20, 1775.
[15] Quoted by Lynn Montross, *Rag, Tag, and Bobtail. The Story of the Continental Army* (New York, 1952), p. 44.
[16] Joseph to Sarah Hodgkins, Prospect Hill, October 16, 20, 1775; January 2, 1776.
[17] William Lincoln, ed., *Journals of Each Provincial Congress of Massachusetts* (Boston, 1838), p. 401.

rank was indicated by a display of ribbons or hat cockades. The commander-in-chief wore a light blue ribbon across his chest, major-generals a purple ribbon, brigadiers pink, and aides-de-camp green. Field officers showed a red or pink cockade on their hats, captains yellow or snuff, and subalterns green. Sergeants wore a red knot on their shoulders, and corporals green.[18]

Fortunately for the army thus sorting itself out, the British proved unwilling in the months after Bunker Hill to test again the strength of American earthworks. Throughout the night of the retreat on June 17th General Israel Putnam had driven his men to the entrenchment of Prospect Hill, on the mainland across Charlestown Neck from Bunker Hill, and in the days that followed the colonial farmers were prodigal with their spadework. By the time the regulars had replaced their losses of June 17th, the Americans were dug in solidly on Prospect and Winter Hills, opposite Bunker, and on a chain of low elevations southeast to Roxbury, opposite Boston Neck. Lieutenant Hodgkins had revealed in his letters the piety and energy with which his company fell to digging at Winter Hill on the night of June 18th and had described their service until they moved back to Cambridge on June 23.[19] The Ipswich men were camped in the town until mid-July when they took up their permanent station on Prospect Hill. Under Washington's command, Colonel Little's regiment served throughout the siege in the American left wing, directed by Major General Charles Lee; and Brigadier General Nathanael Greene led the seven regiments on Prospect Hill. The center at Cambridge was commanded by Major General Putnam, and the right wing at Roxbury by Major General Artemas Ward.[20]

Some 17,000 men were assigned to these commands during the summer and fall months, but the army was so ill-equipped that major movements were impossible. In early August, Wash-

[18] Christopher Ward, *The War of the Revolution*, I (John Richard Alden, ed., New York, 1952), p. 104. See also Aaron Perkins to Joseph Hodgkins, August 2, 1775, for notice of the new insignia. *Essex Institute Historical Collections*, XIV (1878), p. 123.

[19] Joseph to Sarah Hodgkins, Cambridge, June 18, 20, 23, 1775. An order survives in the Wade Papers, directing Captain Wade to quarter his men after Bunker Hill in Francis Moore's house in Cambridge.

[20] Richard Frothingham, *The Siege of Boston*, pp. 218-220.

ington reported that he had no more than nine cartridges to the man, and at no time during the siege were his men equipped with more than twelve or fifteen rounds at a time. Benjamin Franklin's notion that bows and arrows would serve was not judged practical, and the spears or pikes gathered had only limited defensive uses.[21] The British, on the other hand, were well equipped, but their commanders hesitated to pay the price of forcing the American troops to yield yet another set of hills, particularly when the rebel forces lacked the artillery to take advantage of the hills that they had. Of military action, therefore, little occurred that was of significance during the long months that followed. There was skirmishing from both sides and the Americans moved several times to occupy small hills in the area, but the lines were on the whole unchanged until Washington occupied Dorchester Heights, south of Boston, in March of 1776.

The summer and fall brought rapidly pyramiding responsibilities to officers at the company level. Newly commissioned leaders like Wade and Hodgkins took charge without the support of experienced non-commissioned officers, and struggled to combat the disease and disorder that threatened in equal parts the safety of the camp. In July and August, security against the nearby enemy was their first concern. Drill was incessant, the company exercising twice a day, two hours in the morning and three in the afternoon—except on Sundays, when "ye Whole ought to be Ingaged in heavenly devotions."[22] Those at worship, though, were ordered to "take their armes ammunition & Cutrements" and be prepared for immediate action.[23] At evening muster, the captain and his subalterns checked each man's ammunition and read off the lists of men assigned to fatigue parties the following day.[24] The fatigue parties were as important as the drill squads, first in the completion of the entrenchments on Winter and Prospect Hills, and then in the building of barracks as cool weather began to come on. Men on fatigue worked from

[21] Ward, *op.cit.*, p. 108.
[22] Entry of August 21, 1775, Little Orderly Book.
[23] Entry of July 16, 1775, Wade Orderly Book.
[24] *Ibid.*, entry of August 4, 1775.

six to eight and nine to twelve in the morning, and from two o'clock to sunset in the afternoon.[25]

The men rotated constantly from drill to fatigue to duty on the outposts at Plow'd Hill, Cobble Hill, or Lechmere's Point. The captains were warned to put no man on sentry duty who was "not Perfectly Sober and tollerably observing."[26] Since July 8, it had been a standing order that captains assign no man to the outposts "whose carecter they are unacquainted with." The order provided that "no man shall be appointed to those important stations who are not Natives of their Country or have a wife or family in it to whom it is known he is attacht. . . ."[27] From August 22, no officer was permitted to leave camp, even for nearby Cambridge, without a pass.[28]

Meanwhile, for the captain, there was constant paper work. Various receipts have survived, in which Nathaniel Wade signed himself accountable for guns and clothing issued for use by his men. On July 24, it was two guns appraised by the Committee at four pounds, fourteen shillings, and on August 7, "one French Arm sent from Newbury Port," valued at two pounds eight shillings—"which I Promise to Return to ye Colony or Acc't for ye Same. . . ."[29] Captains of companies acted as licensing agents in giving permits to sutlers authorized to sell liquor to their men, it having been found that "some persons are so Daring as to supply the Soldiers with an immoderat quantity of other spirits & Liquors. . . ."[30]

Simply keeping their men alive and decent was a full-time job for the officers. Once they lost their initial fear of sporadic cannon fire from Bunker Hill, men began to make a game of catching cannon balls before they stopped bouncing, a sport at which more than one lost his life.[31] The captains had to keep their men from giving too great offense to the citizens of the surrounding towns. On August 22, General Washington de-

[25] Entry of September 28, 1775, Little Orderly Book.
[26] Entry of August 5, 1775, Wade Orderly Book.
[27] *Ibid.*, entry of July 8, 1775.
[28] Entry of August 22, 1775, Little Orderly Book.
[29] Receipts in the Wade Papers.
[30] Entry of July 10, 1775, Little Orderly Book.
[31] Frothingham, *op.cit.*, p. 231.

clared that he did "not mean to discourage the Practice of Bathing," but it had been observed that "many men lost to all sense of decency & Common Modesty are running about Naked upon ye Bridge Whilst Passengers and even ladys of ye First Fashion in the Neighborhood are passing over it. . . ." Worse, the men seemed "to glory in their Shame."[32] General Greene ordered company officers to go to general headquarters to learn the proper way of building a stove—their cooks were wasting fuel and endangering the camp with fire.[33] It was the officers, too, who had to "surpress the Soldiers Broiling any Meat whatsoever as it much Indangers ye Peoples Health."[34] The men adjusted very slowly to the most elementary rules of camp sanitation, justifying, sometimes, Washington's description of the New Englanders as a "nasty" people. On August 14, Captain Wade recorded in his Orderly Book notice of the "Great Neglect of People Repairing to the Nessesaries"; instead the men voided "Excrament about the fields Pernishously," greatly endangering health in the closely packed camps.[35] A regular minor punishment assigned by regimental courts martial was a tour of duty at covering old vaults and digging new ones for the camp necessaries. The officers waged a losing battle against bad liquor, immoderately consumed, though it was on them that execution of Washington's August 28 order fell: "As nothing is more Pernicious to ye health of Soldiers Nor Certainly more Productive of ye Bloody Flux than drinking New Cyder the Gen'l in a Most Posative Manner Commands an Intire disuse of ye Same . . . such of them as are detected Bringing New Syder into ye Camp After Friday may depend on Having their Casks Stove."[36]

An occasional skirmish with the British must have been a welcome break from the trials of making an army. Every week provided some small alarm, and the threat of larger ones, to keep the camp alert to its dangers. Lieutenant Hodgkins made dutiful report of each skirmish in his letters; on July 8, for

[32] Entry of August 22, 1775, Little Orderly Book.
[33] *Ibid.*, entry of August 21, 1775.
[34] *Ibid.*
[35] Entry of August 14, 1775, Wade Orderly Book.
[36] Entry of August 28, 1775, Little Orderly Book.

instance, when Major Benjamin Tupper and Captain John Crane took a force to burn the guardhouse of the British outpost on Boston Neck, he wrote: "we have had several alarms Latley one this morning about half after two oclock whitch whas occashoned By a party of our men at Rockbury whitch went Down to there garde house at the nek and Drove of the garde & Burnt the house and sume other Bildings there whas Considerable of firing But we left no men at tol they Lost Sume But we no not how many."[37]

Hodgkins appears to have been at home when a more decisive move was made. On the night of August 26, a large force from adjacent Winter Hill marched out to dig throughout the night on Plowed Hill, a low eminence that lay between Prospect and Bunker. The place was in close gunshot of Bunker Hill and controlled the Mystic River approaches to Medford. Thirty-six hundred men were involved in the entrenching operation, and the following day 5,000 more marched out from Prospect and Winter Hills to resist the columns seen forming among the regulars on Bunker Hill. No attack followed, but Plowed Hill was subject to heavy bombardment for several days.[38]

Hodgkins' pen was taken up, during this engagement, by his brother-in-law, Ensign Aaron Perkins, who described the preparations for the Plowed Hill occupation in three letters to the absent lieutenant.[39] By Perkins' account, the American force hesitated

[37] Joseph to Sarah Hodgkins, Prospect Hill, July 8, 1775.

[38] Ward, *op.cit.*, p. 110.

[39] The reasons for Hodgkins' absence are unknown; when he left, in late July, the commander-in-chief was expressing repeatedly his "astonishment" at requests for furloughs by officers. "Brave Men who are Engaged for the Noble Cause of Liberty," said Washington, "Should Never think of Removing from their Camps While the Enemy is in Sight." Possibly Hodgkins was assigned, under General Orders issued on July 10, to recruiting duty for his unit; every Massachusetts company had been ordered to detach one subaltern for this service, preferably men "that are in the most esteem of the District they are sent" to. There is no record of the lieutenant's appointment to the duty, but he was the only subaltern absent from the Ipswich company in August. On the other hand, Perkins, in the three letters referred to above, spoke of Hodgkins' poor health and declared his delight that "you are so much better, as you inform me." The Perkins Letters, according to the transcription in the *Essex Institute Historical Collections*, were addressed to Lieutenant "Jas." Hodgkins, but their context makes it clear that they were written to an absent Joseph, whose duties had fallen on the next subaltern of the company. Perkins was carried on early muster rolls as a sergeant, but

for at least three weeks before it moved to fortify the Hill. On August 2, he expressed his fear that "the Regulars will get Plow'd Hill. I hope not." On Prospect Hill, the Ipswich men were on constant alert: "We have a tough time of it. We are not allowed to leave the Camp. We have to go on duty or fatigue every other day. Our money is gone and we want Rum very much. I have sent home your half barrel, as far as Mr. Nathaniel Appleton's; if you could get some Rum and send it down, it will oblige us very much. We have not more than thirty-five men fit for duty. I expect to go on picket guard to night."[40]

A hundred men from each regiment went down each night to picket duty at Plowed Hill, before the entrenchments of August 26 were undertaken, and "standing on the hill all night" was described by Perkins as "hard duty. I was never used to such hardship before. . . ."[41] With Hodgkins gone, and Captain Wade sometimes absent, the second lieutenant was also obligated to "parade the men" and carry on company affairs. He declared, on August 16, that he was "not afraid of the Regulars getting the Plowed Hill," but he was sure that a major engagement was impending: "The Regulars desert almost every day; they seem to be preparing for a battle, and it is thought by many they will shortly make one violent push with all their forces, which if they do not succeed, they will destroy all they can and push off, and our people heare seem to be allmost anxious to have the time come and I have nothing to fear of sickness, but

---

Peter Force, in his records of participants at Bunker Hill, listed him as a second lieutenant. Earlier references name him an "ensign." Joseph Hodgkins' wife was Sarah Perkins before her marriage, and the use of "Brother" as a form of address between him and Perkins supports the assumption that the first and second lieutenants were brothers-in-law. Hodgkins was back on duty in early September—he wrote from camp to his wife on September 8—and declared, in a letter of October 2, that he had been back for four weeks that night. See the Nathaniel Wade Orderly Book, July 18; Moses Little Orderly Book, July 10; and Joseph to Sarah Hodgkins, September 8 and October 2, 1775. For the Perkins letters, see "Revolutionary Letters and Other Documents, Communicated by F. H. Wade, of Ipswich," *Essex Institute Historical Collections*, XIV (Salem, 1878), pp. 233-236. The Force reference is in *American Archives*, Series 4, II, p. 1,628.

[40] *Ibid.*, p. 233.
[41] *Ibid.*, p. 235.

only our sins which seem to prevail hear very much. We must pray God to give a spirit of repentance and humiliation, which, if he is pleased to do, we shall soon have Deliverance from all our distress."[42]

The British, though, chose not to oppose the occupation of Plowed Hill, and the American camp settled back to the lesser alarms that marked the fall. Hodgkins, after his return, spoke from time to time of a "good many Bums" sent at his lines, but he concluded on September 29 that "the Enemy are Very Peasable at Present."[43] He was witness in late November to General Putnam's occupation of Cobble Hill, a nearby mound, and outlined for his wife the uses of the Hill: "our People went to Cabble Hill & intrenched there & have Ben Very Bisey since a finshing there work & have got Down there several Cannon in order to give the ship a worming that lays up above Chalstown all this has Ben Done & our Enemy hath not fired a gon at our People whitch I think is Very Extrodenery But how Ever there seams to be a grate Probablity of a Movement Very soon But whare I can not tell But I hope we shall be on our garde But our army is Very thin now But in good spirits and I hope we shall Be asisted By him houe is able with a small number to Put thousands to flite"[44]

A few days later, Hodgkins reported that "Part of the famos Prise has arived at Cambridge from Cap ann."[45] This was the treasure from the ordnance brig *Nancy*, captured by John Manley on the *Lee* at the mouth of Boston Harbor. Two thousand muskets, 100,000 flints, 30,000 round shots, and 30 tons of musket bullets were on the *Nancy*, along with an enormous 13-inch, 2,700-pound brass mortar. "Old Put [General Putnam] mounted on the large mortar . . . with a bottle of rum in his hand, standing parson to christen, while god-father Mifflin gave it the name of Congress."[46]

By this time the American army, as Hodgkins had noted on November 25, was growing "Very thin"; the term of enlistment

[42] *Ibid.*, pp. 235-236.
[43] Joseph to Sarah Hodgkins, Prospect Hill, September 8, 20, 23, 29, 1775.
[44] *Ibid.*, November 25, 1775.
[45] *Ibid.*, December 3, 1775.
[46] Quoted in Frothingham, *op.cit.*, p. 270.

for every soldier outside Boston expired by December 31st, and the Connecticut troops marched away a month earlier. Holding the army together for the uneventful siege grew harder as the days grew colder, and nothing revealed its weakness so clearly as did the excuses by which men sought home and fireside in the deepening winter. Lieutenant Hodgkins' irritation at Captain Wade's long furlough mirrors in small detail the massive anger Washington must have felt as he watched his army slowly dissolve. Hodgkins made no complaint when Wade, who he said was "Very Poorly," left camp for home in late September.[47] All the Ipswich men were ailing—"Brother Perkins is got the Rumetis in his neck & shoulders so that he is not fitt for Duty," and "we have not a man hear . . . fit. . . ."[48] The lieutenant had himself been absent through the crucial month of August, and he was magnanimous in urging, on October 16, that Wade not come back "Before he gets Pretty well for we have Cool nights."[49] Within a few days, though, he was anxious: "I hope I shall be able to get a furlow as soon as Capt Wade gets Able to Come hear But I cannot tell how long that will be . . . But I hope it will not be a grate wile. . . ."[50] Sarah Hodgkins had given her husband reason to think that the Captain recovered his health as soon as he arrived at home; she had written, on October 1, that "I have been to See Capt Wade today & he thinks he is a little better . . . I am in hopes he will get it over without being any wors."[51] By early November, Hodgkins was angry: "I whas in hopes when I wrote the last Letter I should Been att home By this time But I Cannot Come home till Capt Wade Come hear and when that will be I cannot tel for some People that Come hear say that he is well others say he is Poorley so you can tell when I shall Come home as well as I. . . ."[52] In December, the lieutenant wrote wearily: "if you see Capt Wade tel him I hope he will com hear soon. . . ."[53]

It was late December before Wade was back, and Hodgkins

[47] Joseph to Sarah Hodgkins, Prospect Hill, September 25, 1775.
[48] *Ibid.*, September 27, 1775.   [49] *Ibid.*, October 16, 1775.
[50] *Ibid.*, October 23, 1775.
[51] Sarah to Joseph Hodgkins, October 1, 1775.
[52] Joseph to Sarah Hodgkins, November 7, 1775.
[53] *Ibid.*, Prospect Hill, December 3, 1775.

home for sight of his three children, wife, and aged father.[54]
The nature of the captain's illness was not specified in the letters, but a postscript on one of Perkins' notes to Hodgkins, back
in August, may hold some clues: "The Capt.'s cockade is so
faded that I believe he will be glad of that young woman's
you spoke of. . . ."[55] Twenty-five-year-old Nathaniel Wade, however, survived as a bachelor until July 1777, and then he married a Gloucester girl, so it may not have been a fresh cockade
that he sought during his three-month absence. Real bitterness
did not enter Hodgkins' letters until February 6, 1776. He had
reported Wade "something unwell" in early February,[56] but he
still hoped to attend the ordination on February 7 of the Reverend Levi Frisbie at the Ipswich church. Unfortunately for
him, this important social function appealed equally to the
Captain:

"My dear having an oppertunity this morning to write a line
By Capt Wade I would inform you that I am well & I hope
these lines will find you the same I should Ben Very glad to
Come home to ordanation and upon my making applycation
to Capt he whent to the Colol & when he found that one officer out of the Company might go home insted of speaking
a word for me he spok two for himself But if you should have
the oppertunity to see him Due ask him to supper with you
though I Due not Expect you will see him. . . ."[57]

For all their readiness to demand furlough time, both Wade
and Hodgkins were more constant in their service than were
many of their fellows. ". . . our People are all most Bewitcht
about getting home," Hodgkins had written early in the fall;[58]
and by the end of 1775, when the Massachusetts enlistments
ran out, the army had shrunk to little more than half of its
peak size. General Greene's brigade on Prospect Hill was down

[54] *Ibid.*, December 31, 1775.

[55] Aaron Perkins to Joseph Hodgkins, August 16, 1775, in *Essex Institute Historical Proceedings*, XIV (Salem, 1878), p. 236.

[56] Joseph to Sarah Hodgkins, Prospect Hill, February 5, 1776.

[57] *Ibid.*, February 6, 1776. Small compensation for missing the ordination lay in Sarah's loneliness at the occasion: ". . . we had a comfortable ordanation but there Seemed to me to be Something wanting I wanted you at home & that would have crowned all . . ." Sarah to Joseph Hodgkins, February 11, 1776.

[58] Joseph to Sarah Hodgkins, Prospect Hill, October 6, 1775.

to four regiments from its original seven by early January; and many of the men on duty were newly recruited green troops.[59] The brigade commander wrote, "We have just experienced the inconvenience of disbanding an army within cannon-shot of the enemy, and forming a new one in its stead. . . . Had the enemy been fully acquainted with our condition I cannot pretend to say what might have been the consequence."[60] Sarah Hodgkins wrote anxiously to her husband, expressing her concern "on account of the army being so thin" and declaring her "fear the enemy should take the advantage."[61]

But the Massachusetts men remained stubborn to the end of the war in their refusal to sign on for indefinite service—"for the duration"—and thousands of them left camp, often carrying their needed guns, on the day their enlistments expired. A new army had been in the process of forming since mid-November, but recruiting for the winter siege went very slowly. A week after enlistment papers for the year 1776 were issued on November 12, Hodgkins was optimistic: "men inlist much faster than I thought for witch I am very glad."[62] A few days later he was worried: ". . . Our men inlist very slow and our Enemy have got a Reinforsement of five Regiments and if the New Army is not Reased in season I hope I & all my townsmen shall have virtue anofe to stay all winter as Volentears Before we Will leave the line with out men for our all is at stake and if we Due not Exarte our selves in this gloris Cause our all is gon and we made slaves of for Ever But I Pray god that it never may Be so"[63]

All three officers of the Ipswich company decided to sign on for another year, promising service to December 31, 1776. "I hope I am in the way of My Duty," Hodgkins wrote.[64] Of the sixty men with the Ipswich company in February, however, only twenty-eight remained from the fifty-one who had marched out to the alarm of April 19, 1775.[65]

[59] Frothingham, *op.cit.*, p. 291.
[60] *Ibid.*, p. 285.
[61] Sarah to Joseph Hodgkins, January 8, 1776.
[62] Joseph to Sarah Hodgkins, Prospect Hill, November 19, 1775.
[63] *Ibid.*, November 25, 1775.
[64] *Ibid.*, November 30, 1775.
[65] See a pay record for the company signed on February 23, 1776, and compare it with the roll of men who went to the Lexington Alarm, Wade Papers.

A factor influencing the officers to sign again was the new pay scale pushed through by southern delegates in the Continental Congress. "The first Leut Pay," Hodgkins hurried to tell his wife, "is advansed to better than four pounds pr Month old tennor. . . ."[66] A captain's pay rose from $20 to $26 2/3 per month, a first lieutenant's from $13 1/3 to $18, and an ensign's from $10 to $13 1/3. To the dismay of equalitarian New England, a private's pay remained unchanged at $6 2/3. This pointed notice of the distinction between officer and man, resolved the town of Harvard, Massachusetts, "much chilled the spirits of the commonalty. . . ."[67]

As important as the raise was the fact that wages were coming with reasonable regularity by the turn of the year. In the confusion of the preceding summer and fall, payment had been uncertain; "as to Money," complained the lieutenant on September 27, "we have none and I Dont know when we shall have any. . . ."[68] By October 6, however, Hodgkins was able to mail eleven dollars to his wife, and he followed with eight dollars on November 17, and forty-nine dollars (for himself and two of his men) on December 31.[69] Last in coming was the full amount due from the Colony of Massachusetts before the Continental Congress began payment to the army on August 1. Captain Wade did not sign until February 26, 1776, the receipt to the Colony acknowledging receipt of money for his men from the time they enlisted to August 1.[70] By the standards of the day for military pay, the delay was tolerable, for American privates got more than five times the wage of their British opposites, before the inflation set in.

In various ways the American troops lived better than did their increasingly hungry enemy in Boston. They were abundantly supplied with food, though the formidable rations prescribed by the Continental Congress were not always available

---

[66] Joseph to Sarah Hodgkins, Prospect Hill, November 19, 1775.

[67] L. C. Hatch, *The Administration of the American Revolutionary Army*, (New York, 1904), pp. 78-79.

[68] Joseph to Sarah Hodgkins, Prospect Hill, September 27, 1775.

[69] *Ibid.*, October 6, November 17, December 31, 1775.

[70] *Ipswich Antiquarian Papers*, II (May, 1881) number 19. As early as August 7, 1775, Colonel Moses Little was beginning a chain of petitions to the Massachusetts General Court, trying to get pay for all his men.

on schedule.[71] The only references to food in the Hodgkins letters throughout the siege indicate his satisfaction with his diet. On October 23, the lieutenant sent home a loaf of bread from the camp ovens to show his wife "what fine Bread we have. . . ."[72] On October 25, he described a feast:

"I would just inform you that the Quarter Master has just Brought into our tent a fine Peas of Beaf and we have got it Down a Roosting for supper and I hop that while we are making our selves merry we shall not forget our Absent wives and friends But for fear you should think that we should be unseasonable in our Devoytion I would Let you Know that I whas on guard all Last night & I Entend to goo too Bead in season to night. I must Conclude for the Beaf is almost Rosted. . . ."[73]

In a postscript added the next morning, Hodgkins, always meticulous in description of his physical state, reported that "My supper sot Very Well on my stummack." Again, on January 2, he declared, "we have just Ben to supper on a fine Turky. . . ."[74] The men in the American camp could always send to their families for extras: Hodgkins requested sugar and coffee on June 20, and Ensign Perkins asked for a "young pig to roast" on August 8.[75]

The Ipswich officers fared less well in their housing; they were among the last to get into barracks that winter. The tent that had made such pleasant "Lodgen" in June[76] "growes Cool," said Hodgkins, on October 6.[77] He reported a soaking time of

[71] The Wade Orderly Book, in an entry of August 8, 1775, says that Congress allowed the following weekly ration per soldier: one pound fresh beef or three-quarters pound of pork or one pound salt fish per day; one pound of bread or flour per day; three pints of peas or beans per week, or equivalent vegetables at five shillings per bushel for peas and beans; one pint of milk per man per day "when it is to be had"; one-half pint of rice or one pint of Indian meal a man per week; one quart of spruce beer per man per day, or nine gallons of molasses for a company of 100 men per week; three pounds of candles for a hundred men per week for guard; twenty-four pounds of soft or eight pounds of hard soap per 100 men per week; one ration of salt and one of fresh fish and two of bread to be delivered on Monday and Wednesday mornings; and on Friday the same plus the salt fish.
[72] Joseph to Sarah Hodgkins, Prospect Hill, October 23, 1775.
[73] *Ibid.*, October 25, 1775.   [74] *Ibid.*, January 2, 1776.
[75] *Essex Institute Historical Collections*, XIV (1878), p. 235.
[76] Joseph to Sarah Hodgkins, Cambridge, June 8, 1775.
[77] Joseph to Sarah Hodgkins, Prospect Hill, October 6, 1775.

it in mid-October, when the tent "smocked very Bad in the storme."[78] In November, he complained, "our houses are Very good in fair weather But in a storm they are Very Bad for the Rane Runs Douen Chimbely so that we Cannot keep any fire But how Ever our Barracks are a Bulding & we hope By the first Day of January to get into them. . . ."[79] Most of his men were in the barracks by January,[80] but the officers were not equipped with their "Pretty Room" there until after February 12, when Hodgkins wrote, "I must Be shor for the weather is Very Cold & our tent smoks so that it is with Defelty that I can stay in it. . . ."[81] It was a cold winter for patriots.

Of other needs Hodgkins had few. Laundry and mending caused him constant difficulty, which he resolved by mailing his problems to his wife. "I fear I shall weary you," he said, "in sending to have so much Done for me But I must tel you we live whare we have no woman to Due anything for us so you must give som Alowance. . . ."[82] His only large complaint was that of all soldiers in all wars—he wanted his own home, fireside, and family. Repeatedly, in his letters, he said, "I whant to see you Very much."[83]

Service on the outposts was constant in the late fall, "By Reason of so many officers Being absent,"[84] but as the winter hardened, the guards "are Redust"; "we go on guard only once in tin Day but we spend a grate Part of our time in Exersising the Regiment. . . ."[85] Passage in and out of the camp was no longer so closely restricted, and there was much visiting back and forth

---

[78] *Ibid.*, October 20, 1775. Hodgkins at least had his wife's sympathy. On October 9, she had written: "I feel Quite concerned about you all these cool nights on account of your haveing no Better habetations to live in but I hope the Same that has preserved hither to will still be with you and preserve you from Cold & Storms. . . ." Sarah to Joseph Hodgkins, October 9, 1775.

[79] Joseph to Sarah Hodgkins, Prospect Hill, undated in November, 1775.

[80] *Ibid.*, January 7, 1776.

[81] *Ibid.*, February 12, 1776.

[82] *Ibid.*, October 16, 1775.

[83] *Ibid.*, November 30, 1775. Two days before, Sarah had demonstrated that loneliness was a shared experience. She wrote: ". . . it is thanksgiving day night tonight and it Seems to be very lonesome and dull I did not know any better way to deverte myself than by writing to you. . . ." Sarah to Joseph Hodgkins, November 28, 1775.

[84] Joseph to Sarah Hodgkins, Prospect Hill, December 3, 1775.

[85] *Ibid.*, January 2, February 3, 1776.

among the regiments. On January 2 an uncle of Sarah Hodgkins stopped at the lieutenant's tent to report friends at Sudbury well,[86] and on January 25 Hodgkins was at Cambridge transacting business for Ipswich friends.[87] Parochial clannishness was dissolving, too, as the Ipswich men sought pleasure in the company of men from other provinces. A man from distant parts was no longer the object of immediate suspicion, as a page from the diary of a Connecticut lieutenant reveals:

"I arose a little after 3 o'clock, attended the alarm post as usual. I then went to Capt. Ripleys barber and got shaved and at 8 o'clock went to the main guard . . . We marched down to the main guard house where we relieved the old guard. I went with Lt. Parker of Col. Brewer's regt to the redoubt, spent some time with him and return'd to the guard house, spent some time with Capt. Wade and other officers of the guard, and then I took charge of the redoubt myself where I was posted until 3 o'clock in the afternoon, when I was relieved by another subaltern and returned to the guard house, drank some brandy, and Cudilla bro't me some dinner."[88]

It was from such encounters as these that Washington might build a true Continental Line, rather than remaining subject to the jealousies and loyalties of the several colonies.

Early in February rumors began to spread of action sufficiently decisive to end the weariness of the siege. Washington was restive with inconsequential raiding,[89] and he was anxious to use his greater manpower to force the British out of Boston. As usual, the camp was discussing his plans before the general met with his Council of War to formulate them: "it

[86] *Ibid.*, January 2, 1776.

[87] *Ibid.*, January 24, 1776.

[88] Diary of Jabez Fitch, Jr., of Colonel Huntington's 8th Connecticut Regiment, Massachusetts Historical Society, *Proceedings*, IX (1894), p. 54.

[89] Such a raid took place on January 8, 1776, when Major Knowlton crossed the millpond dam to Charlestown, burned the houses still standing, and returned with captives. Lieutenant Hodgkins heard the commotion after he had gone to bed and, rising, hurried to the top of Prospect Hill to watch: "we soon got up the Hill and found that the Houses over to Chalstown whare all in flames & since we hear that a number of Generall Putnams men went over & sot them on fire & Brought of one or two Prisnors & they say Brought of one woman." Joseph to Sarah Hodgkins, Prospect Hill, postscript written January 9 to letter of January 8, 1776.

is sayed," wrote Hodgkins, "that the Generals are Determaned to do something very soon But What the event will be god only knows But I hope god will Direct them in there Counsels and order Every thing for his Glory and our good. . . ."[90]

The commander-in-chief, when he met with his generals on February 16, argued for a direct blow at Boston across the neck and frozen harbor, but he was overruled by his cautious advisors. The generals voted to fortify Dorchester Heights, a move that would force the British either to attack or to abandon the city, which lay within range of guns on Dorchester. The occupation of the Heights was to be undertaken, as at Breeds Hill, by night; and elaborate preparations were made to cart in breastworks, impossible to dig in the frozen ground. The camp labored for two weeks preparing gabions, fascines, barrels, and bales of hay for the movement of March 2. When the British waked on the morning of March 3, they were shocked by the new works. General Howe, who now commanded at Boston, eyed the miraculously appeared fortifications and estimated that 12,000 men must have labored out the night to erect them, though the movement in fact had taken only 2,000. The British general laid plans for an attack and ordered one, but then, thinking of Bunker Hill, he decided to leave Boston instead. By unwritten agreement Washington refrained from bombarding the city, and Howe left it unburned when he took ship on March 17, 1776.[91]

On Prospect Hill Hodgkins wrote excitedly of the "grate Movement among the Enemy," and speculated about the prob-

---

[90] *Ibid.*, February 12, 1776. Within four days after the generals had met, on February 16, the news of impending action had spread into the towns. Sarah Hodgkins complained, on February 20, that Joseph was not making good his pledge to come home regularly: "I think you told me that you intended to See me once a mounth & it is now a month & I think a very long one Since you left home as I dont hear as you talk of comeing but I must confess I dont think it is for want of a good will that you dont come home It is generaly thoght that there will be Something done amongst you very soon but what will be the event of it God only knows so that we may be prepared for all events. . . ." Sarah to Joseph Hodgkins, February 20, 1776.

[91] This account of the Dorchester movement, and of Howe's and Washington's decisions, is based on Ward, *op.cit.*, I, pp. 125-134. By some accounts, Howe dropped plans for the attack when a storm prevented execution of his orders, but Ward notes that the battle was called off five hours before the storm came up.

ability that the army would soon be on the march. His company did not enter the abandoned city, for only men who had had smallpox risked contact with the pestilence that had plagued the British through the winter. Hodgkins sent his regards to his brother, and asked his wife to "tell him I whant my Briches Very much for I due not know But we shall march soon."[92] The next day, in his final report from the siege of Boston, the lieutenant wrote to reassure his wife, but he spoke for all patriots: "I would not have you mak yourself uneasy . . . for our Enemye seems to Be a flieing Before us which seems to give a spring to our Spirits."[93]

[92] Joseph to Sarah Hodgkins, Prospect Hill, March 17, 18, 1776.
[93] *Ibid.*, March 18, 1776.

A Soldier and His Family

JOSEPH HODGKINS knew that the evacuation of Boston meant marching; "as our Enemy are gone from us I Expect we must follow them. . . ." He prepared for the movement with "Chearfullness," and declared himself ready "to sarve my Contery in the Best way & mannar that I am Capeble of. . . ." He argued in advance against the protests any wife would make—"I would not Be understood that I should Chuse to March But as I am ingaged in this glories Cause I am will to go . . . with a Desire to Commit myself & you to the care of him Who is able to Carry on through all the Defiltes that we may be Called to."[1] Joseph marched with God for three and a half more years, braving fire and water to escape capture on Long Island, facing the icy Delaware on a Christmas night, conquering "camp sickness" after the victory at Saratoga, and starving at Valley Forge.

His wife sustained him through it all. She was his quartermaster and comforter, his home business agent, and his lover. She buried his son and bore him a daughter, each with praise to God for His awful mercies. Few of Sarah Hodgkins' letters survive, but among those that remain are several that Joseph took from Long Island. He lost his best shirt, breeches, and greatcoat there, but he kept the letters—good evidence that he carried them next to his heart. Sarah wrote more mannered prose than Joseph, but both slipped frequently into the scriptural cadence that proves the eighteenth-century's intimacy with the Bible. "I think as your day is So your Strength Seems to be," wrote Sarah, marveling at Joseph's survival through the chain of battles across Long Island and New York.[2] "I hope God will apear for us & send Salvation and deliverance to us in due time and if you Should be called to Battle again may he be with

---

[1] Joseph to Sarah Hodgkins, Prospect Hill, March 20, 1776.
[2] Sarah to Joseph Hodgkins, October 19, 1776.

you & cover your heads & Strenthen your hands & encorage your hearts and give you all that fortitude and resilution that is left for you and in his own time return you home in Safty. . . ."[3]

Joseph was more matter of fact. Any phrase of his that one might search for second meaning, he quickly modified—"my Candle is almost out so I must Be short . . ." but "I have Leet another Candle so I will write a word or two more."[4] He left an almost clinical record of his physical state. If he suffered from boils, he reported not only their size and his discomfort but also noted their usefulness in releasing bad "humors" from the body—"as People say they are holsome But not Toothsome. . . ."[5] He was stoical about his personal troubles. After Saratoga, observing that he was "Prity Well now," he remarked that "I have had something of the Camp Disorder & Lost most all my flesh but I hope soon to Pick up my . . . [crumbs] again We have had a Very [fatiguing] Campain But as we have Don the Bisnes we came hear for I hope none of us will Complain of a little hardship. . . ."[6]

More than a hundred letters survive from the exchange. Rich in details of battle and life in the camps, the documents are even more valuable as a family record from the Revolution. Joseph faced the British with Ipswich on his mind, and Sarah was distracted in her prayers for him by the countless tasks he set her there. Their letters were rarely intimate, in the modern fashion, but for all their reticence the two found phrases enough to tell their love. "I am on the main Guard," wrote Joseph from Rhode Island, "& have had many thoughts in my head to night But it would Be folly in me to commit all my thoughts to writing. . . . I want to see you Very much. . . ."[7] When Sarah wrote, "give regards to Capt Wade and tell I have wanted his bed fellow prety much these cold nights," Joseph replied, "I gave your Regards to Capt Wade But he Did not wish that you had his Bed fellow but I wish you had with all my heart."[8] Sarah was

---

[3] *Ibid.*, September 16, 1776.
[4] Joseph to Sarah Hodgkins, Providence, Rhode Island, October 13, 1778.
[5] *Ibid.*, Long Island, May 9, 1776.
[6] *Ibid.*, Albany, New York, October 27, 1777.
[7] *Ibid.*, Providence, September 10, 1778.
[8] Sarah to Joseph Hodgkins, February 1, 1776; Joseph to Sarah Hodgkins, Prospect Hill, February 5, 1776.

artful in her appeals for Joseph to get leave. I've "got a Sweet Babe almost Six mounths old but have got no father for it. . . ." She played on Joseph's fears for his children's health: "my Sweet Baby Seems to be Something unwell but I hope it is nothing more than Breeding teeth She longs to See her farder She is a Scolding at me like a dogges tal." A few weeks later, she added, "I must Jest tell you my Baby has got two teeth & she can Stand by things alone . . . if my Leter is not So correct as might be you must consider from whence it came and excuse all thats amis. . . ."[9] Sarah was careful in her role as young second wife to the middle-aged soldier. She apologized for her boldness in urging him not to reenlist: "I dont know but you may think I am too free expressing my mind & that it would have been time enough when I was asked but I was afraid I Should not have that oppertunity So I hope you will excuse my freedom."[10]

When Joseph left home in April 1775 his wife was twenty-four. He had married her in 1772, within a few months of the death of his first wife; and he left in her charge the surviving child of his earlier marriage, Joanna, as well as their own twenty-month-old Sarah ("Salle") and new-born Joseph. He also expected her to look in on his aging father, who at eighty-three counted on his boys for assistance. The excitement of war for the young passed Sarah by, for Joseph sent few presents and reported little detail from the sinful cities through which he passed. For gifts she received a half a box of chestnuts and a loaf of bread (to see how good her man's bread was) in 1775, and three black handkerchiefs in 1776. In the same year Joseph sent a "quire of Paper . . . for I am so fond of Letters that I shall not only Embrase Every oppotunity to write my self But will furnish you wherewith to Do the same."[11]

Letters from home were as necessary as gunpowder to the campaigns. The men slipped away from the camps to check conditions at home if too long a time passed without news; and

[9] Sarah to Joseph Hodgkins, April 26, July 27, September 3, 1778.
[10] *Ibid.*, October 19, 1776.
[11] Joseph to Sarah Hodgkins, October 16, October 23, 1775; March 23, 1776. Of the handkerchiefs Joseph added that the shopkeeper "will Change one for a white one if you are a mind to Part with anv of them the Price is 9/6."

such constant pleas as those of Joseph Hodgkins for more mail make clear the extent to which he depended on Sarah's reassurances.[12] Sarah waited as anxiously for the post, wondering whether her husband lived or died—the news of an engagement was likely to precede a letter from him by weeks. She was as lonely as he, and begged him not to "mis any oppertunity you may have of writing to me sence that is all the way we have to converse together it is much to my greif that it is so."[13]

Correspondence was easy and frequent during the first months of the war when the Ipswich men were near Boston, only a few miles down the road. Towns in Essex County had met at Ipswich on May 4, 1775, to set up a regular post to Cambridge, and the Provincial Congress soon adopted the system.[14] A letter went for 5¼ pence for sixty miles, and a whole ounce of mail for only four times as much.[15] The Continental Congress theoretically made the system country-wide on July 26, 1775, but, once the armies left from their home areas, service was uncertain.[16] Men in the distant camps preferred to rely on some friend leaving on furlough or a visitor from home.[17] Sometimes they burdened passing strangers with their letters; Joseph wrote from Rhode Island, "Now I Do not know Who I shall send this By But hearing of a young man going to the Eastward tomorrow I thought I would write a line. . . ."[18] Many letters were lost, so Joseph frequently repeated the same news in a subsequent letter and enumerated the dates on which he had recently written.[19] Postal charges were a matter for bargaining when the regular mail service was used. When Joseph asked for shirts from home, he warned his wife against giving "more then what is Reaseneble" for sending them. Money by mail posed a greater

[12] See Joseph Hodgkins' letters from Prospect Hill of October 25, November 7, December 3, 1775, and March 17, 1776.
[13] Sarah to Joseph Hodgkins, January 8, 1776.
[14] Thomas Franklin Waters, *Ipswich in the Massachusetts Bay Colony*, II (Salem, 1917), p. 324.
[15] *Journals of Each Provincial Congress* (May 13, 1775), p. 223.
[16] Allen French, *The First Year of the American Revolution* (Boston, 1934), p. 171.
[17] Joseph to Sarah Hodgkins, Long Island, June 10, 1776.
[18] *Ibid.*, Rhode Island, August 18, 1778.
[19] *Ibid.*, New York, April 24, 1776.

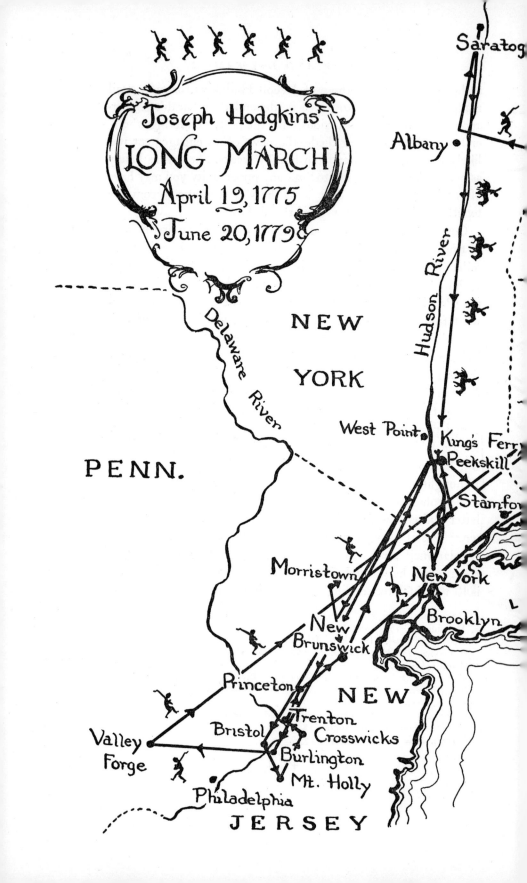

Joseph Hodgkins'
LONG MARCH
April 19, 1775
June 20, 1779

SARATOG

ALBANY •

PENN.

NEW
YORK

Delaware River

Hudson River

West Point •

King's Ferr
Peekskill

Stamfo

Morristown

New York

Brooklyn

New
Brunswick

Princeton

NEW

Bristol

Trenton
Crosswicks

Valley
Forge

Burlington
Mt. Holly

Philadelphia

JERSEY

Ipswich
Cape Ann
Salem
Boston
Worcester
Walpole
home to
Ipswich
June 1779
Providence
RHODE
Tiverton
IS.
New
London
Newport
New Haven
MASSACHUSETTS
NECTICUT
ISLAND

problem—the men had to wait for a safe agent to carry it, or to pay the regular post a shilling on the pound for safe delivery.[20] The post-rider gave his receipt to the soldier and took, in turn, a receipt from the wife at home.[21] The wives watched constantly for a familiar face from the camps, and scolded if a local man came without a letter from the absent soldier:

". . . Cousin Perkins told me he Saw you & you was well but he Says he dont think you will come home so he is but one of Jobs comforters I was very glad to hear you was well but my Dear I must tell you a verbal Letter is what I should hardly have expected from So near a freind at So greate a distance it Seems you are tired of writing I am sorry you count it troble to write to me Since that is all the way we can have of conversing together I hope you will not be tired of receiveing letters it is true you wrote a few days before but when you was nearer you wrote every day Sometimes I was never tired of reading your Letters. . . ."[22]

Sarah Hodgkins was always watching for a chance to send packages free, for Joseph was dependent on her for the clothes he wore in camp.[23] The Continental Army, in Hodgkins' day, was not supplied with uniforms; it was 1781 before Washington's followers looked like "something more than farmers called out of their fields . . ."[24] Even when a colony bought clothing in quantity for its troops, no uniformity was maintained. The Selectmen of Ipswich billed Massachusetts for breeches made by ladies in the town, describing them as "striped, bearskin, ratteen, kersey, swanskin, searge, Blue Broad Cloth, Redish, Leather, Fustian. . . ."[25] Mostly, though, the men depended on the needles of their wives when they wore their clothes to tatters. The Hodgkins correspondence is filled with orders for shirts, stockings, breeches, and the like. "I am afrade that I shall whare

[20] *Ibid.*, Valley Forge, April 17, 1778.

[21] *Ibid.*, Long Island, June 20, 1776.

[22] Sarah to Joseph Hodgkins, February 23, 1778.

[23] Finding a package carrier was difficult, and Sarah often had to wait weeks for such opportunities as that provided by "Mr. Norton in his horse Cart," setting out for Prospect Hill. Sarah to Joseph Hodgkins, December 10, 1775.

[24] John C. Miller, *The Triumph of Freedom* (Boston, 1948), pp. 485-486.

[25] Waters, *op.cit.*, pp. 327-328.

you out," wrote Joseph, "By sending you so much work But I cannot git any thing Don hare so I must Bage your Patience. . . ." When winter came on there were fresh calls for mittens, winter shirts, boot soles—without them, wrote Joseph from Valley Forge, "I must go naked. . . ."[26] Sarah not only kept her husband covered; she was busy sending him paper, candles, equipment for his shoemaking side line, even a pillow for his head.[27]

Money was always a problem. Hodgkins had owned some real estate at the beginning of the war but because of "his necessary expenditures in the army & to subsist his family," he "became empoverished & embarassed by debts, as is well known to the people in his County."[28] Officers were among those hardest hit by the rising prices and depreciated currency of the war years. Paid in continental currency of decreasing value, they had to feed and clothe themselves and maintain their families as well. Men in the ranks were paid less, but they got their keep in the army and their towns often gave relief to their dependents.[29]

Hodgkins, fresh from a village barter economy, did not question the value of his dollars during the first year of the war. He was impressed by their number and asked only that he be paid with reasonable regularity. When he set out from Boston for the defense of New York, he discovered that he had to pay for every meal he ate on the march, and New York shocked him with "Verry Expensive Living."[30] They did not live as they did during the last campaign, he said; "Everything is Excesive Dear 9 shilling now full money a gallon for Rum & Evrything in Preportion."[31] The reference to "full money" is one

[26] Joseph to Sarah Hodgkins, Cambridge, July 8, 1775; Saratoga, September 29, 1777; Valley Forge, January 11, 1778.
[27] *Ibid.*, Prospect Hill, September 19, 25, October 29, 1775; January 2, 8, 1776.
[28] The quoted passage is taken from a copy of Hodgkins' deposition to the Circuit Court of Common Pleas, Middle Circuit, Salem, in 1818. The claim by which an old soldier established his right to a pension is suspect, of course, but the evidence cited in the following pages might have been used to support his application.
[29] John Richard Alden, *The American Revolution, 1775-1783* (New York, 1954), p. 219.
[30] Joseph to Sarah Hodgkins, New York, April 24, 1776.
[31] *Ibid.*, New York, May 9, 1776.

of the few in his letters, in which he customarily complained of price rather than depreciated currency.

He continued to send money regularly to Sarah, in amounts ranging from thirty to a hundred dollars. Two letters suggest that he earmarked a third of his pay for her: this "will Be your third," he wrote of a remittance in 1776, and she replied, "I think if I can get my thirds these times I shall come well off."[32] In none of her letters did Sarah complain about money. She thanked Joseph dutifully for each remittance, and observed on one occasion, "I hope you have not Straitend youself for I was not in Present Want. . . ."[33] Living was harder, though, in 1777. "I wish I could make you . . . Returns," Hodgkins wrote from the Saratoga campaign, "But I cannot Except Love & good will. . . ." He worried about Sarah at home, for "we hear that things are Exceeding Dear & if you meet with any Difflty in gitting the Nesserys of Life Due send me word for I due not mean to Live in the Sarvis my self & have you suffer at home for I think I suffer Enough for us Both on that account. . . ."[34] A month later he advised his wife to get in a good stock of cider, "if you can git any Body to Trust you for it."[35]

The worst pinch came during the winter at Valley Forge. Hodgkins had marched directly from Albany to the winter quarters outside Philadelphia, without a chance to settle his wife for the winter: "I am Very uneasy in my mind about you for I am sarting that you have Long Looked for me home & I am affrade you will suffer for the Nesarys of Life for I am informed that things are as Dear with you as they are hear & if that is the Case I wish you would Let me know it & if you Due suffer I am Determined to come Home and suffer with you I Believe you think I Dont Care much about you as I Do not send any thing home But my Dear you are allways near my hart & in my thoughts But I am sorry to inform you that I am obliged to spend grate Part of my wages or Ells I should suffer. . . ."[36]

[32] *Ibid.*, Fort Constitution, New Jersey, October 1, 1776; Sarah to Joseph Hodgkins, October 19, 1776.

[33] *Ibid.*, July 3, 1776.

[34] Joseph to Sarah Hodgkins, Saratoga, September 28, 1777.

[35] *Ibid.*, Albany, October 27, 1777.

[36] *Ibid.*, Valley Forge, April 17, 1778.

The next fall he joked bitterly from Providence: "I Wish you would Contrive some way or other that I Can Live without work for you know that soldiers Cannot work Espechally Continatal Officers who have Lived so high as we have Don Espechally Last Winter."[37]

Hodgkins, a captain by this time, was also forwarding money for his men. While at Valley Forge he drew money for the soldiers on leave, but decided not to send it until he could bring it in person. His wife was charged with breaking this news to the absent men.[38] Sarah was kept busy with minor business errands. She sold her husband's gun in 1776, after instructions from him as to a fair price: "Brother Heard may have it for 12 Dollars and that is But 2 shillings more then I gave for it Last Whinter and guns have Ben A Rising Ever since."[39] In the same letter she was asked to collect an old debt; Hodgkins had heard that Captain Moses Harris was at home with money: "there is something Due to me from him which you may see By my Book & I would have you . . . Call on him to settle for it is likely that he is able now."[40]

Sarah was of course responsible for provisioning the family, and did man's work in pasturing the cows, buying corn, stocking meat at slaughter time, and laying in rum. In his first letter from camp, her husband inquired anxiously about the pasturing[41] and the next month authorized her to get corn from a neighbor who had some to spare.[42] In the fall it was beef: "I would have you tell Brother Chapman to let you have about two hundred wate of Beaf if he Dose not ask more than the market price."[43] Hodgkins was less specific in his instructions of succeeding years, and his wife grew accustomed to making her own decisions about supply and price.[44] Joseph commented with interest on growing conditions for her garden, and left the management of affairs

[37] *Ibid.*, Providence, October 13, 1778.
[38] *Ibid.*, Valley Forge, February 22, 1778.
[39] *Ibid.*, Long Island, July 17, 1776.
[40] *Ibid.*
[41] *Ibid.*, Cambridge, May 7, 1775.
[42] *Ibid.*, Cambridge, June 23, 1775.
[43] *Ibid.*, Prospect Hill, November 17, 1775.
[44] *Ibid.*, Long Island, June 11, 1776; Sarah to Joseph Hodgkins, May 23, 1776.

at home to her.[45] "I am Very glad to hear that you have so growing a season Likewise that you have Plenty of West India goods I wish we had we are obliged to give 4 shilling Lawfull Money a quart for Rum. . . ."[46]

Sarah shared these responsibilities with her own and Hodgkins' large families, but this fact did not lighten her burdens. Early in the war she thought of moving in with Joseph's father, but soon gave up the idea.[47] Thomas Hodgkins, the father, was eighty-three in 1775, and was to survive until his ninety-sixth year in 1788. "I am concerned about farther Hodgkins," his son wrote, "for I due not know how he will mak out to get wood But I hope Brother John will not see him suffer. . . ."[48] Since wood was scarce Sarah was advised to buy some while the carting lasted. Apparently Thomas Hodgkins was still active, for his son told his wife, "if you have not got our Pertatoes Dug Due get frather Hodgkins to Dig them if he can. . . ."[49] Sarah was expected to share Joseph's salary with her father-in-law—"you may Let Farther Hodgkins have some if he neads and you have it to spair."[50] She also had her own mother and father to think of. She wrote in 1778 that she was with her family; "mother was taken last thursday morning with a terible pain in her Side the pain has Left her but She Seems to be quit weak & poorly I hope She will get better in a few days."[51]

Another Thomas Hodgkins for whom Sarah shared responsibilities was the youngest member of Captain Wade's Company. Thomas, the fifth of his name, went to war at sixteen, apparently as the bound boy of Joseph.[52] Sarah made all his clothes,

---

[45] *Ibid.*, July 27, 1778; Joseph to Sarah Hodgkins, Long Island, August 11, 1776.

[46] *Ibid.*, New York, September 5, 1776.

[47] *Ibid.*, Cambridge, June 15, 1775.

[48] *Ibid.*, Prospect Hill, October 20, 1775.

[49] *Ibid.*, Prospect Hill, October 16, 1775.

[50] *Ibid.*, Fort Constitution, New Jersey, October 1, 1776. In a letter from Prospect Hill, of January 2, 1776, Joseph asked that his father be given money and that Sarah "Charge the same."

[51] Sarah to Joseph Hodgkins, July 27, 1778.

[52] Waters, *op.cit.*, II, p. 323. Thomas was the son of Hodgkins' older brother, John. Sarah to Joseph Hodgkins, May 23, 1776. Joseph to Sarah Hodgkins, Cambridge, June 21, 1775.

and Joseph collected his army pay.[53] Joseph reported at the end of 1775 that he believed Thomas would stay with him, "But he Expects Part of his weages & I am willing to give him what is hadsom and wright."[54] He wrote with pride of the boy's stamina—"there is not a man in our Company that could out Travel Thomas"—and of his behavior under fire: "He whas with us in all the Battle & Behaved like a good solder."[55] Thomas' departure from the company left the officers dismayed, for he had made himself indispensable: "I am dull to think of loosing Thomas who was not only my koock But my wash woman & nus in sickness in short he is good for all most Everything But he is Going home & I wish him well with all my hart."[56]

Sarah, busy with the young and old at home, found time to keep Joseph abreast of important news from Ipswich. The town lay on the sea, and disaster there found frequent place in her letters. ". . . a very melancoly Providence hapened hear last monday night Mr Ringe & Spiler as they were coming in from the eastward Struck upon the Bar & were both Lost. . . ."[57] Cousin Ephraim Perkins, homeward bound from the West Indies, had Cape Ann in sight when he was taken by the *Milford*, man of war, on which "he is with all his hands for ought we know." Captain Holmes, "comeing from the west Indeas founderd at Sea but the men are all got home."[58] Some of the news was social—a banquet, a husking bee, and most of all, religion: "this day was the turn for Mr Danas Lecture he thought the times calld for fasting and accordingly he tirnd it into a day of fasting & prayer and desird our parrish to join with them I have been to meeting all day & heard two as find Sermons as amost ever I heard Mr Frisby preachd in the forenoon and Mr

[53] Sarah to Joseph Hodgkins, October 1, 1775; October 19, 1776. Joseph to Sarah Hodgkins, September 20, November 19, 1775.

[54] *Ibid.*, Prospect Hill, December 31, 1775.

[55] *Ibid.*, New London, Connecticut, April 10, 1776; Fort Constitution, New Jersey, September 30, 1776.

[56] *Ibid.*, Valley Forge, January 11, 1778.

[57] Sarah to Joseph Hodgkins, January 8, 1776.

[58] *Ibid.*, September 16, 1776. Apparently Cousin Ephraim escaped or was exchanged, for two years later Sarah reported his death on another passage from the West Indies. *Ibid.*, February 23, 1778.

Dana in the afternoon next wensday is our ordanation it is apointed a day of fasting I should be very glad if you could be at home. . . ."[59]

Joseph reported encounters with those "Cursed Creators Called Torys." One of them, he said, "was Tried on winsday Condemned on thusday and Executed on friday & I wish Twenty more whare sarved the same. . . ."[60] The two shared news from the public prints, and wrote anxiously of the course of the war.[61]

One constant fear darkened every letter of the exchange. In the first line of his first note home from Cambridge, Joseph Hodgkins wrote, "I am in good health at Presant for whitch I Desire to be thankful."[62] Disease rather than the enemy was their immediate fear when letters were delayed; and death came suddenly by night. To scores of his letters Joseph added postscripts, just before he handed them to the post: "I wrot the above letter Last night I would inform you that I am well this morning."[63] God's aid was sought daily, to "Continnue halth whare it is injoyed and Restore it to those that whant it."[64] Men in the camps depended on Providence for escape, for their hospitals were death traps and sanitary measures primitive beyond belief. They prayed that "god will apear for us and Remove the Pestelance and the swords from us and give us harts & occation to Rejoyce in his salvation."[65]

The camps and towns were first scourged by a "distemper" that appeared among the soldiers in the late summer of 1775. A severe dysentery, it was carried home by men on leave, and was prevalent until the cold weather came on.[66] Sarah Hodgkins wrote on October 1 that "it is a good deal sickly both with grone folk and Children there is three funerals to night old Mr Hovey & William Apletons youngest child & one of Mr Noyes

[59] Joseph to Sarah Hodgkins, Prospect Hill, October 2, 1775; February 5, 1776; Providence, October 13, 1778. Sarah to Joseph Hodgkins, February 1, 1776.
[60] Joseph to Sarah Hodgkins, Long Island, July 17, 1776; Buckingham, Pennsylvania, December 20, 1776.
[61] *Ibid.*, New London, April 10, 1776.
[62] *Ibid.*, Cambridge, May 7, 1775.
[63] *Ibid.*, Prospect Hill, March 20, 1776.
[64] *Ibid.*, Prospect Hill, July 8, 1775.
[65] *Ibid.*, Prospect Hill, January 8, 1776.
[66] Allen French, *op.cit.*, pp. 464-465.

Children the children are crying So I must Leave of for the present. . . ." Mr. Dodge would probably "never go abroad again & old Mr Graves is very Sick."[67] Joseph had heard that "it is very sickly at town and a Dieing Time," and said, of the death of both Graves and Dodge, "a loud call to us all to Be also Ready for a thousand unseen Dangers awate us. . . ."[68]

Hodgkins' health record through the war included a formidable variety of ills. In the first year it was bad colds, stomach aches[69] and rheumatism;[70] in the next it was boils and the "humers" that produced them.[71] He had the "camp fever" at Saratoga, and in 1779 went "laim in one of my Lags By Reason of Braking the skin a little and gitting cols in it. . . ."[72] He was constantly in the presence of death: "I am sorry that I have the occation to inform you that it is a good Deal sickly among us we Bured Willeby Nason last thusday John Sweet is Very sick in Camp and Josiah Persone of Cape ann in our Company is Just moved to the ospittle Capt Parker is a little Bitter Mr Harden is sick in Camp John Holladay Died last thusday night there whas five Buried that Day We Bured Mr Nason from the ospittle Capt. Willm Wade has Lost one man he was Burred a friday I must Conclude at Presant by subscribing myself your Loving Husband till Death.[73]

No disease ran a predictable course. Cousin Abraham Hodgkins, a sergeant in the company, was down with the "Flux" in July 1776, but after three bad weeks was better by mid-August. On August 25, however, he was reported dead, a fact "Lemented Both by officers and men I hope it will be santified to us all for our good." Joseph wrote the news to Abraham's father, and asked his wife to carry the death message to the family.[74] A few days later William Goodhue died from the same malady, and

---

[67] Sarah to Joseph Hodgkins, October 1, 1775.
[68] Joseph to Sarah Hodgkins, Prospect Hill, October 6, 1775.
[69] *Ibid.*, Cambridge, July 3, 5, 1775.
[70] *Ibid.*, Prospect Hill, September 25, 1775.
[71] *Ibid.*, Long Island, May 22, 1776; Sarah to Joseph Hodgkins, May 23, 1776.
[72] Joseph to Sarah Hodgkins, Albany, October 27, 1777; Providence, January 1, 1779.
[73] *Ibid.*, Prospect Hill, January 7, 1776.
[74] *Ibid.*, Long Island, July 22, August 11, August 25, 1776.

again Sarah had to notify his people: "Due let his farther know it as soon as you can he whas Very much like Sargt Hodgkins only had more feavor two of the strongest men in our Company Cut of sudden heavy News to there friends. . . ."[75]

Smallpox was the major pestilence. Hodgkins frequently voiced his fear of the disease and at Valley Forge he used his concern as an excuse to apply for leave so that he could go home to New England to be inoculated against it.[76] Prevention, almost as dangerous as the disease, involved severe illness and a long convalescence.[77] Joseph's scheme for leave backfired; he was given the protection in camp and spent the late winter and early spring recovering from his inoculation. Sarah, meanwhile, suffered several weeks of anxiety; she learned from the post in February that "you was anoculated for the small pox a day a two before he came away you wrote me word you Should come home as soon as you could but did not set any time . . . I concluded you would come as Soon as you got well if you lived to get well & I never heard a word from you Since till about ten days ago which you must think gave me great uneasyness fearing how it was with you." A neighbor got word in mid-April that the whole company had survived inoculation, and Joseph wrote on April 17 that he was "Prety well."[78]

The susceptibility of children to the infections that plagued the towns was the most frightening problem with which parents had to live. Hodgkins rarely wrote a letter in which he did not express concern for Joanna, Joseph, and Sally, and when one of them was ailing he usually feared for the worst. "I want to . . . know how Salle Dose I feel uneasy about her," he would write; and he was delighted when Sarah could report: "Salla Seems to be got fine and well for which mercy I desire to be thankful God has been pleased to deal more favorablely with us in respect to her than he has with many others in this town who

[75] *Ibid.*, Long Island, September 5, 1776.
[76] *Ibid.*, Prospect Hill, March 18, 1776; Worcester, Massachusetts, undated in July 1777; Valley Forge, January 5, 1778.
[77] Miller, *op.cit.*, p. 488.
[78] Sarah to Joseph Hodgkins, April 26, 1778; Joseph to Sarah Hodgkins, Valley Forge, April 17, 1778.

have had their Children taken from them by Death."[79] Another time it would be Joanna—"Due send me word how Joanna Dos as soon as you can."[80] When Sally scraped her arm, Joseph asked that Sarah tell her "Dady is Verry Sorry for it and whants to see her. . . ."[81]

The daily activities of the children who were well went unreported in the exchange. Sarah, in a postscript, would add that "Joanna sends her duty to you"; but there was no account of two-year old Sally's first words, nor of the precocity that put her "to scool" before she was three.[82] Nor did Hodgkins ask after the details of their days, though he closed his letters repeatedly with the sentence, "Tell Joanna and Salle to Be good gals and that Dady whants to see them."[83] His inquiries after Joseph were a little more intimate—he referred to him as "my little son" and expressed his pleasure that "Joseph is a good boy I whant to see the Littel Roog. . ."[84]

Joseph fell sick in early July 1776. His father, in a letter of July 17, referred casually to news that "Jose . . . Seems to be Something unwell now but I hope he will be better in a day or two. . . ."[85] A month passed before he learned that the matter was serious. On August 8, he wrote:

"My Dear I Received yours by the Post Last night in witch you informed me that my Little son whas Verry Low and not Like to Live I am afrad that he is not Living now But I must hope that it will Pleas god to spair his life But that we may Be Prepaired for all Events I whas afrad I should hear some Bad News from home But I hop god will Do Better for us then our fears he is able to Raise him Even from the gates of the grave

[79] Ibid., Prospect Hill, September 8, 19, 27, 29, 1775; Sarah to Joseph Hodgkins, October 1, 1775.
[80] Joseph to Sarah Hodgkins, Prospect Hill, November 17, 1775.
[81] Sarah's report of minor illnesses have a familiar sound to parents of several children—it was a rare thing when only one child was down at a time. "I would inform you that Joanna is a good deal better Salla was taken not well that day after you went away and has been very poorly ever Since but I hope she will be better in a few days Jose Seems to be got pretty well again. . . ." Joseph to Sarah Hodgkins, Long Island, June 20, 1776; Sarah to Joseph Hodgkins, November 19, 1775; June 2, 1776.
[82] Ibid., May 23, July 3, 1776.
[83] Joseph to Sarah Hodgkins, Peekskill, December 3, 1776.
[84] Ibid., Long Island, May 22; Cambridge, June 15, 1775.
[85] Ibid., Long Island, July 17, 1776; Sarah to Joseph Hodgkins, July 3, 1776.

But I am sinseble that god will Due what is write and Just and I hope god will seport you & I under all our Trobles and Carry us through all the Difiltes we have to meat with in this world and if we should not Live to see one another again in this world may we Be Prepaired to meat in a Better whare there will Be no more Sorrow nor morning the Loss of friends it is with a heavy hart that I now write to you But it is a grate Comfort to me to hear that you and the Rest of our Children are well what would I give to see you I hope god will Presarve us and give us harts and occasion to Prase his name together ...."[86]

By this time the child was dead, but nearly a month passed before Joseph received further word from home. He wrote repeatedly, on August 11, August 12, and August 25, his mood alternating between hope and despair. "My Dear I cant healp hoping But I Dont know whare I have any Room for my hope...."[87] He tried to put his son out of his mind: "being at Leashur this afternoon I thought I would write a line or two more to Let you know that I am well I would also inform you a little about Publick afairs...."[88] "... though I never Expect to hear that my little Son is alive But I want to hear Verry much yet I am afrade But I hope god will Prepair me for all that I am to met with in this world and santify his Varrious Dealing with us for our good...."[89] Through the same days, Hodgkins survived the most dangerous military actions of his career. He barely escaped capture with a foraging party on the eve of the Long Island engagement; he was with the forward unit at Flatbush Pass when Howe executed his brilliant flanking movement at Washington's expense; and he left his gear behind when the army escaped Long Island by night. He got the news of his son's death on September 1, just after the battle:

"the goodness of God ... has Ben grate towards me I wish I whas more sensible of it and had a harte to Live Answreble for all gods Mercys I Received your Letter ... By which I whas informed of the Death of my Little Son it is heavy News to me But it is god that has Dun it therefore what can I say I hope it

[86] Joseph to Sarah Hodgkins, Long Island, August 8, 1776.
[87] Ibid., Long Island, August 11, 1776.
[88] Ibid., Long Island, August 12, 1776.
[89] Ibid., Long Island, August 25, 1776.

will Pleas god to santifie all these outward aflictions to us for our Best good we are all in a Troubblesom world and we in a pertickler manner which are Exspossed not only to these axidents which are Common to all men But to Fire & sword and many hardships which Before now I whas a stranger to and which are too many to Be Numbered. . . ."[90] He closed his letter with "Love to my two children . . . tell them to Be good galls and that Dady whants to see them."[91]

Hodgkins had buried four children and a wife already, and he was to outlive his second wife and six more children. His son Joseph's place was taken by a new daughter the next year.

Hodgkins resumed a more normal relationship with his family through the spring of 1777, being posted for several months as a recruiting officer with headquarters near home. When he marched off to stop Burgoyne in July 1777 he left his wife carrying their third child, the Martha he was not to see until she was seven months old. The child was born in early November 1777 while her father was on his way from the victory at Saratoga to winter quarters at Valley Forge. He got news of her birth on New Year's day 1778 and rejoiced that Sarah had "Been cumfortebley Carred through all the Defelties that you have Ben Called too in my absents . . . you say you have Named your Child Martha & you Did not know weather I should like the name But I have nothing to say if it suts you. . . ." The baby had a distressing cough, but "I hope god will apear for it & Rebuk its Disorder & Restore it to health again. . . ."[92]

No subsequent calamity nor any sign of grace changed the confidence with which the family submitted to "the same god who is Every whare Prisant and at all Times the same We have had Experiences of gods goodness to us. . . ."[93] Sarah Hodgkins resisted each of Joseph's reenlistments; she wanted her husband at home. She was "contented to Live a widow for the present but I hope I shant always live so. . . ." She protested when Joseph engaged for his first full year in the fall of 1775. Failing in her plea for his permanent return, she hoped that he would at least

[90] *Ibid.*, New York, September 5, 1776.
[91] *Ibid.*
[92] *Ibid.*, Valley Forge, January 5, 1778. Sarah did not report her "Babe . . . well of her coff" until February 28, 1778.
[93] *Ibid.*, Fort Constitution, New Jersey, September 30, 1776.

get leave: "I look for you almost every day but I dont alow my-self to depend on any thing for I find there is nothing to be de-pended upon but troble & disapointments. . . ."[94] During the fol-lowing summer she began to urge that the Long Island campaign be his last, a notion that Joseph found tempting during the hot days on the island: "I think so much of this Presant Campean that I have not spent any time Thinking about another But I will Ventur to say if I Live to see this out I think I shall Be intierly willing to Rest a spell at Least. . . ."[95] In the Fall, Sarah put the matter more strongly: "I dont know what you think about Stay-ing again but I think it cant be inconsistant with your duty to come home to your family it will troble me very much if you Should ingage again I dont know but you may think I am too free in expressing my mind & that it would have been time enough when I was asked but I was afraid I Should not have that oppertunity So I hope you will excuse my freedom."[96]

Joseph quickly forgave her forwardness: "My Dear you are Verry Excusable for I am Senseable that my Being Absent must of nesesity Create a great Deal of Troble for you. . . ." He evaded a direct promise to come home, though; "as to ingaging again I have no thoughts of ingaging in the Capacity that I now Sistane and as for anything Better I shall not Seek after it neither Due I Desire it. . . ." There were many officers fonder of the serv-ice than he, and "Perhap more Caperble of Sarving the Cause. . . ."[97] When the year's end came, however, Joseph changed his mind. He accepted a captaincy in Colonel Timothy Bigelow's Massachusetts battalion, and was assigned to six months of re-cruiting duty near his home. It was July before he was march-ing again, so he may have felt that he had the best of both the civil and military worlds.[98] This enlistment, dated from the end of a month's leave in the winter of 1777, was for three years or

[94] Sarah to Joseph Hodgkins, November 19, December 10, 1775; July 3, 1776.

[95] Joseph to Sarah Hodgkins, Long Island, July 17, 1776.

[96] Sarah to Joseph Hodgkins, October 19, 1776.

[97] Joseph to Sarah Hodgkins, Phillips Manor, New York, November 15, 1776.

[98] *Ibid.*, Worcester, Massachusetts, undated in July, 1777. See also a sur-viving muster roll, dated September 1, 1777, for Hodgkins' company, Bigelow's battalion, Brigadier John B. Glover's brigade, taken at Van Schaicks Island, New York.

the duration, and carried Joseph to Valley Forge in the winter of 1777-1778, an experience that very nearly cured him of further military ambitions. He wrote angrily that spring of plans for reorganization of the army that threatened to interfere with his free choice in the matter: "Leaving the sarvice Dos not troble me for it will Be my Choice to Leave it But to Be sent home without any Reason why is not agreable to me and if it should Be the Case I Believe I shall not troble the army much more But when I think how I have spent three years in the war have Ben Exposed to Every hardship Venterd my Life & Limbs Broke my Constitution wore out all my Clothes & . . . got knothing for it & now not to be thanked . . . seams two much for any man to Bare. . . ."[99]

Sarah, by this time, had almost given up hope of having her husband at his fireside: "I am very low in Spirits allmost despare of your coming home when I began I thoght I would write but a few lines & begun on a Small piece of paper but it is my old friend & I dont know how to leave off & Some is wrong end upwards & Some wright if it was not that I have Some hope of your coming home . . . I should write a vollum I cant express what I feal but I forbear disapointments are alotted for me. . . ."[100] It was in this letter that Sarah reminded her husband in a postscript of the child he had not yet seen—"I have got a Sweet Babe almost Six mounths old but have got no father for it."

Two months' leave after the long winter restored Joseph's patriotic spirit, and by midsummer he was off to rejoin his unit just after the engagement at Monmouth Courthouse, New Jersey. By this time he was thinking forward to the end of the war, and was reluctant to sacrifice his growing hope of half pay or a pension in the years to come.[101] The fall campaign in 1778 was not hard; he was at Providence most of the time, and in closer touch with affairs at home. Sarah still hoped and Joseph argued: "you say in your Letter that you are afraid that I shall stay in the Cause of Liberty till I . . . mak my self a slave att my Day I have two much Reason to fear that will Be the Case But if it should I have no body to Blame but the Continent in general

[99] *Ibid.*, Valley Forge, April 17, 1778.
[100] Sarah to Joseph Hodgkins, April 26, 1778.
[101] Joseph to Sarah Hodgkins, Valley Forge, February 22, 1778.

Who will Ever Be guilty of Ruening thousands unless they Due something more for them then what they . . . have Don yet and now as I have spent so much time in the sarvice & Now to ask a Discharge when to apperence the war is most to an end would Debar me from Expecting any further Compensation . . . But I hope to see you in a short time and then we Consider further of these Matters. . . ."[102]

Sarah won her battle in these further conversations, for, after the Rhode Island campaign, Joseph went no more to the wars. He resigned his commission in June 1779 after service for more than four years.[103] He had earned his retirement, and Sarah had earned twice over his pledge of love and affectionate companionship "till Death." To every plea for his return, she had added two prayers for his safety, and in not a single one of her surviving letters did she complain of the heavy load she carried alone. When he survived death and disaster, she admired his bravery and sympathized with his hardships: "I was grately rejoiced to hear that you was So well . . . I think as your day is So you Strength Seems to be . . . it greives me to think what you have to undergo but I hope it will be for our good . . . I Should be glad if you could have more of the Comfortable nesecaries of Life than you have but I hope you will be carried through all you are to meet with in the way of your duty & in Gods good time be returned home in Safty."[104]

Joseph Hodgkins never turned a moment from what he conceived to be the "way" of his duty; he trusted God, and gave his health and substance to "this glories Cause." When he heard of heroism in distant places, he hoped that it would animate him "to act in like manner."[105] When sudden marching orders extended his absence from home to nearly a year, he said "Soldiers must not Complain."[106] The aging shoemaker of Ipswich was a sturdy patriot.

[102] *Ibid.*, Providence, October 13, 1778.
[103] Hodgkins' name appears for the last time on the payroll of Bigelow's regiment in an entry of June 20, 1779.
[104] Sarah to Joseph Hodgkins, October 19, 1776.
[105] Joseph to Sarah Hodgkins, Long Island, July 22, 1776.
[106] *Ibid.*, Albany, October 27, 1777.

CHAPTER IV

Retreat

NATHANIEL WADE AND JOSEPH HODGKINS enjoyed their passage from Boston toward the New York campaigns. Marching, said Hodgkins, "Dos not worry me so much as I Expected. . . ."[1] The movement resembled a grand parade, as New Englanders turned out to welcome the triumphant army; and the wide-eyed Ipswich men found much to praise in the new country they were seeing for the first time.[2] Wade's company, still organized with Little's regiment in Greene's brigade, got its orders on March 29, and set out from Cambridge on April 1, 1776. The captain, made answerable by general orders for any damage done by his men as they broke camp, had to control the company alone, for Hodgkins did not get back from leave until the unit was departing.[3]

At the company level men marched without knowledge of their destination—they did not learn until they reached Providence that New York, rather than Newport or some other New England town, would be the scene of their next camp. The lieutenant was hard put to find time for writing on the march; he broke off his note from Walpole "to get a Mouthfull of Vittles" and posted his letter as the afternoon march began.[4] At Providence, Little's regiment was given the honor of escorting Washington into the town. The colonel prohibited the appearance of any man who did not have some semblance of a uniform,[5] and

[1] Joseph to Sarah Hodgkins, Providence, April 4, 1776.

[2] *Ibid.*, Providence, April 4; New London, April 10; New York, April 24, 1776. Nathaniel Wade to Mrs. Ruth Wade, New London, April 10, 1776.

[3] Peter Force, ed., *American Archives*, Series 4, V, p. 757.

[4] Joseph to Sarah Hodgkins, Walpole, April 2, 1776.

[5] Washington had been struggling with little success since January to clothe his army in a brown fabric provided more cheaply than other cloth available, as "uniformity and decency in dress are essentially necessary in the appearance and regularity of an army. . . ." Apparently the New Englanders who joined the new army of 1776 were equipped with a brown outfit for parade occasions, but the rigors of the campaigns soon returned them to their work-

urged that "none . . . turn out except those washed, both face and hands clean, their beards shaved, their hair combed & powdered, & their arms cleaned. The General . . . wishes to pay the honours to the Commander in Chief in as decent & respectable a manner as possible."[6] Hodgkins reported that the reception was "Done with a great Deal of Pleasuer and Honnor to Both general & officers."[7]

Marching on at the rate of about twenty miles a day, the brigade arrived at New London on April 9. There it took ship on April 14, and sailed down Long Island Sound to New York. The passage took a week, but was found "very Pleasant." The lieutenant reported that "we saw several Pleasant Towns Newhaven in Pertulare. . . ." Nothing, though, prepared him for New York —"I think this City York Exceeds all Plases that Ever I saw. . . ." In this letter he added to his customary invocation of God's blessing, a plea that he be saved from "Every Evil Especialy from sin. . . ."[8] But the sights of the town were not adequate reward for expensive living there, and the unfriendly population shocked the New England patriots. Wade and his men were glad to move to permanent camp on Long Island on May 2, even though Long Islanders were, if anything, less friendly to the troops than were the New Yorkers—"it is sayd that seven eights of the People are Torrys & I fear that one half in York are not much Better . . . our People are not alowed to tread on the ground scarcely. . . ."[9] It seems that the American army was not a good neighbor, nor did a local citizen have to be a Tory to resent its depredations. General Greene pleaded repeatedly with his men to "behave themselves towards the inhabitants with that decency & respect that becomes the character of troops fighting

ing clothes. Henry P. Johnston, *The Campaign of 1776 Around New York and Brooklyn* (Vol. III, *Memoirs of the Long Island Historical Society*, Brooklyn, 1878), pp. 122-123.

[6] Moses Little's Orderly Book, quoted in *ibid.*, p. 62. The Johnston account of the battles around New York is not only the standard account of the campaign; the documents printed in Part II of the work have been source materials for most recent accounts of the battles. In particular, the orderly books of Col. Moses Little are reproduced among the documents, giving a running account of orders through the summer of 1776.

[7] Joseph to Sarah Hodgkins, Providence, April 4, 1776.

[8] *Ibid.*, New York, April 24, 1776.

[9] *Ibid.*, Long Island, May 22, 1776.

for the preservation of the rights & liberties of America."[10] Thus when forbidden by property owners to take oysters from the Cove, or even to catch eels, Hodgkins admitted that there might be some justice in local complaints: "it is Enough to mak anybodys Blood Boyl . . . to think what Destruction was made . . . By our army. . . ."[11]

Active Tories, however, were a constant danger to the camp. When the abortive "Hickey" conspiracy was discovered, Hodgkins expressed great satisfaction with the trial of a conspirator on one day, his sentencing on the next, and his execution on the third—"I wish Twenty more whare sarved the same."[12] Lieutenant Colonel William Henshaw, second in command of Little's regiment, gave the camp version of the incident in a letter to his wife on June 22: "My Dear - Last evening a Conspiracy of the Tories was discovered; their plan was to murder Gen'l Washington, seize on the Persons of the other General officers, & blow up our Magazines, at the Instant of Time the King's Troops should Land. A number of our Officers rode last night to Flatbush on this Island, & seiz'd the Mayor of the City [New York], who is now in safe Custody & suppos'd to be in the Conspiracy—several others are also taken & the Names of others we have. . . ."[13] The execution Hodgkins witnessed was that of Thomas Hickey, a member of Washington's personal guard, who was hanged before the assembled regiments on June 28.[14]

Captain Wade's company built its permanent camp in Brooklyn, near the center of the earthworks being constructed from Wallabout Bay to Gowanus Creek. The line faced south across Brooklyn Heights, and had the East River and the ferry to New York about a mile and a quarter to its rear. The generals had ample time to prepare their ground, for it was July before the British began to arrive at Staten Island in full force, and

[10] Little Orderly Book, Johnston, *op.cit.*, Part II, p. 7. This order continued: "The General would have the troops consider that we came here to protect the inhabitants & their property from the enemy, but if instead of support & protection, they meet with nothing but insult & outrage, we shall be considered as banditti & treated as oppressors & enemies."
[11] Joseph to Sarah Hodgkins, Long Island, May 22, 1776.
[12] *Ibid.*, Long Island, July 17, 1776.
[13] William Henshaw to his wife, Johnston, *op.cit.*, Part II, pp. 44-45.
[14] *Ibid.*, pp. 129-130.

late August before they were ready for attack. New York was obviously the key to full-scale invasion of the American states, and the town of Brooklyn commanded the city. Washington fortified both sides of the East River, from the Battery to Hell Gate, and put guns on Governor's Island, Red Hook, and Paulus Hook. Positions were also erected on the northern spine of Manhattan Island, near Kingsbridge—Fort Washington went up on the York side, and Fort Constitution opposite on the Jersey shore. Hulks were sunk in the East and Hudson Rivers to block passage by the British men of war. The attack, when it came, would thus be turned to Long Island, where the major defenses were being raised at Brooklyn. The wisdom of trying to hold an island in the face of the British navy was dubious; but the decision to make a stand there was strategy no worse than other American blunders in this campaign.

Little's regiment was assigned to hold the center of the main line at Brooklyn. Five of his companies manned Fort Greene, and three were assigned alarm posts in the oblong redoubt between Fort Greene and Fort Putnam, on the left. Company camps were pitched to the rear of these action posts.[15] Fatigue, guard, drill, and discipline posed problems similar to those that company officers had met outside Boston, for the camp was not under pressure of the enemy until August. Wade and Hodgkins showed themselves veterans by the dispatch with which they violated orders against officers sleeping out of camp, and took a room in a farmhouse until their bell-shaped tents were floored with wood. Their memory of Boston was green, the weather was "Cool & the Tents . . . verry Bad. . . ."[16]

The officers slipped comfortably into the camp routine. On May 11 both Hodgkins and Wade were assigned to a regimental court martial,[17] and on May 15 Captain Wade drew pay for his men, claiming £147 15s 6p of the £1998 received by Colonel Little for the Twelfth Regiment of Foot.[18] Colonel Little was particularly insistent on the attention of "officers &

[15] Little Orderly Book, June 1, 1776, *ibid.*, Part II, pp. 5-6.
[16] Little Orderly Book, May 4, 1776, *ibid.*, Part II, p. 6; Joseph to Sarah Hodgkins, Long Island, May 9, 1776.
[17] Little Orderly Book, May 11, 1776, Johnston, *op.cit.*, Part II, p. 9.
[18] Manuscript pay record, Document 4969, New York Public Library.

men to the duties of religious worship," for "we are all engaged in the cause of God & our country," and it was the duty of all "in a social way to wait upon God in the way of his appointment. . . ." When the Continental Congress appointed a day of fasting and prayer, all but guard duties were suspended, and the men ordered to attend to their prayers in "a devout and cleanly manner."[19]

Captain Wade had the usual difficulties in persuading his men to present a military appearance. Privates were asked not to go on picket guard without shoes,[20] and the theft of watermelons brought threat of severe punishment. General Greene warned that "A few unprincipled rascals may ruin the reputation of a whole corps of virtuous men. The General desires the virtuous to complain of every offender that may be detected in invading peoples property in an unlawful manner, whatever his station or from whatever part of the country he may come."[21] Later, when Greene was removed from camp by malaria, General Sullivan after him found the same problems: "It is a very scandalous practice unbecoming soldiers whose duty it is to defend the liberty and property of the Inhabitants of the country to make free with and rob them of that property; it is therefore ordered that no person belonging to this army do presume on any pretense whatever to take or make use of any Corn, Poultry, or Provision, or anything else without the consent of the owners nor without paying the common price for them. . . ."[22]

The seniority of the captains in Colonel Little's regiment was undetermined when the companies came to Long Island, and twice the colonel ordered courts to establish the rank of the several captains in his command. If the matter was resolved before the battle, the order has been lost, but at the end of the campaign, Wade was one of the two men recommended for majorities.[23] The officers were under constant pressure to keep

[19] Little Orderly Book, May 15, 16, 1776, Johnston, *op.cit.*, Part II, pp. 10-11.

[20] *Ibid.*, p. 11.

[21] *Ibid.*, July 28, 1776, p. 24.

[22] Little Orderly Book, August 25, 1776, Johnston, *op.cit.*, Part II, p. 30.

[23] Little Orderly Book, June 17, 20, 1776, *ibid.*, pp. 17-18. See also letter of Timothy Danielson to Major-General Heath, dated at Peekskill, December 5, 1776, in Force, *American Archives*, Series 4, III, p. 1084.

their men healthy, as well as law-abiding; General Greene kept urging that the success of the campaign depended on the health of the troops: "The good officer discharges his duty not only in one but in every respect. It is a mistaken notion that the minutiae of military matters is only an employment of little minds. Such an officer betrays a want of understanding and showeth a person ignorant of the necessary dependence and connection of one thing upon another. What signifies knowledge without power to execute? He who studies the Branches of military knowledge relating to Dispositions, & neglects to preserve the health of his troops will find himself in that disagreeable situation."[24]

The "sickly season" was coming on, with August heat, and the officers had a clear memory of the toll taken by disease at Boston. Even with all precautions, Wade and Hodgkins had more than one death letter to write to Ipswich parents of men taken by the flux and fevers.[25]

Digging up New York and Brooklyn from the northern tip of Manhattan to Brooklyn Heights with side excursions to the Jersey shore was a labor of Hercules. Washington's plans for defense of the area were ambitious in the extreme, and his 10,000 Continentals were called on for every talent at their command. Working parties were formidable, numbering upwards from 900 men on a given day[26] and specialized skills were constantly in demand. Grindstone operators were called on May 10 to sharpen the hundreds of spears that pointed outward from the works,[27] and on July 19 a half pint of rum per day was offered to men who could lay turf speedily on the slopes of the raw earthworks.[28] Wells had to be dug in the main forts in case of siege,[29] and the works had to be heightened and ditched.[30] Orders repeatedly took notice of the fact that the duties were "exceedingly heavy on the men," and General Sullivan, on August 21, apologized for the labors he demanded: "Nothing can be more disagreeable to the Genl. than to call upon the men to

[24] Little Orderly Book, July 28, 1776, Johnston, *op.cit.*, Part II, p. 24.
[25] Joseph to Sarah Hodgkins, Long Island, August 25, September 5, 1776.
[26] Little Orderly Book, May 25, 1776, Johnston, *op.cit.*, Part II, p. 12.
[27] *Ibid.*, May 10, 1776, p. 9.   [28] *Ibid.*, July 19, 1776, p. 23.
[29] *Ibid.*, June 21, 1776, p. 18.   [30] *Ibid.*, July 19, 1776, p. 23.

be so constantly on fatigue, but their own salvation, and the safety of the country requires it. He hopes that in 2 or 3 days more the encampment will be so secure that he can release the men from fatigue and give them an opportunity to rest from their labors."[31]

Rest was not to be given, however, for within a week the island was abandoned, and the army faced the enemy, as Hodgkins ruefully observed, without "one shovell full of Durte to Cover us. . . ."[32] The first British sails had appeared on June 25, when General Howe came down from Halifax to wait the arrival of the largest expeditionary force that had ever embarked from the British Isles. Sails crowded the harbor in succeeding weeks, until there camped on Staten Island a 32,000-man army. Hessians freshly hired, the defeated troops of Clinton and Cornwallis, from Charleston, the evacuees from Boston, newly recruited men from England—it was an army of "trained, disciplined, professional soldiers, completely armed, fully equipped, abundantly supplied." Ten ships of the line, twenty frigates, and hundreds of transports added 1,200 guns to the British force.[33] Colonel Moses Little made regular reports to his son on the gathering forces. On July 6 he reported that 160 ships and transports had brought in 10,000 redcoats: "I am of opinion our hands will be full—hope we shall do well." On July 31, reporting more British arrivals, he declared that "This island is a place of great importance, & if possible must be defended. We are five small reg'ts, are scattered, & have 10 forts to defend. . . . I am of the opinion my reg't will stand fast in the cause of the United States." On August 9 the colonel noted that General Greene thought the enemy 20,000 strong, but he estimated 16,000. He cleared up his debt to the quartermaster general, "which will square all accounts." On August 22 he wrote: "I have thought fit to send you my will—you will take all charge necessary. . . ."[34]

Hodgkins was not afraid. He estimated that 25,000 redcoats

[31] *Ibid.*, August 21, 1776, p. 27.
[32] Joseph to Sarah Hodgkins, New York, September 5, 1776.
[33] Christopher Ward, *The War of the Revolution*, I, (John Richard Alden, ed., New York, 1952), p. 200.
[34] Colonel Little to his son, Johnston, *op.cit.*, Part II, pp. 42-43.

were before him, but "I hope with the Blesing of god we shall
Be able to keep our ground and let them know that yankeys
can fite." His optimism rested, in part, on a gross exaggeration
of American strength: "our numbers fair Exceed theirs for we
have 42000 men now and thay are Coming in Every Day."[35]
The lieutenant was wrong, for Washington had come to New
York with nearly 10,000 American regulars, and with militia
reinforcements his paper force was at 28,500. Fewer than 20,000
were actually available, on the lines, and of these General
Greene had only 4,000 on Long Island.[36] Three times as many
were posted around Manhattan, on the Jersey Shore, and on
the line of possible retreat at Kingsbridge.

The men on Long Island were on constant alert. Long before
the British arrived, Greene was exerting constant pressure to
keep his men in a state of battle readiness, for "bad habits once
contracted are difficult to get over, & doing duty in a slovenly
manner, is both disgraceful & dangerous to officers & men."[37]
Each man's twenty rounds, issued when the troops reached the
Island, were constantly checked by the company officers.[38] From
mid-June, the lines were manned each day from morning light
to sunrise, and the troops were exercised at parapet firing.[39] On
July 1 the company commanders drew a deadline to mark the
points, eighty yards from the ramparts, at which an attacking
enemy would meet the first volley from the troops inside.[40]

Lieutenant Hodgkins felt that the Americans were "Prety
well fortyfyed," and promised that the British would "meat with
a Wharm Reception for our men are in good Spirits and seem
to be impatient & sick a waiting for them. . . ."[41] On July 9 the
army was assembled at sunset parade to hear the lately adopted
Declaration of Independence read, an "incitement," as General
Greene put it, "to every officer & soldier to act with courage &
fidelity. . . ."[42] The camp was cheered by the news on July 21 of

[35] Joseph to Sarah Hodgkins, Long Island, July 17, 1776.
[36] Ward, *op.cit.*, I, pp. 207-208.
[37] Little Orderly Book, May 29, 1776, Johnston, *op.cit.*, Part II, p. 14.
[38] *Ibid.*, May 10, 1776, p. 8.
[39] *Ibid.*, June 17, 1776, p. 17.
[40] *Ibid.*, July 1, 1776, p. 19.
[41] Joseph to Sarah Hodgkins, Long Island, June 20, 1776.
[42] Little Orderly Book, July 9, 21, 1776, Johnston, *op.cit.*, Part II, p. 21.

the successful defense of Charleston, South Carolina—"I hope this will anemate me if Called to it to act in like manner," wrote Hodgkins.[43] Captain Wade was sick early in August, and the lieutenant had double duties at a time when news of his sick son left him frantic with worry. "I am obliged," he told his wife, "to Be hear & Bare it all alone for you have friends to Comfort you But I have nobody to speak with hear and can hardly have the Privilege of thinking my one thoughts. . . ."[44]

Lieutenant Hodgkins, along with his military superiors, missed the point of the incidents he described in a letter of August 12. In mid-July two British ships of the line had sailed comfortably through the fortifications designed to close the Hudson, and had anchored in Tappan Zee, forty miles above New York. In early August galleys were sent by the defenders to attack the *Phoenix* and the *Rose*, but "one of the galles split her Best guns and another received a shot Between wind & wharter so thay thought Best to Retreat. . . ."[45] Apparently the British might have used their command of New York's deep waters to land north of Manhattan and to finish the rebellion then and there. Even if they chose to begin with an assault on Long Island, their potential command of the East River threatened Washington's troops with easy capture.[46] Five hundred British ships lay in the harbor, and only Howe's caution delayed the beginning of the engagement until August 22.

Hodgkins was far down the Island when Howe landed unopposed with 15,000 of his best troops on the shores of Gravesend Bay. He had been detached for duty with a party of 200 men and a troop of horse with orders to drive cattle from the south side of the Island and to destroy all boats that might serve the enemy. When news of the landing was brought by an express at noon on August 22, the party was forty-two miles from camp, in the midst of territory that was almost wholly Tory. "I whas not without some happrehentions," observed Hodgkins, "But through the Blesing of god and the asistance of the Troops

---

[43] Joseph to Sarah Hodgkins, Long Island, July 22, 1776.
[44] *Ibid.*, Long Island, August 8, 11, 1776.
[45] *Ibid.*, Long Island, August 12, 1776.
[46] Ward, *op.cit.*, I, p. 210.

Fort
Lee

Fort
Washington

Harlem

NEW YORK

Kips Bay

Flushing

LONG ISLAND

Brooklyn

Bedford

Brooklyn Heights

British Army

Flatbush

Flatland

of hors we [made] ... Camp that night about one oclock. ... ."[47]

Major changes had been made in the command of the army to which Hodgkins returned. General Greene, sick, had been relieved by Major General John Sullivan and on August 24 Major General Israel Putnam had taken general command of the Island. Neither Sullivan nor Putnam was familiar with the topography of the Island, a grave fault before a battle that was to turn on Howe's shrewd use of the terrain over which he attacked. The American fortifications looked south to the British camp across a thickly wooded ridge that rose sharply to a height of 150 feet from the flatlands around Gravesend Bay. The ridge was cut by four "passes," depressions through which roads passed toward Brooklyn and the northern side of the Island. One road hugged the harbor, running past the Narrows; two cut the center between Brooklyn and Flatbush; and the fourth, the Flatlands-Flushing road, crossed three miles farther to the east. Putnam, maintaining dispositions ordered by Sullivan, who arrived before him, guarded the first three, but left the fourth watched only by five young militia officers. Putnam had 7,000 men on the Island, by the time of the engagement, and of these he sent 2,800 forward to the three eastern passes. A detachment from Little's regiment, commanded by Lieutenant Colonel William Henshaw, was part of 1,000 assigned to defend Flatbush Pass, the second of the four roads. On the plain below the Americans were seven times their number.[48]

Captain Wade's company was ordered to the guard at Flatbush Pass on the evening of August 26, the day before the battle. Events of the following day were settled by movements in the night, for while the American right, on the Narrows Road, was engaged by diversionary fire, 10,000 redcoats marched silently to the east from Flatlands and crossed the ridge through the fourth pass before dawn. The American patrol there was surrounded and captured, and by 9 a.m., on August 27, the main British force was close on the rear of the American outposts at the ridge. Two heavy guns were fired by this flanking

[47] Joseph to Sarah Hodgkins, Long Island, August 25, 1776.
[48] Ward, *op.cit.*, I, pp. 212-215.

force to signal an all-out attack by the Hessians on the plain before Flatbush Pass. Captain Wade gave a confused account of the Hessian attack: "Morning coming on the Enemy was Seen all on a Move, when we Expected them up the Road where we ware posted. But being informed (as I suppose) that the Road was so Fortified that they could not Pass the Way We ware posted Without Great Difficulty we had a brest work of trees falen a Cross the Road upon a Steep Hill and two Brass Six Pounders; we Perceived their Plan was to Surround us Kept our Post till the fire Got a Cross the Road in the Rear betwixt us and our Lines; and Not a Sufficient Number to make a Stand; or fight the Way through the Commanding officer Gave orders to Retreat and ascending the hill, found there ware a Vast Body of the Enemy Betwixt us and the Lines. . . ."[49]

Hodgkins had a somewhat clearer idea of the battle—"in the Night the Enemy marched out two Deferant ways and got amost all Round our Division . . . after hearing a very hot fire for some time we whare ordered to march for the fire But we found the Enemy whar Endevering to Cut of our Retreet and in a grate measure did. . . ."[50] General Sullivan, who took personal command of his forces at Flatbush Pass just before the engagement, was among the men captured there. The attack was particularly terrifying, for the Hessians advanced across the ridge without firing a shot, and rammed into the defenders with fixed bayonets. Caught between the British at their rear and the trained mercenaries before them the Americans turned their guns first forward, then backward, and soon fled in total disorder.[51] There was no way of escape, said Wade, "but Crossing a Piece of Marsh and through a Creek Breast high, Near Which was a Redout Well Manned Els we should have Been all Cut of; there were a Continual fire kept up the Whole of our Retreat, wherever we thought to get any advantageous Post in the Bushes or Elsewhere they Lay in ambush for us in Cornfield and Behind Walls and the like Places. . . ."[52] Hodgkins, more eloquent, declared "we whar obliged to go through fire

[49] Nathaniel Wade to Mrs. Ruth Wade, New York, September 5, 1776.
[50] Joseph to Sarah Hodgkins, Long Island, August 28, 1776.
[51] Ward, *op.cit.*, I, p. 223.
[52] Nathaniel Wade to Mrs. Ruth Wade, New York, September 5, 1776.

& wharter But through the goodness of god we got cheafly in. . . ."[53] The Ipswich company fared better than most of the men trapped on the ridge; it lost only one man—Arkelus Pulsifer was wounded and captured—and William Allen took a ball through his wrist. Six men lost their guns in the retreat through the marsh and across Gowanus Creek, and most of the company left the gear they had carried to the forward camp.[54]

The escape of the men at Flatbush Pass to the main lines at Brooklyn was not duplicated by the detachment on the Narrows Road; there hundreds were killed and captured, along with another American general. By noon of August 27 the extent of the disaster was clear; only Howe's curious caution prevented his eager subordinates from storming the breastworks on Brooklyn Heights, where the defenders were demoralized by the panic-stricken flight from the ridge. As it was, American losses were critical, not so much for the 1,000 men left killed and captured on the field, but rather for the corroding fear of open battle with the British that survivors took from the engagement.[55] The defeat was the fault of American leaders. Howe's flanking movement was executed perfectly, but had the Flushing Road been adequately guarded it would have been no surprise. Washington had surveyed the field in person on August 26, and had left Putnam's dispositions unchanged; such honor as the American commander was to take from the engagement would come from the brilliance of his retreat rather than from his strategy of defense.

Howe approached the American lines deliberately during the next two days. Hodgkins, reporting the British within a mile and a half of his position, wrote on the day after the battle that a further engagement was expected momentarily: "it seams the Day is Come . . . on which Depends the Salvation of this Countery . . . it is the Determination to Defend our Lines till the Last Extremity. . . ."[56] Washington remained committed to the defense of Brooklyn through August 28, bringing over

---

[53] Joseph to Sarah Hodgkins, Long Island, August 28, 1776.

[54] A list of the guns lost and taken in the engagement, in Wade's hand, is filed with the Wade Papers.

[55] Ward, *op.cit.*, I, pp. 226-227.

[56] Joseph to Sarah Hodgkins, Long Island, August 28, 1776.

reinforcements until 9,500 men were in the forts.[57] The commander-in-chief revised his strategy, though, on the stormy night of the twenty-eighth. Rain and a northeast storm prevented the British from cutting his East River supply line that night, and the next day he began to assemble all the boats he could lay hands on.

The retreat was beautifully executed. Conscious of the fact that his troops would desert the lines in a race for the boats if his intentions were known, Washington declared in general orders that he was preparing for removal of the sick and wounded, and anticipated relief of battle-weary regiments with fresh men.[58] The lines were manned while the troops were withdrawn; so carefully were plans for retreat concealed that Lieutenant Hodgkins thought, when he was ordered out at seven o'clock on the evening of August 29, that he was mustering "to go out aganst our Enemy." But at "about nine oclock the orders whare to strike our Tents and Pak al up and march to the ferry as quick as Possible and we made al the Dispatch we could But I cant tel you how I felt. . . ."[59] The retreat, wrote Captain Wade, "Was Nobly Effected Without the loss of a man, though our Boats ware so few that it Was from before Sun Down till after Sun Rise Before they Ware all Brought. . . ."[60]

The army thus snatched from disaster was a thoroughly dispirited force. Moravian Pastor Shewkirk, in his diary, observed that "the merry tones on drums and fifes had ceased." The Americans looked "sickly, emaciated, cast down, &c. . . ."[61] Lieutenant Hodgkins had lost all his optimism by this time. On September 5, he wrote:

"we have moved three times since we Left the Island and now we are about 6 or 7 miles above the sity of york near the North River to garde a Landing Place But how Long we shall stay hear is unsarting for the enemy are getting up there ships on Each side of this Island for york is an Island Parted from the

---

[57] Ward, *op.cit.*, I, p. 231.

[58] Orderly Book of Colonel William Douglas, August 29, 1776, in Johnston, *op.cit.*, Part II, pp. 30-31.

[59] Joseph to Sarah Hodgkins, New York, August 31, 1776.

[60] Nathaniel Wade to Mrs. Ruth Wade, New York, September 5, 1776.

[61] Pastor Shewkirk's Diary, in Johnston, *op.cit.*, Part II, p. 115.

Main Land By a River about 14 miles from the sity which is
caled Kings Bridge it is Verry Diffelt to gard Both sides of this
Island against a Numeras Enemy and a large fleet of ships as
Ever whas in america it is Expected they will Land from Longisland over hear at a Place called hellgate this Place is not far
from us only across the Island there is a grate Number of our
People there and I hope thay will be able to anoy the Enemy
But as for hindering there Landing I Do not Expect they Can
and when thay Come we must Either Beet them or they us and
if it should Be the former hapy for us But if the Latter the
Concequiances will Be shocking to All But Let us not Be Discorredged for if god is for us we ned not fear what man Can
Do unto us you may think that I write tu Discorredging But
only Considder aminuet we have Ben all this Summer Digging
& Billding of foorts to Cover our heads and now we have Ben
obliged to Leave them and now we are hear and not one shovell
full of Durte to Cover us But in all Probability we must met
them in the oppen field and Risk our Lives and Countery on one
single Battle . . . I Dont write this to Discorrege you or to
Encrees you Trobble But only to Let you know as near as I can
of our Circumstances . . . As to our Leaving Longisland I Dont
know what most People think of it But if the wind had not
hinderd the shipps from Coming up we must Been all mad
Prisoners But Lucky for us the wind held to the Norred for
some Days. . . ."[62]

The events of the following days were not calculated to lift
American spirits. The American Command, still indecisive,
scattered its force down the length of Manhattan, and left the
detachment in the city completely vulnerable to capture should
the British cross the East River north of the town. Howe made
his move on September 15, landing at Kip's Bay (East River at
34th Street) after savage bombardment. Militiamen assigned to
prevent the landing broke and ran at the first sight of the
British, and Washington himself narrowly escaped capture as
his panic-stricken men streamed past him. Hodgkins wrote that
two brigades had been assigned to oppose the landing, "But
they Being Cheafly Milisha it whas said that Two Hundred of

[62] Joseph to Sarah Hodgkins, New York, September 5, 1776.

the Enemy made them all Run so thay Landed with out much Resistance. . . ."[63] The lieutenant was by this time in command of his company, for Captain Wade "was taken Verry Unwell." In a letter to his mother, Wade wrote, "Being to sick to tarry in Camp, the Col thought twas Best for Me to Go into the Country, as they ware Removing the Sick from York and other Hospitals, they Carried us to tappan a town about 27 Miles up the River on the Jersey shore. . . ."[64] The captain did not return until September 30, when he found his men off Manhattan and camped on the Jersey Shore.

The Ipswich men were not among the troops routed at the landing; they had moved the day before to a camp on Harlem Heights, nine miles north of the city. They were soon in active contact with the enemy, however, for by the end of the day, the British had swept the Island as far north as the present site of Columbia University. The American camp was a little farther up the Island, on the heights looking down to the "Hollow Way" (the depression below Riverside Drive at 130th Street). The position was a strong one, but the conduct of the American troops had been such that little confidence was felt by their commander. "I should hope the Enemy would meet with a defeat in case of an Attack," wrote Washington, "If the generality of our Troops would behave with tolerable resolution, But, experience, to my extreme affliction, has convinced me that this is rather to be wished for than expected."[65]

Within a day, the tables were turned. Of September 16, Hodgkins was able to write proudly that the British did not have "the Milisha to Deal with . . . this time." The Battle of Harlem Heights began before the dawn of the 16th as a reconnaissance action, but as the engagement developed, it proved to be much more. By night, the British pursuit of the American forces had been halted, and the morale of Washington's army restored.

The battle was born of Washington's need to see beyond the dense woods screening Morningside Heights, south of the Hollow Way. There, for all he knew, Howe might be preparing to

[63] *Ibid.*, Fort Constitution, New Jersey, September 30, 1776.
[64] Nathaniel Wade to Mrs. Ruth Wade, Fort Constitution, October 1, 1776.
[65] John C. Fitzpatrick, ed., *Writings of Washington*, VI, p. 59.

push forward to completion of his victories of the preceding day. Therefore Lieutenant Colonel Thomas Knowlton was sent forward with 120 Connecticut volunteers to get knowledge of enemy intentions. The party encountered the British advance lines (in the neighborhood of what is now 126th Street), and after a brief skirmish retired in good order across the Hollow Way. At this point the enemy, reinforced when the firing began, signaled pursuit of the scouts by sounding the call for a fox chase, and Washington, infuriated when he heard the bugles cry a fox gone to earth, decided instantly to play the fox indeed. He ordered a feinting force, under Lieutenant Archibald Crary, into the Hollow Way to lure the British deeper into the valley, and at the same time sent Knowlton and Major Andrew Leitch off to the left to cut across the attackers' rear. Crary, with 150 men, was given hidden support by Nixon's brigade, including Little's regiment, posted in the woods behind the frontal feint. The British hurried into the trap, and the flanking party had nearly crossed to their rear before they realized their danger. Nixon's men were firing by this time, and the fox chase reversed direction. Both commanders of the flanking party fell in the first few minutes of the enlarged battle, but their men drove on to force the British back toward their lines. The redcoats did not turn for a stand until they reached a buckwheat field at the crest of the heights (the present site of Barnard College at 116th Street). Reinforcements brought their numbers up to 5,000, but Washington was ordering regiment after regiment into the battle. Generals Israel Putnam, Nathanael Greene, and George Clinton hurried to the fight, and even the brigade disgraced the day before at Kip's Bay was given a chance to redeem itself. Eighteen hundred Americans fought the British at forty yards for nearly two hours, and then the enemy, low on ammunition, began to retreat again. The Americans pursued almost to the main British lines (at 105th Street), and were called off only with great difficulty.[66]

Hodgkins, in the absence of Captain Wade, commanded the

[66] The foregoing account of the battle is based on Johnston, *op.cit.*, pp. 246-262. Ward, *op.cit.*, I, pp. 246-252; and Willard M. Wallace, *Appeal to Arms, A Military History of the American Revolution* (New York, 1951), pp. 117-118.

Ipswich company through the battle. He was with Nixon's brigade in the woods behind Crary, and he joined in the pursuit to Morningside Heights. A subaltern's impression of a complicated battle provides interest:

". . . on monday morning thay thought thay would attak us with about six thousand men and Drive us all over Kingsbridge But thay whare much mistaken But however as soon as we heard that thay whare advancing towards us the general sent out 200 Rangers under the Command of Coll Knolton who soon met the Enemy and fired on them and fote them on the Retreet Till thay got Pretty near us then the Enemy Halted Back of a hill and Blood a french Horn which whas for a Reinforcement and as soon as thay got itt thay Formed in to two Coloms But our Brigade whas Posted in the Eadge of a thick woods and By some Climing up a Tree could see the Enemys motion and while they whar aforming the general sent a Party to attack them which answred the eand for which they whare sent for our People made the atack and Retreeted towards us to the Place whare we whanted them to Come and then the Enemy Rushed Down the Hill with all speed to a Plain spot of ground then our Brigade marched out of the woods then a very hot Fire Began on Both sides and Lasted for upward of an hour then the Enemy Retreated up the Hill and our People followed them and fote them near an hour Longer till they got under Cover of the ships which whas in the North [*Hudson*] River then our People Left them the Loos on our side is about 40 killed and 60 or 70 wounded there Whas none killed in our Regt and But about 20 wounded one of our Corpl whas Badly wounded through his knees But I hope he will Due well the Loss on the Enemy side is not sarting But according to the Best accounts that we have had thay had near 500 killed and near as many wounded they whare seen to carry off several wagon Loads Besides our People Burryed a good many that they Left we whar informed By two Prisonors that thay found that they had not the Milisha to Deal with at this Time they said the surgone swore that they had no milisha to Day this whas the first time we had any Chance to fite them and I dout not if we should have another oppertunity But we should give them another Dressing. . . ."[67]

Hodgkins' estimate of American losses was reasonably accurate, but like his superiors he exaggerated the enemy casualty list—the British and Hessians had 14 killed and 165 wounded, as compared with 30 American dead and 100 wounded. The satisfaction with which the lieutenant described the battle was justified; the day had proved to Howe that the remainder of the New York campaign would not be a succession of Kip's Bays, and invited from the British general nearly a month of the cautious inactivity for which he was notorious. He spent the next several weeks fortifying and garrisoning the Island, while Washington waited his next move with a reinvigorated army, confident once more in its power.

The Ipswich men, always kept "on the advanced Post next to the Enemy," were relieved on September 20, and ferried to the opposite shore of the Hudson. There they hoped to make Fort Constitution (in a few days to be renamed Fort Lee) a permanent camp: "I hope," wrote Hodgkins, "we shall stay hear the Rest of the Campan as I have Ben at the Truble of Building a Log House with a ston Chimny I got it fit to live in 3 days ago Before which time I had not Lodged on any thing But the ground since we Left Longisland. . . ."[68] Captain Wade returned to his company on September 30, relieving his subordinate of the "grate Deal of Troble and Care" borne during his absence. Wade told his mother that many of the men were sick, but the rest were in "Good Spirits though they have Been Much fatigued."[69] The losses of the company had been light, considering the dangers it had faced. William Allen, wounded at Long Island, later "had his Arm taken of & is since Dead." Arkelous Pulsifer was captured on the Island, but none of the men were killed or taken on Harlem Heights. Many could boast narrow escapes; the lieutenant, on Long Island, "had my sleave Buttin shot out of my sleave and the skin a little

[67] Joseph to Sarah Hodgkins, Fort Constitution, September 30, 1776.
[68] Ibid.
[69] Nathaniel Wade to Mrs. Ruth Wade, Fort Constitution, October 1, 1776.

grased But through mercy Received no other hurt."[70] The record of the company suggests that war in the eighteenth century was not usually carried on very efficiently, and that battles, though noisy, were sometimes resolved with a minimum of bloodshed. Yet the engagement at Flatbush Pass, the retreat from Long Island, the rout at Kip's Bay, and the recovery on Harlem Heights were attended by as much gallantry and courage as any campaign offers, and each encounter was decisive in its outcome. General Howe was awarded the Order of the Bath for his victories around New York, and Washington fought on.

[70] Joseph to Sarah Hodgkins, New York, September 5, 1776.

CHAPTER V

Winter Soldier

THERE WAS no rest for the weary. The American success on Harlem Heights forced time on General Howe for thought, and thought revealed to him the strategy that geography had begged since he first set foot on Staten Island. After the fact, the matter seems simple. The British controlled the waters around New York: the Hudson, East River, and the pass through Hell Gate into Long Island Sound. So long as Washington waited, incomprehensibly, at the north end of Manhattan Island, common sense required a British landing on the mainland, north or east of his lines. Howe chose the eastern approach, and on the evening of October 12, 1776, put 4,000 men on ship for a landing on Throg's Neck, Westchester County, perhaps the only point at which failure of his operation was possible. Throg's Neck (sometimes Frog's Neck, in contemporary letters) was more nearly an island than a peninsula, and twenty-five American riflemen firing from behind a woodpile prevented the British army from crossing the next morning over the causeway that bridged the marsh and creek cutting the neck from the mainland. Howe landed more men on the 13th, paused, and decided that beachheads farther north were more inviting. On October 18 he moved his men three miles to Pell's Point at New Rochelle. Here American opposition was unsuccessful and one of the more deliberate flanking movements in military history began to grind forward.[1]

The week was useful to Washington, permitting conference, decision, and movement. Across the Hudson at Fort Lee the hope of Wade's company for peaceful enjoyment of its new log huts was dissolved by the British advance. On October 13 Gen-

[1] The most complete account of Westchester County movements is in Otto Hufeland, *Westchester County during the American Revolution, Publications of the Westchester County Historical Society*, III (White Plains, 1926), pp. 102-153.

eral Greene ordered General Nixon's brigade back to Manhattan, and Nixon urged Little to "hurry the march as fast as possible, as they must cross the ferry this night. . . ." Rations for three days were drawn and cooked, and baggage was left to follow later.[2]

Once over the river, Nixon's brigade was assigned to the newly created division of Major General Charles Lee, who ordered the unit northward with the bulk of Washington's army. On October 14 the brigade was stationed west of Williamsbridge at the Bronx River on the Boston Post Road.[3] Apparently the Ipswich men were in this vicinity for several days for on October 25 Francis Cogswell, a private in Wade's company, was taken prisoner at Miles Square.[4] The armies maneuvered for ten days after Howe moved from Throg's Neck to Pell's Point. The British pushed farther and farther north, driving to cut across Washington's straggling column; but the Americans, west of the Bronx River, marched parallel with and a little ahead of the enemy and turned east above Howe's advance to the ridges north of White Plains. Howe tested the position on October 28 and paid heavily in casualties for his occupation of Chatterton Hill, which was held by the right wing of Washington's army. The encounter was not quite a battle, for the British leader shrank from an assault across the whole line, and gave the Americans three days to withdraw to North Castle, five miles to the north behind the Croton River. With Washington thus clearly free of the trap that Manhattan or the Bronx might have been, Howe broke off the engagement and turned west to Dobbs Ferry on the Hudson.[5]

Colonel Little's Massachusetts men skirmished their way north with the army, but were not involved in any decisive moment of the retreat. Lieutenant Colonel William Henshaw,

[2] Greene's and Nixon's orders as recorded in the Little Orderly Book, October 13, 1776, Johnston, *op.cit.*, Part II, p. 144.

[3] *Ibid.*, October 16, 18, 1776, pp. 144-145.

[4] A manuscript note in Wade's hand, undated, listing casualties and material losses for the campaign, Wade Papers. Nixon's brigade led Lee's corps north from Miles Square on October 25, 1776, according to a transcript of John Glover's Orderly Book, in the manuscript room of the New York Public Library.

[5] Wallace, *op.cit.*, pp. 120-121.

Little's second in command, outlined the two weeks in a letter
to his wife:

". . . we have had several Skirmishes. I was not in them,
though I saw several of them. One of them last Week was fought
by Reed's & Learned's Reg'ts., where we had six—kill'd & a
number Wounded; the Enemy had Kill'd & Wounded, about
200—the same Week a Scouting Party came across the famous
Rogers Scouts, with a scouting party of the Enemy, took 30 of
them Prisoners, & kill'd a number of them—This Week we
had some Battles with them. Monday the 28th Ins't. about 2000
of them came on a height of Land on these Plains, Attacked
our Picquet, & after some time forced our People to give Back.
The Loss on either side I cannot ascertain, but suppose we had
Kill'd & Wounded near 100, as the Fire of Cannon & Small
Arms was heavy for some time. . . . The Enemy are now Encamp'd within Gun shot of us, so that there is a continual firing
of Small Arms. . . . We daily expect an engagement with the
Enemy. . . ."[6]

For men on the march the retreat to the New York Highlands was bewildering. We have been much "harriet" about,
wrote Lieutenant Hodgkins on November 15; "we Expect to
move soon But Cant Tell whare as the Enemy Some time ago
Drue Back from us & moved to the North River at a Place
Called Dobbs Ferry But what there Desine is we Cant Tell. . . ."
By this time, even subalterns could anticipate the next move
open to Howe—"it is thought they will attak fort Washington. . . ."[7] Washington, persuaded against his will by General
Greene and by the pleas of the Continental Congress, had left
3,000 men and valuable stores at the fort that carried his name
on the north end of Manhattan Island. At the very moment, on
November 15, that Hodgkins was committing his speculations
to paper, the British were turning back toward the city, and by

[6] William Henshaw to his wife, October 31, 1776, reprinted in Johnston,
op.cit., Part II, p. 46. The skirmish "last week" fought by Reed, etc., was the
American effort to resist the landing at Pell's Point; and the engagement with
Roger's rangers took place on the night of October 22. Hufeland, *op.cit.*, pp.
119-130.

[7] Joseph to Sarah Hodgkins, Phillipse Manor (North Castle), November 15,
1776.

the end of the day, the 3,000 defenders of Fort Washington were killed or captured and the stores lost.[8] Five days later General Greene abandoned Fort Lee across the river to avoid a similar fate at the hands of Lord Charles Cornwallis, who had crossed the Hudson above the fort with 4,000 men.[9]

General Washington was eye-witness to the first of these twin disasters that brought the campaigns around New York to a sorry close. He divided his army in the Westchester Highlands after Howe withdrew from White Plains, and took a substantial force across the Hudson to Hackensack near Greene at Fort Lee. He persisted in the indecision that left the forts occupied while reason demanded evacuation, and when they fell, he dropped down to Newark, where he remained until November 29, his force augmented by the men who escaped with Greene. He made no effort to give battle in the face of Cornwallis' leisurely pursuit; the most he could do was to keep his men between the British and Philadelphia, which he judged to be the enemy objective. As he fell back through New Brunswick, Princeton, and Trenton, his command shrank by desertion to the shadow of an army. On the night of December 7 he crossed from Trenton into Pennsylvania, having offered no more than token resistance to the English and Hessians who were enveloping New Jersey behind him.[10]

Behind, in the highlands above New York, the story was the same. October snow brought the promise of a hard winter, the campaign was a failure, and the men waited impatiently for the end of their enlistments on the first of January. "I hope I Shall have the Pleasure of facing you & all frinds in a fue weaks more," Lieutenant Hodgkins wrote his wife; "I have no thoughts of ingaging again in the Capacity that I now Sistane. . . ."[11] Little's regiment, steadfast since Bunker Hill, was fast dissolving. When General Lee began his belated march to Washington's support on November 29, the colonel remained in camp with

---

[8] Ward, *op.cit.*, I, pp. 267-274.   [9] *Ibid.*, pp. 276-277.
[10] William S. Stryker, *The Battles of Trenton and Princeton* (New York, 1898), pp. 2-28. Stryker, like Hufeland, Johnston, and Frothingham, in the works already cited, added to his book a voluminous documentary appendix useful to every scholar who walked after him the ground he described.
[11] Joseph to Sarah Hodgkins, Phillipse Manor, November 15, 1776.

three-quarters of his men. The "12th Continental Foot," commanded now by Lieutenant Colonel William Henshaw, arrived
in Pennsylvania with 18 officers and 108 men.[12] The general
was glad to abandon some of the men; as one sergeant observed,
"all the Lame & Lasy & the Faint Hearted & all that had no
shoes nor Clothes to keep them warm was Drafted out, to Be
Left Behind. . . ."[13] Colonel Little was ill, and according to
General William Heath the men who remained with him were
the "naked convalescents and sick."[14]

Captain Nathaniel Wade lingered on the Highlands in one
of these categories, for Joseph Hodgkins led the remnant of
Ipswich men through the crucial weeks that followed. Apparently
Wade was in reasonable health, for he was one of three captains
recommended for a vacant majority on December 5.[15] He was
not awarded the promotion, however, and he decided against
reenlistment. There is evidence that he remained on active duty
through January; he signed as president the verdict of a regimental court martial held at Phillipse Manor on February 4,
1777.[16] After a season of civilian life, during which he was married, he returned occasionally to the war as a colonel in the
Massachusetts militia.

Joseph Hodgkins, to be sure, marched with Lee into the occupied Jerseys with no special sense of zeal. He had only a
month left to serve, but "the way of my duty" meant for him
that he serve out those thirty-three days as a fighting man. He
did not for a minute give up his plans for an early return to
his home. "I did expect," he wrote to his wife from Peekskill,
to have been "home By ye 20 of January if it had not Ben for
this movement But now I expect it will Be Longer. . . ."[17] Hodgkins' company of Henshaw's regiment marched with a con-

[12] Peter Force, ed., *American Archives*, Fifth Series, III, p. 1401.
[13] Louise Rau, ed., "Sergeant John Smith's Diary of 1776," *Mississippi
Valley Historical Review*, XX (1933-1934), p. 262.
[14] William Heath to George Washington, December 26, 1776, Heath
Papers, *Collections of the Massachusetts Historical Society*, Seventh Series,
IV (Boston, 1904), p. 46.
[15] Timothy Danielson to General William Heath, December 5, 1776, Force,
op.cit., Fifth Series, III, p. 1084.
[16] *Massachusetts Soldiers and Sailors of the Revolution*, XVI, p. 374.
[17] Joseph to Sarah Hodgkins, Peekskill, New York, December 3, 1776.

Peekskill

White
Plains

Fort
Lee

Fort
Washington

New
York

Long
Island

Morristown

Newark

Staten
Island

Millstone R.

New
Brunswick

Rocky Hill

Kingston

Princeton

Delaware R.

American
Army
Christmas 1776

Trenton

Crosswicks

Bordentown

Bristol

to
Philadelphia

Burlington

Mount Holly

N

solidated "New England Brigade," composed of units from Rhode Island, Massachusetts, and New Hampshire. Colonel Daniel Hitchcock, the Rhode Islander who commanded the brigade, was in the last stages of consumption and was to die within ten days after the exertions of the ensuing campaign.

The lieutenant ordered his company from the camp at Phillipse Manor, North Castle, on November 29 and marched north and west to Peekskill, New York, where he crossed by ferry from Verplancks Point to Stony Point on December 3.[18] General William Heath, who watched the crossing, said that Lee was entering the Jerseys with "as good troops as any in the service; but many of them were so destitute of shoes that the blood left on the rugged, frozen ground, in many cases marked the route they had taken. . . ."[19] Undoubtedly shoemaker Hodgkins took care of himself as far as his feet were concerned. General Lee, who took the news of Washington's precipitate retreat as a signal for independent movement on his own, lingered in northern New Jersey through the following week. He wrote from Morristown on December 11 that he had "three thousand men here at present; but they are so ill-shod that we have been obliged to halt these two days for want of shoes."[20]

Apparently Lee was toying with the idea of a march across the rear of the British army, which was by this time around Princeton and Trenton, when his considerable vanity was punctured as a result of his own foolishness. On the night of December 12 he slept away from his army, enjoying the comforts of White's Tavern at Basking Ridge. The next morning, just after he had written a celebrated letter criticizing Washington, he was surrounded and taken by a small troop of British.[21] A great many people regarded his capture as a disaster, for after the New York campaign it was easy to share Lee's doubts of Washington's

[18] *Ibid.*

[19] Rufus R. Wilson, ed., *Heath's Memoirs of the American War* (New York, 1904), p. 107.

[20] George Henry Moore, *The Treason of Charles Lee, Major General Second in Command in the American Army of the Revolution* (New York, 1860), p. 54.

[21] Lee's letter, addressed to General Horatio Gates, observed that *"entre nous,* a certain great man is most damnably deficient. . . ." Wallace, *op.cit.,* p. 126.

capacity. In the lines, the men knew that Lee had only himself to blame for his discomforts. "Doutles you will want to hear how genl Lee whas Taken," wrote Hodgkins to his wife. "I will Tell you that general Lee whas invited by a gentleman to Put up with him that night & weather that man or another informed the Enemy I Cant say But some Body Did so about sixty of the Lite hors Came ye nex morning & surrounded the house . . . ye genl whas five miles from whare the army inCampd that night."[22]

Lee's second in command was General John Sullivan, who had been exchanged since his capture on Long Island. Sullivan wasted no more time in hurrying his army across the Delaware; he joined Washington in the midst of a snowstorm on December 20. Hodgkins' company crossed the river at Phillipsburg on December 15, and marched down the Pennsylvania side to join the main force. His men were "Very Much fatagued with a long March . . . the gratest Part of the way whas Dangrus By Reason of the Enemy Being near & . . . the Contry is full of them Cursed Creaters Called Torys."[23] Only 2,000 men remained of the 5,000 that Lee had led into the Jerseys, and the enlistment time of these was fast running out. "I Expect to Lay my head to the Eastward in aBout" a fortnight, the lieutenant promised.

By mid-December, few remained to dispute the conviction that the patriot cause was lost. Washington himself said that without reinforcements "the game will be pretty near up"; and every fact that presented itself confirmed his gloom. Howe had taken Newport, Rhode Island, with one hand while he swept Washington across New Jersey with the other. New York was completely lost, and there was little to prevent the 10,000 victorious Englishmen and Hessians camped around Trenton from marching the last thirty miles to Philadelphia, the largest city in America. The Congress had fled to Baltimore; New Jersey had ignored Washington's call for militiamen; and the troops that he had were his for but two weeks more. Some 6,000 men were camped in the brush west of the Delaware—the men Washington had brought out, Sullivan's 2,000, 500 who had

[22] Joseph to Sarah Hodgkins, Buckingham, Pennsylvania, December 20, 1776.
[23] *Ibid.*

come with General Horatio Gates from the north, and 1,000 Pennsylvania militiamen who had just come in. But with the completion of enlistments on December 31, no more than 1,400 would remain. The infant republic might expire, it appeared, within a half year of the Declaration of Independence. History found its caption for the moment in *The Crisis,* a new pamphlet by Thomas Paine. The author had shouldered a musket for the retreat from Fort Lee but he took his pen too and his words, scribbled on drumhead desks across the Jerseys, once more flashed through the camps and electrified the land: "These are the times that try men's souls: The summer soldier and the sunshine patriot will, in this crisis, shrink from the service of his country; but he that stands it Now, deserves the thanks of man and woman. Tyranny, like hell, is not easily conquered; yet we have this consolation with us, that the harder the conflict, the more glorious the triumph."[24]

The very extremity of the crisis revealed the beginning of hope. Washington had nothing more to lose, so he could gamble without thought of the odds. He abandoned the panoply of commander-in-chief, which he had worn uncomfortably and with little distinction, and played for ten days the irresponsible role of a field officer. He met chance and change on the gallop, and waited uncommitted to try the promise of each new day. Fortunately, Sir William Howe remained his most effective ally. With victory almost in his grasp, Howe decided against an unfashionable winter campaign; John R. Alden has observed that "it was not in him to push the sword to the hilt if the blade were clouded with frost."[25] He halted his army at Trenton and sent his men into winter camp at Burlington, Bordentown, Trenton, Princeton, New Brunswick, and Amboy. Fourteen hundred crack Hessian troops remained opposite Washington at Trenton, and as many more were six miles to the south at Bordentown. The British line was gravely extended, if Washington's ragged band could be considered any threat to its security.

[24] This estimate of the crisis, and the quotations from Washington and Paine, are from Ward, *op.cit.,* I, pp. 285-290. See also Fitzpatrick, *op.cit.,* VI, p. 347.
[25] John Richard Alden, *The American Revolution, 1775-1783* (New York, 1954), p. 106.

Howe and his subordinates belittled their dangers and made no plans that took account of the possibility that the patriots might rise again.

When Washington crossed the Delaware on Christmas night 1776 his plans were more ambitious than the actual events of the following morning. He crossed and, in every schoolboy's phrase, "fell on the Hessians," capturing or killing more than 1,000: the story is familiar through many tellings. But of three crossings planned only the one that he led personally was undertaken. Brigader General James Ewing had orders to cross directly at Trenton and take a station to cut off the retreat of the Hessians who might escape Washington's movement, but Ewing judged the river too dangerous, and waited indecisive through the night. To the south, below Bristol, Brigadier General John Cadwalader put 600 of his 2,000 men across and then decided that ice piled on the east bank made completion of the movement impossible, and hauled his advance guard back again. The southern force had been assigned to engage the enemy at Bordentown and Mount Holly, to divert them from the main attack at Trenton. So Washington, instead of gambling his whole army on a general attack along the Delaware, had conducted a raid; and lack of intelligence about British movements in the country beyond forced him to cross with his captives back into Pennsylvania late on December 26.[26]

The events of the next morning were almost comic. General Cadwalader, his backbone stiffened by news of Washington's victory, crossed successfully with his whole division, only to learn on the eastern shore that Washington had retired and that he, Cadwalader, was alone in New Jersey. Lieutenant Hodgkins was beyond comment on the antics of his superiors; his report to Sarah on the moves and countermoves was without editorial asides. The New England brigade, according to his letter, had joined Cadwalader at Bristol on December 22—he did not add that Colonel Hitchcock's tattered men were the only veterans with the southern unit.[27] Nor did he make reference to the fact that his colonel was forced to advise the division com-

[26] Ward, *op.cit.*, I, pp. 291-305.
[27] Joseph to Sarah Hodgkins, Crosswicks, New Jersey, December 31, 1776.

mander that the New England men would refuse to cross without shoes. Shoes, stockings, and breeches were rushed from Philadelphia, home of Cadwalader's militia, and were distributed on the 26th.[28] If this problem in supply was in part the cause of the general's delay, Hodgkins made no mention of it: "we marched to Bristol & in Camped in the woods near the Town & on Christmas night we marched with about 2000 Men to a ferry about 7 miles from Camp in order to Pass over to the Jersey side of the River to atack a Party of the Enemy that Lay at a Place Called Mount Holly But the Ise Prevented our Crosing that night But the Troops that Lay up about 20 miles . . . got across. . . ." Half of the letter is missing; the part that survives breaks off with a description of the Trenton affair: "this gave the Enemy a grate shock so they soon Retreated from the other Places whare they intended to stay. . . ."[29]

This last news was the important intelligence won by Cadwalader's belated movement. He reconnoitered Burlington on the night of December 27, and found the enemy gone. Soon his scouts reported that the British had drawn back from Mount Holly and Bordentown, and the next morning he marched his column north as far as Crosswicks, eight miles southeast of Trenton.[30] When Washington learned that the enemy had abandoned the whole Trenton area, he ordered his divisions to their boats once more, and began crossing back on December 29. He persisted in the movement even after he learned that the enemy was regrouping at Princeton. Howe, shocked from his lethargy by the news of the raid at Trenton, recalled Cornwallis from a winter's leave, and hurried him back toward central New Jersey with 8,000 men.[31]

Before Washington could deploy his force to face this approaching column, he had to give precious hours to the reenlistment crisis. The last day of the year marked the end of the service his men had pledged; and the officers of the patriot army, from commander-in-chief to subaltern, rode from regiment to regiment pleading with the men to stay for the pending

[28] Stryker, *op.cit.*, pp. 423-424.
[29] Joseph to Sarah Hodgkins, Crosswicks, December 31, 1776.
[30] Stryker, *op.cit.*, pp. 238-243.
[31] Ward, *op.cit.*, I, pp. 306-308.

engagement. At Crosswicks, General Thomas Mifflin, "mounted on a noble-looking horse and clothed in an overcoat made up of a large rose blanket," begged the New England brigade to hold firm; he came "to harangue our brigade," said an eyewitness, and "did it well." The most impassioned appeal of the day was made by the dying Hitchcock, and after him the Massachusetts regiment heard the words of Lieutenant Colonel Henshaw: "At present this is our business, let us not forsake it. It is you and I, brave boys, who are banded together in one common cause. We scorn the thought of flying from it." Speeches and the promise of a ten-dollar bounty carried the day; the ragged New Englanders renewed loyalty "by our unanimously poising the firelock as a signal. . . ." To one observer, the brigade seemed to be composed of "animated scarecrows," but within four days it had proved itself the elite corps of Washington's army.[32]

Washington knew that the fate of the Republic lay with the loyalty of his veterans; he valued their services so highly that he pledged the ten-dollar bounty from his own private fortune. "I feel the inconvenience of this advance," he reported to Congress, "and I know the consequences which will result from it; But what could be done? Pennsylvania had allowed the same to her militia. The troops feel their importance, and would have their price." He was surprised that so small a bounty served: ". . . as their aid is so essential and not to be dispensed with, it is to be wondered, they had not estimated it at a higher rate." "I thought it no time to stand upon trifles," he told Robert Morris, "when a Body of firm Troops inured to danger, were absolutely necessary to lead on the more raw and undisciplined."[33] A Rhode Island sergeant of the brigade described the day in his diary:

". . . in the Afternoon our Brigade was sent for into the field where we Paraded Befor the General who was present with all

[32] C. C. Haven, *Thirty Days in New Jersey Ninety Years Ago: An Essay Revealing New Facts in Connection with Washington and His Army in 1776 and 1777* (Trenton, 1867), p. 36; Stryker, *op.cit.*, pp. 254-256; Benjamin Cowell, *The Spirit of '76 in Rhode Island*, p. 307; Ward, *op.cit.*, I, p. 308; Thomas Jefferson Wertenbaker, "The Battle of Princeton," *The Princeton Battle Monument. The History of the Monument, A Record of the Ceremonies Attending Its Unveiling, and an Account of the Battle of Princeton* (Princeton, 1922), p. 58.
[33] John C. Fitzpatrick, *op.cit.*, VI, pp. 461, 464.

the feild Officers & after meaking many fair promises to them he Begged them to Tarey one month Longer in the Scervice & Almost Every man Consented to stay Longer who Received 10 Doler Bounty as soon as Signd their names then the Genll with the soldiers gave three Huzzas & was with Claping of hands for Joy amongst the Specttators & as soon as that was over the Genell ordrd us to heave a gill of Rum pr man . . . we was Dismisd to Goe to our Quarters with great Applause the inhabitents & others saying we had Done honour to our Country viz New England. . . ."[34]

The brigade had but a night in quarters; on the afternoon of January 1, 1777, it got orders for a night march from Crosswicks to Trenton. When the New Englanders arrived on the morning of January 2 the American advance guard was already disputing the march of the British over the road from Maidenhead (now Lawrenceville) to Trenton. Cornwallis had assembled a formidable force, composed of nearly all the British and Hessians in New Jersey. Six hundred had been left to guard stores and treasure at New Brunswick, and Lieutenant Colonel Charles Mawhood remained with the Fourth Brigade at Princeton. The rest, 5,500 strong, set out with a powerful artillery train to put an end to the untimely disorders around Trenton. Washington could claim an equal number, but of his 5,000 only 1,400 were veterans of the Continental Line, the rest being hurriedly raised militia of varying experience.[35] He posted his main line on the south bank of Assunpink Creek, a small stream flowing west through Trenton into the Delaware. When Hitchcock's men came in on the morning of the 2nd, they were ordered to the left flank at the bridge over the creek at the foot of Queen Street (now Broad Street).[36]

A heavy rain had fallen the night before, and a January thaw mired the Post Road from Maidenhead to Trenton. It was four in the afternoon before Cornwallis drove through mud and sniper fire to the outskirts of Trenton, and there he was held for nearly an hour by a desperate stand of the American advance

---

[34] Louise Rau, ed., "Sergeant John Smith's Diary of 1776," *loc.cit.*, pp. 269-270.

[35] Wertenbaker, "The Battle of Princeton," *loc.cit.*, p. 59.

[36] *Ibid.*, pp. 60-61.

guard. Then the British surged over the defending line and began hot pursuit of the men retreating down Queen Street through the village. Here Hitchcock's men showed what it meant to be veterans: marching over the bridge toward their retreating fellows they opened ranks to let the weary men through, then closed up and contested every foot of the street in a slow march back to the bridge. Queen Street was roaring with fire by this time; British units on King Street (now Warren Street) were racing to cut across the rear of the New England brigade, and heavy cross fire poured out from the side streets. The brigade made the bridge in the nick of time, and as it pounded across the single arch to the far side of the creek each man passed close to Washington, who sat with the breast of his great white horse pressed against the rail of the bridge. One of the men trotting into the winter dusk remembered the face of his chief as "firm, composed, majestic."[37]

The battle thus hung in the balance at the edge of dark but when the New Englanders beat off an effort to ford the creek west of the bridge, Cornwallis decided to delay his victory till the following morning. For once, British confidence seemed reasonable. Washington had no place to go—he could not operate his shuttle over the Delaware under enemy guns, and a retreat south down the Jersey peninsula would only delay his capture. To the British general, therefore, morning seemed time enough to "bag the fox."

But the American chief had no stomach for a disastrous battle or hopeless retreat. Since the country behind would soon be untenable, he decided to occupy British territory instead. At midnight his force began to peel off to the east around the British left flank. A handful of men were left in the lines to keep the campfires high, and a noisy show of activity was continued in the earthworks on the creek. Baggage and heavy guns were sent back to Burlington, while most of the army marched out the Sandtown road (along the line of the present Hamilton Avenue) to its intersection with a little back road, long since obliterated, that ran from the Quaker Meeting House at Crosswicks northwest to the Meeting House at Stony Brook, two miles south of

[37] Haven, *op.cit.*, pp. 37-38.

Princeton. The unseen dangers of the night were too much for some of the militia—1,000 Pennsylvanians bolted to the south and formed themselves as an unnecessary guard for the baggage train.[38]

In circling behind the British army, Washington had more in mind than a retreat. With the bulk of the enemy waiting for day at Trenton, only small detachments remained at Princeton and New Brunswick; and the latter town held vast quantities of stores, along with a £70,000 pay chest, treasury for the invading army. New Brunswick was twenty-five miles away— more by the back road along which the army marched—but rapidly falling temperatures hardened the ground and raised hopes for a quick march. By sunrise the head of the column had reached the Quaker Meeting House at Stony Brook, and swung right along the now forgotten road that led along the low ground past the present Institute for Advanced Study, Olden House, and on past the Graduate College and Prospect, south of Princeton. From the Meeting House, the men could look up a deserted slope to the brow of Mercer Heights, scene within the hour of one of the decisive battles of the war.[39]

As Washington approached Princeton, the British in the town were already astir. Lieutenant Colonel Charles Mawhood commanded the three regiments of the Fourth Brigade there, and was under orders to bring two of them to Maidenhead at morning light. As Washington's column passed the Quaker Meeting House, Mawhood was crossing Stony Brook on the Post Road (Stockton Street), a half mile to the north. From the top of the steep hill west of the brook, Mawhood's men looked back and caught glimpses of the American army toiling along in a parallel but opposite direction. The British commander immediately turned his men about and hurried them back across the brook toward Mercer Heights, a hill that separated the Post Road from the little-used road along which Washington marched. As he approached the height he became aware of another threat. Washington, after the van of his army turned up

[38] Stryker, *op.cit.*, pp. 274-276; Leonard Lundin, *Cockpit of the Revolution. The War for Independence in New Jersey* (Princeton, 1940), p. 207.

[39] A painstaking and accurate review of the order of march is offered in Wertenbaker, "The Battle of Princeton," *loc.cit.*, pp. 64-74.

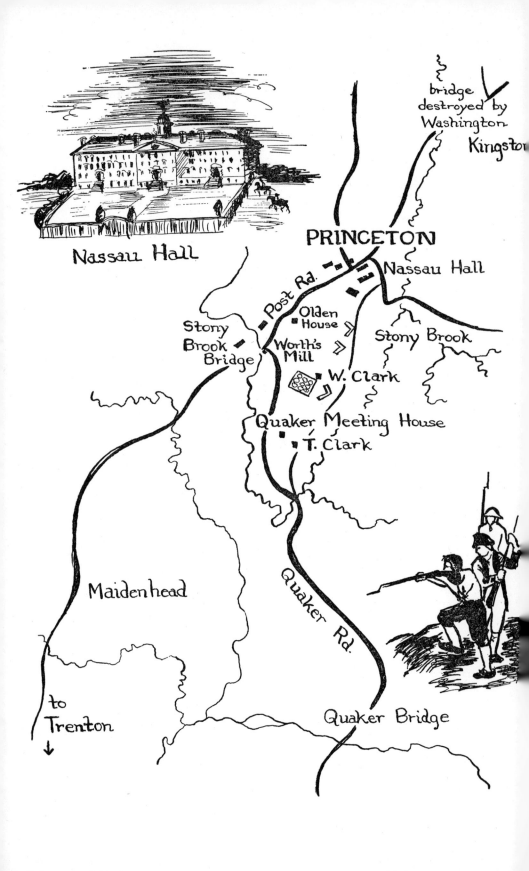

Nassau Hall

bridge destroyed by Washington

Kingston

PRINCETON

Nassau Hall

Post Rd.

Olden House

Stony Brook Bridge

Worth's Mill

Stony Brook

W. Clark

Quaker Meeting House

T. Clark

Maidenhead

Quaker Rd.

to Trenton

Quaker Bridge

the back road, had detached General Hugh Mercer's brigade, and ordered it north along Quaker Road to cut the Post Road Bridge at Stony Brook. At some point in his race for the heights, Mawhood spotted this column. He instantly ordered his 55th Regiment to continue to the brow of the hill, and he sent out units of the 17th to intercept Mercer's column, now on his right.[40]

General Mercer, marching north along Quaker Road, apparently spotted Mawhood's men at about the time his own presence was discovered. He wheeled his 350 men sharply to the right, led them up out of the ravine through which the road passed, and marched southeastward across the higher ground in an effort to rejoin the van of his army, now nearing the

[40] The following account of the battle depends heavily on the work of Wertenbaker and Bill. The field is difficult to visualize now, for in well-groomed western Princeton stately houses and towering trees have filled more than half of the cultivated fields that covered the western slopes of Mercer Heights on January 3, 1776. The cleared oval now preserved as the site of the battlefield covers only the ground of the close fighting; the key roads and paths over which the several detachments maneuvered lie outside the Memorial Park. A tortured metaphor, nevertheless, may discipline to words the rolling terrain that the armies contested. The pattern containing the movements approximates the shape of a huge baseball diamond, about a half mile square. The Quaker Meeting House, still standing a few rods from the intersection of Mercer Street with Stony Brook, was home plate. Quaker Road, along which Mercer's men were marching, was the left foul line, following Stony Brook north to the point where the Post Road, or Stockton Street, crossed. The left field fence, beginning at the Stony Brook Bridge, followed Stockton Street back to the point at which it turns sharply toward the north, then crossed the ravine there and mounted in a straight line to the hilltop south of the road. The center field fence turned east by southeast from the Thomas Olden House, then standing 300 yards south of its present location, near the stone tablet that today marks the common grave of the day's dead. The back wall crossed behind the north end of oval Memorial Field; and the right field fence fell south by southwest from the point where Mercer Street (not in existence then) enters the park. This fence passed below the brow of Mercer Heights, and intersected the right foul line between the Olden House and the Institute for Advanced Study. The line back west to the Quaker Meeting House marked the now forgotten back road over which the van of Washington's army was passing; his advance guard was nearly out of the park when the action began. The orchard in which the troops first collided lay high in center field, near the line now made by Mercer Street across the cleared area. The Thomas Clark House, in front of which the battle ended, still stands well out into the infield, halfway down the line from the pitcher's box to first base. This line marked a low crest between the Meeting House and the higher slopes on which the orchard lay. Beyond this infield crest was a dip, crossed then by a fence between the Clark House and the orchard.

Olden House. As he cut through the orchard that lay across his path he was surprised by fire from Mawhood's advance guard on his left flank. The 17th Regiment was not yet to the brow of the hill that rises from Stockton Street, and when the Americans turned left to meet the unexpected fire they were able to force back the enemy detachment and take stations on the fence that bounded the north side of the orchard. In a few minutes the whole British regiment crossed to the brow of the hill and after point-blank fire Mawhood led his men in a charge into the orchard. Mercer's men got off three volleys before the redcoats were on them with cold steel; they held for a moment, then broke through the orchard toward the Thomas Clark House. Mercer fell in the melee with bayonet wounds that were to prove mortal and the retreat of his brigade soon turned to full flight.

The engagement to this point had two audiences: Mawhood's 55th Regiment had gained the top of Mercer Heights, but it dared not turn back to its commander's aid, because the van of Washington's army had been spotted near the Olden House below. Similarly, General Sullivan, who commanded the American advance, could not turn back to help Mercer; he too would expose his rear to the waiting British regiment on the Heights if he crossed into the field. Reinforcement for the remnants of Mercer's brigade had to come from the column just moving up the road to the Quaker Meeting House, Cadwalader's Pennsylvania militiamen. The Pennsylvanians hurried over the low crest by the Thomas Clark House, where they faced the unexpected turmoil of the fleeing veterans. They entered the field in column and their courage failed as Cadwalader tried to form them into line. Most of them broke and began to cross back down the hill with the fugitives from the orchard; only a battery of artillery and a handful of riflemen held firm to a place before the Clark House. Washington had galloped to relieve his brigadiers by this time; he crossed repeatedly through fire of the opposing forces in an effort to rally the demoralized men. Mawhood had paused at the fence before the Clark House when the militiamen came over the crest, but it began to appear that with one regiment he would sweep the Americans from the field, brigade by brigade, with the disciplined fire of his trained men.

Washington had only his rear guard to add to the fray; the day would turn on the courage of the last men to enter the battle.

Hitchcock's New England brigade, stationed on the left flank at Trenton, had fallen into column at the rear of the army during the night march. The New Englanders came up past the Clark House while the issue was in doubt, and swung briskly on Washington's order to the right flank of the American line. Two hundred yards from the action they shifted from column into perfect lines—Henshaw's Massachusetts men were closest to the Clark House at the center. They advanced a hundred yards, halted and fired a volley, reloaded and held firm in their line as they marched forward again. After another round they charged, and it was Mawhood's turn to retreat with the steel of the enemy at his back.[41] The action became a rout; the Pennsylvanians who had held firm at the left joined the charge and the day was carried. From then on it was a chase—"a fine fox chase it is, my boys," cried Washington. The British were pursued far up Stony Brook north of the Post Road and south along the road almost to Maidenhead.[42]

Mawhood's 55th Regiment, shaken by the fate of the 17th on the slopes below, quickly dropped back toward Princeton, and there joined the other regiment, the 40th, to attempt a stand outside the village. The two units formed on the hill that drops from the Theological Seminary toward the Princeton Inn, above Frog Hollow, the ravine that runs from Mercer Street past the Springdale Houses down through the Golf Course. Sullivan's men, near the Olden House, took up their march once more, and managed to round the hill below the Graduate College and get within 60 yards of the waiting line before they were detected. The British had had enough, and bolted on first sight of the advancing Americans. Many hurried out to the north, but 200 were foolish enough to take refuge in Nassau Hall, where they were soon forced to surrender. Official accounts disputed the number of those captive or killed but Englishman and American agreed that the crack Fourth Brigade had been destroyed.

[41] Wertenbaker, "The Battle of Princeton," *loc.cit.*, pp. 103-105.
[42] *Ibid.*, p. 108.

The whole action was carried off with remarkable speed; no more than forty-five minutes were spent in the main engagement, and the rout of the 40th and 55th took little more time. The next two hours were required to tend the wounded and round up the units still pursuing remnants of the Fourth Brigade. Princeton was no place to remain, for the troops of Cornwallis, puffing and blowing up the road from Trenton, were soon close at hand. The main British force was delayed by cannon fire from the head of Nassau Street; a few stragglers turned the redcoats' own guns on them, from a redoubt the British had built between the present site of the Battle Monument and the Second Presbyterian Church. By the time Cornwallis entered the town, Washington was out the Kingston Road and over the Millstone River. There he destroyed the bridge, and turned left along the north bank toward Rocky Hill. He dared not continue his race for New Brunswick: his men had been under arms for forty hours and were exhausted by the sharp engagements—the New Englanders, as a matter of fact, arrived at Princeton after their second night march.

The Americans therefore crossed Rocky Hill toward Somerset Court House (now Millstone) and proceeded behind the shelter of the Watchung Mountains to Morristown. They were not pursued, for Cornwallis, no longer confident of anything, hurried on to guard his precious stores at New Brunswick. After January 3, Sir William Howe made no effort to hold any points in the Jerseys except for the eastern corner at Brunswick and Amboy; the patriots were soon in possession once more of Hackensack, Newark, and Elizabethtown. Washington's ten days in the saddle had changed the course of the war.[43]

As the army hurried north from Princeton, Washington took Colonel Hitchcock by the hand and expressed "his high approbation of his conduct and that of the troops under his command."[44] The brigade got generous praise from all who remembered the day; Dr. Benjamin Rush told Richard Henry Lee that the "New England men . . . are entitled to a great share of the honour . . . at Princeton."[45] The men in the ranks were

[43] Ward, *op.cit.*, I, pp. 306-318.
[44] Haven, *op.cit.*, p. 53.   [45] Stryker, *op.cit.*, p. 298.

pleased and proud but Joseph Hodgkins, for one, did not waver for a moment in his determination to get on home as soon as he could. The thirty-three days he owed his country when he set out from the highlands of New York had stretched to thirty-eight before he demanded his discharge at Morristown. But somewhere along the road he had changed his mind about quitting the war for good—at Morristown he signed on for three more years as a captain in the Continental Line. He made a good thing of his reenlistment; when he left camp in January 1777 he had wangled assignment to recruiting duty near his home. His superiors had no reason to doubt that he would pay for the spring at home, just as he had earned the ten-dollar bounty he took for his march from Crosswicks through Trenton and Princeton to North Jersey. He must have reached Ipswich in early February; his third child by Sarah Hodgkins was born on November 9, 1777.[46]

[46] *Vital Records of Ipswich, Massachusetts To the End of the Year 1849*, I, *Ipswich Births* (Salem, 1910), p. 189.

CHAPTER VI

The Turning Point

SINCE the regiment to which Captain Joseph Hodgkins was
posted did not exist when he accepted his new commission,
his first duty was to find men who wanted him as their captain
for the next three years. While Washington wintered with a
handful of men at Morristown, many of his officers scattered
to their homes to find an army for the next campaign. Hodgkins
labored to enlist his company for Colonel Timothy Bigelow's
"Fifteenth Massachusetts Battalion," a paper regiment with
headquarters at Colonel Bigelow's home in Worcester, Massachusetts.

Bigelow's battalion was one of eighty-eight such units ordered
raised by the Continental Congress in September 1776.[1] Yielding
to Washington's desperate pleas, and to common sense, the
Congress had attempted to eliminate the annual reenlistment
crisis. To every man willing to enlist for the duration, it promised
a substantial bounty: twenty dollars in cash, a suit of clothes, and
a hundred acres of land. But generous gifts could not attract men
to a lost cause; no more than 1,000 continentals reenlisted during
the fall. Congressional hopes for a regular army of 75,000,
pledged for the duration, had to be shelved until the victories
at Trenton and Princeton revived flickering patriot hopes. Even
victory in New Jersey failed to overcome the reluctance of recruits to agree to indefinite service, so the obligated term was
reduced to three years.[2] The promise of a land grant was dropped
but cash and clothes were still offered, the "suit" to consist
of "two pair of overalls, a leathern or woollen waistcoat with
sleeves, one pair of breeches, a hat or leathern cap, two shirts,
two pair of hose, and two pair of shoes."[3]

---

[1] L. C. Hatch, *The Administration of the American Revolutionary Army*
(New York, 1904), p. 73.

[2] Lynn Montross, *Rag, Tag, and Bobtail. The Story of the Continental
Army, 1775-1783* (New York, 1952), p. 146.

[3] Quoted in Hatch, *op.cit.*, p. 73.

Officers on recruiting duty were offered adequate incentives for their service. For every able-bodied man enrolled they got ten shillings, but the recruit had to pass muster in camp before they were paid. Soldiers who were "only Food for Worms ..." would do little to advance the cause, so regulations required inductees to be at least sixteen years old, healthy, and not under five feet two inches in height.[4] The bounties to both officer and man were modest in comparison with payments of succeeding years; with inflation a private soldier demanded hundreds of dollars and hundreds of acres before he would sign on for a campaign.

Competition for Massachusetts men was fierce in the spring of 1777, for the state was attempting to raise fifteen of the battalions planned for the three-year army. Enlistment went so slowly that the General Court decided in April to draft for eight months' duty enough men to fill out any regiment not complete by May 15. Nearly half of the recruits in Joseph Hodgkins' company were draftees, apparently. Of the fifty-five non-commissioned officers and privates he mustered at the beginning of the fall campaign, only thirty-one were three-year men; the other twenty-four were enrolled at once on May 19 for eight months' service.[5] The struggle to keep the Continental Line filled was unending; when Captain Hodgkins marched to the Saratoga campaign he left his first lieutenant behind to look for more men. Massachusetts' peak contribution to the regular army came this year, when 7,816 of her men were by one means or another persuaded to the duty.[6] Congress had hoped for an army of 75,000 but raised in all no more than 34,000 men in 1777. But from this time forward, though the numbers were to shrink, Washington could always count on the presence of seasoned veterans for each campaign.[7]

[4] John C. Miller, *Triumph of Freedom, 1775-1783* (Boston, 1948), p. 502.
[5] Muster of September 7, 1777, Colonel Timothy Bigelow's Fifteenth Massachusetts Battalion. All the muster rolls reported in this chapter are from photostats taken of surviving documents maintained in the Adjutant General's Office, War Department, during the 1920's. For enlistments and the draft in Massachusetts, see Jonathan Smith, "How Massachusetts Raised Her Troops in the Revolution," *Proceedings, Massachusetts Historical Society,* LV (1921-1922), pp. 351-352.
[6] Smith, *loc.cit.*, p. 356.
[7] John R. Alden, *The American Revolution, 1775-1783* (New York, 1954), p. 120.

The interlude during which Captain Hodgkins gathered his company, from February through June, was undoubtedly the most pleasant period of his military career. Apparently Ipswich was his base for duty: no letters to his wife exist for these months and most of his men came from the town or from villages of the area to the west.[8] The specialized skills required of a recruiting officer were more easily come by than were the arts of camp and field. The local tavern was the favored hunting ground for recruits, and officers soon learned to spot the moment to push for a signature on enlistment papers just before the candidate slipped from their grasp and disappeared beneath the table. Tavern keepers were willing allies of the recruiting officers; they hoped to get a piece of the new soldier's bounty before he set out for camp. Most old soldiers had the recruiting officer's talent—it took only colorful yarns of past victories, enthusiasm for the peculiar virtues of leaders in the regiment being formed, and a good head for rum.[9]

Colonel Bigelow, to be sure, wondered from time to time where his regiment might be: on April 8, he demanded that "both officers and soldiers immediately . . . repair to Worcester. . . ."[10] All good things have to end; in early July Captain Hodgkins made his reluctant way to join the men he had been forwarding to Worcester.[11] By this time the unit had been assigned to the brigade of General John Glover of Marblehead. General Glover had distinguished himself in lower ranks through each of the battles that Hodgkins had fought; the Marblehead fishermen whom he led to the siege of Boston had proved to be the invaluable amphibious branch of the patriot army. Glover's fishermen had launched attacks by water on British outposts at Boston; they had evacuated the army in the retreat across the East River from Long Island; and they poled the river boats that carried Washington across the Delaware. Colonel

[8] Hodgkins' company included seven Ipswich men, and others from Topsfield, Lunenburg, Lancaster, Westminster, and Winchington. The largest group was from Lancaster. See muster roll, Bigelow's regiment, taken at Van Schaick's Island, New York, on September 7, 1777.

[9] Miller, *op.cit.*, p. 502.

[10] Ellery Bicknell Crane, *Services of Colonel Timothy Bigelow in the War of the American Revolution* (Worcester, 1914), p. 39.

[11] Joseph to Sarah Hodgkins, Worcester, Mass., undated, July 1777.

Bigelow was a veteran of even harder campaigning; he had marched with Benedict Arnold to Quebec in the winter of 1775-1776. Taken prisoner at Quebec, he had been exchanged the following September.

Captain Hodgkins forfeited to training and skill any chance he might have had to linger at Worcester; his company was among the first ready for service in Bigelow's regiment. "I am to march from hear toMorrow with the first Devision of the Regt . . . " he wrote to Sarah, "Which I whas in hops I should not have Don But as I had not But one Lieut appointed & he is not able to march so there is nobody Else to Take Care of the men But myself. . . ."[12] The company was thirty days on the march from Worcester to the mouth of the Mohawk River, a few miles above Albany on the Hudson. The distance was less than 200 miles, but the days were invaluable. The captain's obligation "to Take Care of the men" involved lending them a veteran's experience in survival on the march.

Hodgkins had the knack of serving only at occasions that would become historic; the engagements around Saratoga, like the battles at Trenton and Princeton, were high moments of the war. At about the time the captain left Ipswich, Gentleman Johnny Burgoyne, the most colorful general of the British army, was pushing up the Richelieu River, the traditional route over which an invasion from Canada could be launched across Lake Champlain. Just before Hodgkins reached Worcester, Ticonderoga passed back into British hands; during his thirty days on the march Herkimer was ambushed at Oriskany; and shortly after he joined the growing American army at the mouth of the Mohawk River, General John Stark routed the foraging British force at Bennington, Vermont. By the time Bigelow's regiment was mustered for battle in early September 1777 the structure of the northern campaign was clear. The American army of General Horatio Gates was growing by the day and Burgoyne, after early triumphs, was in trouble. His western expedition under St. Leger had failed; his search for desperately needed supplies had been rudely interrupted at Bennington; and the

[12] *Ibid.,* This letter, if inferences drawn from the content of the next note are employed, was probably written on July 11, 1777.

column that Clinton might have sent up from New York was lingering below the Highlands.[13]

Gates, on the other hand, was by no means sure that he was safe from an attack from the south; the American high command, from Washington down, was puzzled by Howe's failure to send aid to the invading army. Further, though many men were coming, few regiments had anything like their full strength by early September. The weakness of Bigelow's Fifteenth Battalion, revealed in musters taken at Van Schaick's Island between the first and seventh of September, was probably typical of many regiments on whose presence the battle would turn. Colonel Bigelow himself was not yet present, and would not arrive until October 4. Of his 27 commissioned subordinates, only 8 were on the ground; the "Battalion" actually consisted of 4 half-full companies. Captain Hodgkins' company, 57 strong at Worcester, reported only 36 officers and men ready for duty. The first lieutenant was still recruiting, 7 men had been detached to other posts, 8 were sick, one had died, one had deserted, and one had gone lame on the march. "I do Swaer," wrote Hodg-

[13] Burgoyne had undertaken the campaign full of confidence, despite knowledge that General Howe planned no more than an amusement to aid him from the south. Howe by this time was en route by sea for Philadelphia, and had left Clinton in command of the forces at New York and Newport. It was June 15 when Burgoyne left Fort St. John, on the Richelieu, for his journey across Lake Champlain; his army, with its infantry, artillery, and auxiliaries, amounted to 9,500 officers and men. A few days later Lieutenant Colonel Barry St. Leger, with 900 regulars, tories, and scouts, set out from Montreal for a march from the west by way of Lake Ontario and Oswego; Burgoyne expected St. Leger to sweep the Mohawk Valley and join him at Albany. St. Leger was at Oswego in late July and, reinforced by a thousand Indian allies, he moved toward Fort Stanwix, the western outpost of the patriots. Meanwhile Burgoyne had taken Ticonderoga without a battle; General Arthur St. Clair, exposed to fire from a hill that no one had ever occupied before, on July 6 left the fort in time to fight again. King George III, by various reports, rushed to his wife's bedroom with news of Ticonderoga, shouting, "I have beat the Americans." In the west, St. Leger surrounded Fort Stanwix, and on August 6 ambushed at Oriskany the relief column led by General Nicholas Herkimer. Inside Stanwix, Colonel Peter Gansevoort and Lieutenant Colonel Marinus Willet were unimpressed by this adventure, and held on until General Benedict Arnold came to relieve them in late August. American success in the west was matched by British disaster in the east. As Burgoyne toiled down the route he had selected below Ticonderoga, he sent powerful foraging parties into Vermont for stores and horses. He lost a tenth of his army in the stunning defeat inflicted on August 16 by General John Stark at Bennington. Alden, *op.cit.*, pp. 131-142.

kins on the face of his report, "that the within Muster Roll is a true State of the Company without Fraud to these United States or to any Individual to my Best Knolidge."[14]

For all the raggedness of company, battalion, and brigade, Gates could command more than 7,000 men by September 8, when the general muster of his army was completed. General Benedict Arnold had returned with the expedition that relieved Fort Stanwix, and Colonel Daniel Morgan's invaluable riflemen had arrived in camp. The army moreover was still growing; while Burgoyne, forced to garrison Ticonderoga and suffering from heavy losses at Bennington, was pushing down the east bank of the Hudson with no more than 5,500 regulars and 800 tory and Indian auxiliaries.[15] The patriot force was, as usual, barefoot and tattered but was fully equipped, for a change, with arms and ammunition. Supplies in great quantity, given secretly by France and Spain, had been landed in New Hampshire the preceding spring.[16]

The "Battle of Saratoga" began when Burgoyne decided to cross to the west bank of the Hudson on September 13 and 14. Crossing eliminated any chance of retreat; he would have to conquer or face humiliating defeat. The British general, a gambling man, chose to continue his southward march against mounting odds that he would fail. General Gates, anticipating this decision, moved forward from his camps at the mouth of the Mohawk and at Stillwater to fortify Bemis Heights on the Hudson south of the plains of Saratoga. In the month that followed there were only two days of battle, though constant skirmishing eliminated Burgoyne's scouts and auxiliaries. On September 19, at Freeman's Farm, a whole day of battle closed with the British in possession of the field, but sorely wounded. On October 7, again near Freeman's Farm (northwest of Bemis Heights; the second day, for clarity perhaps, is known as the "Battle of Bemis Heights"), Burgoyne was forced back with staggering losses to his camp at Saratoga. By the seventh Gates had an army of 11,000; militiamen were pouring in from New

[14] Muster of Hodgkins' company, Bigelow's battalion, Van Schaick's Island, September 7, 1777.

[15] Alden, *op.cit.*, pp. 142-143.

[16] *Ibid.*, p. 120.

York and New England. The British camp was effectively surrounded by October 13, and Burgoyne committed himself to the convention negotiations with a Gates who by then commanded 14,000 men.[17]

Captain Hodgkins' 36 effectives were drifting about somewhere in this cloud of patriots, but no one seems to have noticed them passing. Indeed the only direct assertion that the captain fought at Saratoga at all was not made until 1829, when the unknown author of the inscription carved on his tombstone said: "He was also . . . at the capture of Gen. Burgoyne and his army."[18] However, a muster of the company reported on December 10, 1777, surviving in the National Archives, lists Amos Spring, a private in the unit, as "killed September 19"—the date of the first engagement at Freeman's Farm.[19] It is possible that Hodgkins was there, for some units of General John Glover's brigade were among the 3,000 Americans fighting by the close of the day. By Glover's report of September 21, the fighting was fierce:

". . . The battle was very hot till half past 2 o'clock, ceas'd about half an hour, then renewd the attack, both armies seem'd determin'd to conquer or die.

"One continual blaze, without any intermission till dark, when by consent of both parties it ceased, during which time we several times drove them, took the ground, passing over great numbers of their dead and wounded, took one field piece, but the woods and brush was so thick, and being closely push'd by another part of the enemy coming up, was oblig'd to give up our prize.

"The enemy in their turn sometimes drove us. They were bold, intripid and fought like heroes, and I do assure you, Sir, our men were equally bold and couragious, and fought like men fighting for their all. . . ."[20]

[17] Christopher Ward, *The War of the Revolution*, ii (John Richard Alden, ed., New York, 1952), pp. 524, 535.
[18] Hodgkins' stone, with the inscription, stands in the High Street Cemetery at Ipswich, Mass.
[19] Muster of Bigelow's battalion, December 18, 1777, Gulph Mills, on the Schuylkill River, Pennsylvania.
[20] John Glover to General William Heath, September 21, 1777, *Heath*

There is no reliable evidence at all about the location of the company on October 7, the day of the second major engagement. Colonel Timothy Bigelow, who did not join his men until October 4, was, according to his biographer, praised by Washington for his role at Saratoga. The commander-in-chief, by this account, rose when Bigelow attended his first staff meeting at Valley Forge, and introduced the colonel to his officers, saying: "This, gentlemen ... is Col. Bigelow ... who ... joining the northern army under Gates, participated in the struggle with Burgoyne, and shares largely in the honor of that victory."[21]

Joseph Hodgkins, who almost never let a battle pass without regaling his wife with tales of his escapes, wrote home on September 28, October 17, and October 27. The first letter, full of personal detail, touched on the campaign only in his request for winter clothing; it was a "Cool Country & I should Be glad of a pr Mittens. . . ." He referred Sarah to "Brothers Letter for some Pertickelars that I have omitted in this."[22] Sarah Hodgkins was great with child by October; perhaps the captain, not normally a sensitive man, chose in this letter to leave out reports of the dangers to which he had been exposed. In October, after the victory was won, he reported that "we have had a Very fartagueing Campain But as we have Don the Bisnes we Came hear for I hope None of us will Complain of a little hardship." As usual, he wrote "in hast I have nothing new to write as the Compleet Victory gained over our Enemy in this Part of the world is By this time an old story it will Be Needles for me to say much about it Espechaly as you will have the Perticklers By them that whare hear on the spot But I think there is a Remarkable hand of Providence in it & we shall Due well to acknowledge it."[23] If Joseph Hodgkins was at Freeman's Farm or Bemis Heights he exercised great forbearance; he was a man who revelled in the detail of boils, bowel obstructions, and battles.

Hodgkins' letter from Albany, after the battle, carried hard

Papers, Part II, *Collections of the Massachusetts Historical Society*, 7 Series IV (Boston, 1904), pp. 156-157.
[21] Crane, *op.cit.*, pp. 50-51.
[22] Joseph to Sarah Hodgkins, camp near Saratoga, September 27, 1777.
[23] *Ibid.*, Albany, October 27, 1777.

news for Sarah. "I wish I Could inform you that I thought our fartague was over for this year But to the Contray I Expect we shall march to Morrow Morning Down the River to wards the Pakskills & I expect we shall Be ordered towards Philledalpha to Take another winters Camppain in the Jerseys Soldiers must not Complain."[24] Captains may not have complained but the men must have been thoroughly dispirited as they turned from their victory at Saratoga to retrieve Washington's southern defeats. General Howe, while Burgoyne ground forward toward defeat in the north, had landed at the head of the Chesapeake in late August with the main army from New York and East Jersey. In early September he had moved forward through Kennett Square to Chad's Ford, on the Brandywine, and had successfully dislodged the American forces there. Philadelphia fell to the British on September 25, and the battle at Germantown, Pennsylvania, in early October, demonstrated once more the dangers of relying on American militia for a complicated maneuver.[25] Captain Hodgkins, leaving Albany in early November with an army urgently needed by his commander-in-chief, hoped that he could complete the business before spring: "if Genl Washington is But Able to Take Care of Gel How I hope we shall get into winter Quarters in season But we must Leave the Event with him who knows what is Best for us."[26]

The movements of the next two months must have proved disconcertingly familiar to the captain. Once again he crossed the Hudson at Peekskill, and marched toward winter in the Jerseys to reinforce a defeated commander-in-chief. Indeed, if the march had been delayed two weeks, he might have counted each day's progress an anniversary of the same movement during the preceding December and January. Before he reached the dubious security of Valley Forge, he had marched and countermarched over the very ground of the earlier campaign. Even men in the ranks, though, knew that the winter of 1777, for all its hardships, held greater promise than that of the year before. The news of Saratoga brought recognition of the United

[24] *Ibid.*
[25] Alden, *op.cit.*, pp. 121-126.
[26] Joseph to Sarah Hodgkins, Albany, October 27, 1777.

States by France; and the disciplined veterans of the Continental Line who waited with Washington north of Philadelphia were worlds apart from the crew in his camp on the Delaware at Christmas 1776.

General Glover's brigade marched south from Albany early in November and reached Peekskill by November 16, a Sunday. The "Brigade is now Crossing Kings farry," wrote Hodgkins; "we shall Take the Best Rode to Philadelphia hope we shall Be able to Give some good account of Genl How Before we Return." The captain was a new father when he wrote this letter, but he did not find this out until New Year's. "I hear that it is thanksgiving with you this weak," he told Sarah. "I wish I Could Be with you. . . ."[27] Somehow it was never permitted for Captain Hodgkins to take the "Best Rode" anywhere; Glover's brigade was scarcely into New Jersey before it was ordered left from its planned route and dispatched to the support of General Nathanael Greene, south of Trenton at Burlington. Greene had entered the state to resist the last phase of the movements by which General Howe secured control of Philadelphia. The British had entered the city from landings at the head of the Chesapeake Bay, bypassing the fortified water approaches to the city on the Delaware River. After Washington had been pushed to the north of the city, Howe turned to reduce the river forts so that he would have a free supply line by water. By the time Glover's brigade entered the area, only Fort Mercer, on the Jersey shore opposite the mouth of the Schuylkill River, remained in American hands. When Cornwallis approached the fort with overwhelming numbers on November 20, Greene decided to evacuate the place without further resistance. Glover's column had not yet joined him; it was November 24 before the unit arrived at Burlington, a week from its crossing at King's Ferry.[28] Two days later the united force decided to quit New Jersey, and marched for Washington's headquarters at Whitemarsh, north of Germantown, Pennsylvania. When Greene reported to his chief on November 30[29] there was still threat

---

[27] *Ibid.*, Peekskill, November 16, 1777.
[28] G. W. Greene, *Life of General Nathanael Greene*, I (Boston, 1867), pp. 514-522.
[29] *Ibid.*, I, pp. 528-533.

of action from the British. Howe marched up from Philadelphia on December 5 with 14,000 men to tackle the willing army at Whitemarsh, but two days of skirmishing failed to develop into a general engagement. Washington began to move west toward Valley Forge on December 11, and established his winter camp there on December 19.[30]

Captain Hodgkins survived the march with 33 effectives in his company. He reported a formal muster of his men on December 18, at Gulph Mills, west of the Schuylkill; 21 were sick or on leave, and the remainder ready for duty included the captain, a second lieutenant, two sergeants, a corporal, 27 privates, and a drummer.[31] The first concern in the new camp was shelter for the men. A formal military city was erected at Valley Forge, with huts for each unit built along company streets and officers' huts in a line behind. The individuality and imagination that had flowered in the last such city Hodgkins had occupied, outside Boston in 1775-1776, was a thing of the past. Regulations provided a common design: "Plan for the Construction of Hutts dimensions 14 by 16 Foot, Sides Ends & Roof made of Logs, the Roof made light with Split Slabs, the sides made tight with Clay; the fire places made of wood & secured with Clay in the Inside 18 Inches thick, this fire place to be in the rear of the hutt, the door to be in the end next to the Street . . . Side Walls 6½ feet high, the Officers Hutts to form a line in the rear of the Whole. . . ."[32] Officers of a company had a hut to themselves, while each cabin on the street ahead was occupied by 12 non-commissioned officers and men. By January 5, 1778, Hodgkins wrote that "we have got our hutts allmost Don for the men But its Reported that Genl How intends to Come & See our new houses & give us a House warming But if he should I hope we shall have all things Ready to Receive him & treet him in Every Respect according to his Desarts."[33]

Protected from the elements and under no real threat from General Howe, the captain was able to turn to the principal business that occupied him in the early weeks at Valley Forge.

[30] Montross, *op.cit.*, pp. 240-241.
[31] Muster of Bigelow's battalion, Gulph Mills, December 18, 1777.
[32] Quoted in Montross, *op.cit.*, p. 244.
[33] Joseph to Sarah Hodgkins, Valley Forge, January 5, 1778.

He wanted to go home. He learned on New Year's Day 1778 that his wife had delivered another daughter, and in his letter of January 5, he approved the name "Martha" that had been selected ("if it suts you I am content"). Apparently Sarah begged urgently for his return, for in answer to her letter, which has not survived, Hodgkins said, "But My Dear I thought when I wrote Last that I should not Try to get home this winter & wrote you some Reasons why I should not But since I have Received your Letters & seeing you have made some Dependance upon my Coming home therefore out of Reguard to you I intend to Try to get a furlough. . . ."[34] His scheme for getting leave was quite elaborate: he planned to petition his superiors for leave to retire to New England to be inoculated against smallpox—"if this Plan fails me I shall have But Little or no hope. . . ." The plan failed, for he and his whole company were inoculated at Valley Forge in February—perhaps as a misfired result of his stratagem.

Hodgkins did not need Sarah's appeal for his return; "I Believe I have as grate a Desire to Come home as you can Posibly have of having me for this winters Camppain Beats all for fatague & hardships that Ever I went through. . . ."[35] Valley Forge was a nightmare from the start. The army reached the camp half-frozen, starved, and exhausted. On the eve of the abortive engagement at Whitemarsh on December 5, Washington had sent tents and baggage far to the rear, and the succeeding march through days of snow and sleet, the nights on wet ground, took a toll from which the force did not recover for months. A quarter of the 9,000 men were reported "barefoot and otherwise naked"; Washington understated the literal fact when he said, "you might have tracked the army from White Marsh to Valley Forge by the blood of their feet." Further, the army, chopping its huts from standing timber, was as hungry as it was cold. The camp, which took its name from a forge at the junction of Valley Creek with the Schuylkill River, lay on ground over which the armies had been foraging since August. Days passed when the only food available was "fire-cake"—a thin wafer baked from a paste of flour and water. "Fire Cake

[34] *Ibid.*   [35] *Ibid.*

and water for breakfast!" wailed one observer. "Fire-cake and water for dinner! Fire-cake and water for supper! The Lord send that our Commissary for Purchases may have to live on fire-cake and water!"[36] The wonder was that disease and desertion cut the army so little; some 5,000 to 6,000 hung on until spring. The hunger and nakedness were the harder to bear for the fact that they were suffered in a fat, agricultural land. Provisions went begging for buyers at Philadelphia, for producers simply preferred gold to Continental promises.

Captain Hodgkins resented all this and put the blame where it belonged, on the New England towns on which his own men depended: "I must just inform you that what our soldiers have suffred this Winter is Beyond Expression as one half has Ben Bare foot & all most Naked all winter the other half Very Badly on it for Clothes of all sorts and to ComPleat our misery Very shorte on it for Provision not Long since our Brigade drue But an half Days aLownce of Meat in Eight Day But these Defeltis the men Bore with a Degree of fortitude Becoming soldiers But I must say one word to the people at home who I fear have Lost all Bowles of Compassion if they Ever had any for the Contry Towns have Provided Clothing for there men and Brought them to Camp But as there has Ben none from the seeport Towns I fear they have Lost all there Publick Spirit I would beg of them to Rouse from there stupedity and Put on som humanity and stir themselves Before it is too Late I would not have them think hard of maintaining there soldiers for what the soldiers has sufferd the past year Desarves a Penshon During Life. . . ."[37]

Perhaps Captain Hodgkins did the only sensible thing when he submitted in late February to smallpox inoculation and retired to the dark of his smoky hut to fight the fever that followed.[38] He was reported present on musters of Bigelow's regi-

---

[36] The facts and impressions of the above passage on Valley Forge are based on Ward, *op.cit.*, II, pp. 543-545.

[37] Joseph to Sarah Hodgkins, Valley Forge, February 22, 1778.

[38] Sarah to Joseph Hodgkins, Ipswich, April 26, 1778. In this letter Sarah Hodgkins outlined the fear she had felt when the post who brought Joseph's letter of February 22 told her that Hodgkins had been inoculated before he left the camp to bring the letters north.

ment of February 19 and March 5, and "Sick in Camp" on the report of April 4.[39] At least he was spared the torrent of activity that engulfed Valley Forge when that fabulous impostor, Baron Von Steuben, came in March to refine the veteran army in its mastery of formal drill and marching order. His illness undoubtedly helped him get his overdue furlough (Bigelow reported him on leave in returns of May 2 and June 2),[40] and by the time he was on his feet, in mid-April, supplies were flowing again and the army was gathering strength for the next campaign.

Before setting out on the long journey to Ipswich, he found cause for one more burst of anger at the thankless Republic. Rumors had circulated through the spring to the effect that the army would be reorganized along lines of its actual strength, rather than continuing with its half-full paper divisions. If companies and regiments were combined until each remaining unit had its full complement, there would be many an unemployed officer. Hodgkins did not mind the thought of giving up a soldier's life, "But to Be sent home without any Reason why is not agreable to me and if it should Be the Case I Believe I shall not troble the army much more But when I think how I have spent three years in the war have Ben Exposed to Every hardship Venterd my Life & Limbs Broke my Constitution wore out all my Clothes & has got Knothing for it & now not to be thanked for it seams two much for any man to Bare. . . ."[41] The new arrangements were not announced until general orders of June 7, after Hodgkins was at home, but he need not have worried; no one suggested that he give up his command.[42]

While the captain was enjoying his two months at home, news of momentous change began to filter out of Philadelphia. The belated honors done by succeeding generations to the heroes of Valley Forge has sometimes obscured world events of the winter and spring that were of greater consequence. The whole

[39] Musters of Bigelow's battalion, Valley Forge, February 19, March 5, and April 4, 1778.
[40] *Ibid.*, May 2 and June 2, 1778.
[41] Joseph to Sarah Hodgkins, Valley Forge, April 17, 1778.
[42] W. T. R. Saffel, *Records on the Revolutionary War* (Baltimore, 1894), p. 376.

character of the war was altered with the signing of the Franco-American alliance; the turning point was reached, and England practically abandoned any further effort to win or even hold the ground in the northern states over which she had fought for three years. The resignation of General Howe was accepted in February, and in May Sir Henry Clinton came from New York to Philadelphia to take the supreme command of the army in America. More important, Clinton brought secret orders for abandonment of the city, and of New York too, if necessary. The important front for England now lay east of the American mainland; and her troops hurried to find strong defensive positions from which they could look out to the sea, where the greater dangers lay. The American frontier against France and her allies bounded Georgia and crossed into the Indies; and it was in the south and on the islands that the remainder of the war was to be fought. Newport, Rhode Island, was to be held at all costs, according to Clinton's orders, while the fate of New York was left to his discretion. The evacuation of Philadelphia was but an incident in the developing world war, but it was something else as well. The two costly campaigns that Howe had waged to take the American capital only proved, in the end, that war in a rural underdeveloped land is different from war in a complex modern nation. Americans had not yet so entangled their lives with cities, commerce, and governments that the loss of a capital could paralyze them—there must have been times, as a matter of fact, when Washington was relieved to have the threat of Congress removed from his rear.[43]

The logic of grand strategy is apparent only in retrospect, however, and to men in the Continental Line, the British march from Philadelphia back across New Jersey was for the moment an invitation to renew the annual series of Anglo-American engagements there. Clinton left Philadelphia on June 18, and Washington set out the same day for a crossing farther north on the Delaware. The columns slowly converged in familiar territory, the British moving through Mount Holly, Cross-

[43] The large British strategy for 1778 is outlined in Alden, *op.cit.*, pp. 196-197; and the fate of Philadelphia is discussed in Ward, *op.cit.*, II, pp. 567-569.

wicks, Allentown, toward Cranbury and New Brunswick, and the Americans hurrying to intercept through Kingston and Rocky Hill. The indecisive battle at Monmouth Courthouse was fought on June 28. The American attack under General Charles Lee was made half-heartedly, a result of divided counsel on Washington's staff, and before the American chief could renew the engagement the next day Clinton had stolen a leaf from his book. At midnight on June 28 the British column slipped from its camp and by dawn was well clear of the scene.[44]

Bigelow's regiment was in the thick of the fighting at Monmouth Courthouse, but Joseph Hodgkins' company fought without its captain through this last major engagement in the northern theatre. Apparently Hodgkins met his men in northern Jersey, for he arrived at Peekskill with the regiment on July 15.[45] No report of casualties in the company has survived, but Hodgkins met news, on his arrival, that two fellow captains in Bigelow's command had been killed in action. Sarah Hodgkins, commenting on the loss "of your old Companions in the late Battle," said "a Loud Call my Dear may we take Sutable notice of it had you been there it might have been your Lot but Blessed be God it is otherwise. . . ."[46]

Hodgkins had not dawdled on his return; tired of trudging so frequently the whole length of the eastern seaboard, he had bought a horse. Unfortunately the beast was stolen at Peekskill, and he had to travel on foot "till I got so Laim I could not Travel then I was obliged to By another which I have got now But I intend to seel him the first oppertunity for it took all my money to By him But I hope I shall not Loose anything By him."[47] Sarah was sympathetic: "I am sorry for the Loss you met with in Loosing your horse it Seems to be rather against us. . . ."[48]

For the most part, the couple found more cheerful phrases

---

[44] Ward, *op.cit.*, II, pp. 576-586.

[45] The diary of Sergeant Ebenezer Wild, in one of Glover's Massachusetts regiments, lists the itinerary of the brigade after Monmouth. It was at Brunswick on July 2; Newark, July 7; Kings Ferry, July 13; Peekskill, July 15. *Proceedings, Massachusetts Historical Society*, 2 Series, VI (1890), p. 91.

[46] Sarah to Joseph Hodgkins, Ipswich, July 27, 1778.

[47] Joseph to Sarah Hodgkins, Rhode Island, August 18, 1778.

[48] Sarah to Joseph Hodgkins, Ipswich, September 3, 1778.

for their summer letters of 1778; the sense that American fortunes were on the rise was widespread by the time of the Newport campaign. Sarah expressed hope that "the enemy will be defeated this year,"[49] and Joseph answered with talk of the pleasures of "Seeing our friends in Peas."[50] By October he was beginning to consider seriously Sarah's plea that he quit the war for good.[51] He would fight until death for his nation in crisis, but indefinite service on garrison duty was no sensible calling for a middle-aged man with a family to keep. The year had begun poorly, but as the months passed the promise of a happy ending seemed brighter and brighter.

[49] *Ibid.*, Ipswich, July 27, 1778.
[50] Joseph to Sarah Hodgkins, Rhode Island, August 18, 1778.
[51] *Ibid.*, Providence, October 13, 1778.

CHAPTER VII

Citizen Soldiers

I⊤ WAS probably a thin line, no more than a shadow of meaning, that separated the definitions given "duty" by Joseph Hodgkins and Nathaniel Wade when they parted at the camp above White Plains in November 1776. Hodgkins turned south to serve out the thirty-three days for which he was obligated, and found himself on the bloody road that wound through Trenton, Princeton, Saratoga, Valley Forge, and Monmouth Courthouse toward freedom for the Republic. Wade, on the other hand, waited out his term in the New York camp, went north, and found himself favored at home with increasing responsibility, recognition, and honor, to a degree that Hodgkins would never achieve. He walked all one stormy night with Lafayette and earned a place in the Marquis' memory, and he was entrusted with a crucial command by Washington's personal order. After the battle of Long Island, he was in only one brief action but he emerged from the war as the eminent soldier of Ipswich.

Wade discovered, while Hodgkins was making his second laborious round trip through the middle states in 1777-1778, that an experienced officer could rise fast in the Massachusetts militia. He was commissioned on May 8, 1777, as a major in Colonel Danforth Keyes's Middle Essex Regiment, and before the unit was fully organized he was advanced in July to a lieutenant colonelcy.[1] He was ordered to active duty on June 27, 1777, but while his regiment slowly formed in Essex County he found time to marry Mary Foster of Gloucester on July 17. He was soon off again to the wars but his first militia campaign developed as a comic affair in which valor was not required.

[1] *Massachusetts Muster Rolls,* XL, p. 325. For a detailed review of Wade's day-to-day orders in the Rhode Island campaigns, see Herbert T. Wade, "Colonel Wade and the Massachusetts State Troops in Rhode Island—1777-1778," *Essex Institute Historical Collections,* LXXXIX (1953), pp. 357-375.

Keyes's regiment had been called to service as an incident of New England's reaction to the occupation of Newport by the British on December 8, 1776.[2] The following May, Massachusetts sent a secret committee to confer with the governor of Rhode Island on the possibility of dislodging the invaders and, during the summer, an ambitious expedition was planned.[3] Wade's unit went to Rhode Island late in the summer to prepare the way for the 9,000-man force that a one-month draft on the militia of Connecticut, Rhode Island, and Massachusetts was expected to bring out in October. The four Hessian and three British regiments at Newport numbered fewer than 4,000 men; the New Englanders were confident that sheer manpower would sweep them from the Island. General William Heath, writing from his Boston headquarters, promised in late September that there would soon be "news from this quarter, as a secret expedition is just undertaken."[4]

The rendezvous for the American force was set for October 1 at Tiverton on the mainland east of the upper end of the Island, but it was October 13 before the whole army had arrived. The highest returns of the campaign were reported that day; General Joseph Spencer, who commanded, found 8,333 men waiting for his orders. After a few days of drill the army was poised to cross to the Island on October 19, but one of the chaplains argued against a Sunday movement, Spencer was uncertain about the readiness of his men,[5] and it was evident from British preparations on the opposite shore that the secret expedition was not exactly secret any more. Storms prevented action during the next few days and as the end of October approached a good part of the one-month army began to leave. When a muster revealed that the army had shrunk to 5,000 men, the generals decided that their cause was hopeless and released the

[2] Ward, *op.cit.*, I, p. 281.

[3] *Acts and Resolves of the Province of Massachusetts Bay*, XIX, p. 226.

[4] Samuel Greene Arnold, *History of the State of Rhode Island and Providence Plantation, from the Settlement of the State, 1636, to the Adoption of the Federal Constitution, 1790*, II (New York, 1860), pp. 406-408. William Heath to John Glover, September 29, 1777, "Heath Papers." *Collections of the Massachusetts Historical Society*, 7 Series, IV (Boston, 1904), pp. 160-161.

[5] Franklin Bowditch Dexter, ed., *The Literary Diary of Ezra Stiles*, II (New York, 1901), p. 221.

remaining short-term troops from service. Nathaniel Wade's six-month men retired to a camp near Providence until their term was out.[6]

Legislators were dismayed by the unhappy news: the assemblies of Massachusetts, Connecticut, and Rhode Island investigated the fiasco, and the Continental Congress sent a mission to seek the causes of the failure.[7] Wade noted later in his Orderly Book that the citizens of the area had complained "Loudly of the Disorderly Behaviour this last Campaign in Robing and Defacing the houses and Plundering them. . . ."[8] Everyone was disgruntled. One New Englander observed: "The 9000 Men lately raised to go upon a Secret Expedition returned home without effecting any Thing. The public Expence attending this Manoevure has been computed at 35000 dollars pr. day."[9] President Ezra Stiles of Yale College jotted down his impressions after talking with General Spencer, who lost his military reputation along with the campaign: "This unhappy Event teaches two Lessons, that Generals commanding Amer Militia must watch the critical Moment when the Patience & Spt & Confidence of their men is exhausted; 2nd it will teach Militia not to be so infinitely impatient for runng home when Enlistmts are out. Had they tarried one week longer, they would have succeeded, taken R. Isld. and returned with Honors."[10] To General William Heath, the lesson was somewhat different: "We must have a permanent army. Promiscuous crowds . . . cannot be called soldiers. . . ."[11]

Nathaniel Wade was one of the state soldiers who struggled earnestly to find a third course, between the Continental Line and the occasional soldiers of the Newport campaign. His men remained on active duty and in training until the first of the year; and many of his subordinates elected to remain in service the following year, when Massachusetts decided to keep several

[6] *Massachusetts Soldiers and Sailors of the Revolution*, IX, p. 150. Felt, *op.cit.*, p. 189.
[7] Edwin Martin Stone, *Our French Allies* (Providence, 1884), pp. 53-54.
[8] Nathaniel Wade Orderly Book, June 24, 1778.
[9] "Boyles Journal of Occurrences in Boston, 1759-1778," *New England Historical and Genealogical Register*, LXXXV (1931), p. 131.
[10] Dexter, *op.cit.*, p. 223.
[11] Heath to George Washington, March 21, 1778. "Heath Papers," p. 221.

militia regiments activated in preparation for another attempt on Newport. Apparently Wade had attracted favorable notice, for he was given the command of one of these units and promoted to full colonel on March 2, 1778.[12]

The struggle for Newport, a minor sideshow among the large events of 1777, developed as a major campaign of 1778. The British troops defending there were among those eventually captured at Yorktown, and the attacking Americans were joined by the same French fleet that in similar circumstances made possible the later decisive victory. Newport was the one point on the American mainland that Clinton had been ordered to hold at all costs; and Washington later observed that the failure of the joint expedition there "blasted . . . the fairest hopes that ever were conceived. . . ." The battle is almost forgotten now, but in the opinion of the commander-in-chief: "If the garrison of that place (consisting of nearly 6000 Men) had been captured, as there was, in appearance, at least a hundred to one in favor of it, it would have given the finishing blow to British pretensions of sovereignty over this country; and would, I am perswaded, have hastened the departure of the Troops in New York, as fast as their Canvas Wings could carry them away."[13]

Newport came into focus tardily as the city in which independence might be secured. The radical change in British strategy, turned by the circumstances of world war from general invasion to a narrow holding operation, was not fully evident until the summer of 1778 was well along. Washington, back in the old camp at White Plains in late July, was increasingly optimistic— the war had come a full circle and the armies appeared to have exchanged the roles they had played on the same ground in the campaigns of '76. Now it was Washington who had the choice of offensives, and he could exult over the fact that the enemy in New York were "reduced to the use of the spade and pick axe for defence."[14] Further, on July 8, 1778, Charles Henri Théo-

[12] The letter from the Council of Massachusetts, notifying Wade of his appointment, is dated March 2, 1778. Wade Papers, Ipswich Historical Society.

[13] Fitzpatrick, *op.cit.*, XII, p. 488.

[14] *Ibid.*, p. 343.

dat, Comte d'Estaing, had arrived off the American coast with a powerful French fleet and 4,000 seasoned troops. One decisive joint operation might guarantee the success of the Revolution.

New York was the most obvious target but while Washington moved an army grown to 13,000 men to points north of the city d'Estaing decided against the risks of an attack on the smaller British fleet in the bay at New York. The French commander argued that his larger ships drew too much water to cross the bar off Sandy Hook, a matter over which historians have argued ever since. In any event Washington, sensitive to the diplomacy of a joint campaign, did all he could to insure the success of the alternative course, the August assault on Newport. He detached two of his best brigades, those of John Glover and James M. Varnum, for a quick march to Providence, where General John Sullivan had been in command since mid-March, and authorized General Sullivan to issue an appeal for New England militia. Command of the Continental detachment was given to Lafayette, in order to insure smooth relations with the French; and a few days later General Nathanael Greene, a native Rhode Islander, followed to assist General Sullivan in coordinating his fast-growing army.[15]

For Joseph Hodgkins the orders to Glover's brigade probably represented an exasperating but welcome about-face—he was no eager campaigner but he preferred action in New England to duty in the siege at New York. Sarah Hodgkins, at any rate, ought to have been pleased. Before she got news of the new movement, she acknowledged Joseph's report of a safe return to his company in the Jerseys, but said, "I should be glader if you were a going to take the Same journey again as Soon as you had rested yourself. . . ."[16] Her wish was realized before it was expressed. Hodgkins returned from leave to find his men marching for the north. They left New Brunswick on July 5, crossed the Hudson at King's Ferry on July 15, and then, after a four day rest, marched on through Stamford and New Haven toward Providence.[17]

[15] Montross, *op.cit.*, pp. 288-293.
[16] Sarah to Joseph Hodgkins, July 27, 1778.
[17] "Journal of Ebenezer Wild," *Proceedings, Massachusetts Historical Society,* Second Series, VI (1890-1891), pp. 110-114.

The men of the Continental Line made a considerable impression on the towns through which they passed. President Ezra Stiles of Yale College counted them as they entered New Haven on July 26, entertained Lafayette and other high officers, and recorded in his diary an impression of the optimism with which the second Newport campaign was launched. "General Greene," he noted, "says we never had so good an Army as now—we have had more men—but these are *healthy* & well *disciplined* & *full of Life*."[18] The column coming up from New York, composed of men hardened and unified by the winter at Valley Forge, confident after the retreat of the British at Monmouth Courthouse, and elated by the arrival of the French, had every reason for optimism. Unhappily, though, the impending engagement would turn on the skill of the men hurrying south out of New England to join the approaching veterans. Some were relatively well-disciplined militiamen, enlisted for six months or more, like the troops Nathaniel Wade commanded. More were short-term soldiers, responding to General Sullivan's mid-July call on all the New England states.

The first of consecutive entries in Colonel Wade's Orderly Book, made on June 24, suggests the recurring problems faced by militia commanders: the men were congratulated for avoiding plunder of the neighborhoods through which they passed and for refraining from "Riot, Disorders or abuses. . . ."[19] Succeeding entries were remarkably similar to those in the orderly books of 1775; the nation had been at war for three years but raw troops could not borrow the experience of veterans. On July 1 each man in Wade's regiment was issued fifteen rounds of "Sporting Cartriges," and a "firing" was scheduled "for the Purpose of Enuring the troops to firing. . . ."[20] Drill was incessant, as Wade exhorted company officers to "see that their men Scoure their Arms that they May Not appear so Disgraceful when they appear upon the Parade. . . ."[21] Enforcement of elementary rules for camp sanitation was difficult, the colonel

[18] Dexter, *op.cit.*, pp. 290-291.
[19] Wade Orderly Book, June 24, 1778.
[20] *Ibid.*, July 1, 1778.
[21] *Ibid.*, July 17, 1778.

being moved repeatedly to express his "surprise to see the men appear so Beastly and have No more Regard for their own health. . . ."[22] Wade hoped for officers with "so much ambition" as to enforce his orders, but he found it necessary to dismiss a number of captains and subalterns for incompetence.[23] This was a risky procedure in a political army, and the colonel found himself the subject of an investigation by the Massachusetts legislature. On September 26 the General Court took notice of the fact that various officers assigned "to do duty . . . in Wade's and Jacobs' regiments till the first day of January next, by a Resolve of this Court June 12th last, have been in a singular manner sent home, after their men in like manner were put under other officers by the order of said Colonels Wade and Jacobs, to the injury of the Common Cause in the great discouragement of the Militia of this state . . . when again their aid may be requested. . . ." On October 8 the dismissed officers were reinstated but by this time the campaign was over.[24] General Sullivan had similar problems to settle at the regimental level. On August 12, for instance, he announced in general orders that a colonel commanding a Massachusetts regiment had pled "his inability and inexperience in Military Affairs and begs to Be discharged from his Com'd—he is accordingly Discharged . . . the Gen'l wishes that this example May Determin those who have Neither firmness or knowledge for the Military Life, from Excepting Offices which they Cannot Discharge—and at the Same time be a Caution to those who have the appointment of Officers, first to know the Charactors of Men Before they Intrust them with Commands of Such Consequence. . . ."[25]

Leaders with Colonel Wade's experience were invaluable in this army, and the men Wade commanded were afforded vital weeks of training before the bulk of the militia turned out for the August descent on Newport. Wade had been on active duty since February 27, moving back and forth between Massachusetts and Rhode Island as he gradually organized his unit. He

[22] *Ibid.*, August 16, 1778.
[23] *Ibid.*, July 17, 1778.
[24] *Acts and Resolves of the Province of Massachusetts Bay*, xx (Boston, 1918), pp. 490-491, 511.
[25] Wade Orderly Book, August 12, 1778.

was probably at Ipswich on May 3 when his first child, Nathaniel Wade, Jr., was born—at any rate a letter dated May 25 from the Massachusetts Council to General Sullivan refers to his being ordered out to move toward Providence.[26] He was on continuous service with his men from July 24, according to the entries in his Orderly Book. His regiment reached peak strength in August, when he reported 837 privates, 21 drum and fife, 77 sergeants, an adjutant, quartermaster, surgeon, surgeon's mate, 15 second lieutenants, 16 lieutenants, 19 captains, 1 major, and 1 lieutenant colonel.[27] While the colonel struggled to prepare this force for battle, he met unfamiliar responsibilities in planning the campaign. He met with General Sullivan's Council of War on July 25 and agreed with the group's decision to delay action until the Continental force under Lafayette arrived.[28] The same day he sat as president of a court martial that sentenced a spy to death by hanging.[29]

The campaign began to unfold on July 29 when the French fleet arrived off Point Judith; d'Estaing easily destroyed the handful of British ships at Newport and forced a passage on both sides of the Island. The Continentals reached Providence on August 3, and continued around Mount Hope Bay to Tiverton, the selected staging area for the American force. Rhode Island proper, on which Newport lay, was shaped like a narrow-based isosceles triangle seven or eight miles long, pointing north into Mount Hope Bay. Newport was at the southwestern corner and Tiverton was east of the northern tip. According to the plan of action agreed on by d'Estaing and Sullivan, the 4,000 French troops would be landed on the western side of the tip, while the American force crossed from Tiverton. The two armies would then march in parallel columns down the island to undertake the siege. August 9 was chosen for the landings—Sullivan hoped that his militia levies would have arrived by that day.[30]

[26] *Massachusetts Archives, Letters, 1676-1780*, II, p. 4.
[27] Return dated August 25, 1778, Wade Papers.
[28] Otis G. Hammond, *Letters and Papers of Major-General John Sullivan, Continental Army*, II (*Collections of the New Hampshire Historical Society*, XIV, Concord, 1931), pp. 113-114.
[29] Wade Orderly Book, July 24, 26, 1778.
[30] Ward, *op.cit.*, II, pp. 588-590.

Newport

Butts Hill

Tiverton

American
Lines

American
advance

British
Lines

Newport

French Fleet

Execution of the joint operation proved to be a more delicate matter than planning it. On August 8 Sullivan discovered that the British defenders had abandoned fortifications on the northern tip and had concentrated their forces around Newport, so he crossed and occupied the abandoned forts a day ahead of schedule. This action by the American major general without ceremonial consultation with the French lieutenant general soured relations between the allies. The next day it was the turn of the French to offend. Already disgruntled, they had just begun putting troops ashore when the sails of Admiral Richard Howe's fleet were sighted off Newport; Howe had been reinforced since d'Estaing left New York and was hurrying to reinforce the garrison at Newport. The French troops were reembarked despite American protest, and on August 10 the French fleet sailed out to engage the British.[31] Since by this time Sullivan's whole force, 10,122 men, had crossed to the island, he decided to continue the operation as planned, while he waited the return of the French.[32] British General Robert Pigot had only 6,679 men at Newport, so Sullivan could keep the initiative without risk.

The forts abandoned by the British at the northern tip of the island were a substantial base for the American movement—apparently they consisted of both earthworks and barracks. The Reverend Mr. Manasseh Cutler, a volunteer chaplain attached to a Massachusetts regiment, referred in a diary entry of August 10 to the fact that he had found lodging "in the officer's room in the barracks in the fort taken up by Colonel Wade."[33] Wade enjoyed only one night under adequate cover, for on the next he was assigned to duty on the lines through the violent storm that was to prove disastrous for American hopes. August 11 was a cold grey day marked by fairly high winds. Sullivan, nonetheless, was determined to begin his advance at dawn of the following morning. Ammunition was issued, the troops formed for the approach to Newport, and the whole army was mustered

[31] Montross, *op.cit.*, p. 294.
[32] Returns as stated in William Heath, *Memoirs of the American War* (New York, 1904), pp. 202-203.
[33] The sections of Cutler's diary covering the Rhode Island campaign are reprinted in Stone, *op.cit.*, pp. xv-xix.

at 4 p.m. for the readings of general orders describing the advance. General Sullivan, in calmer times a lawyer, outdid himself in the splendid "after-orders" with which he sought to charge the spirit of his inexperienced army; the official prose that day was not to be matched in American military annals until the era of General Douglas MacArthur.[34] But the wind kept on rising. During the night it reached gale proportions and was accompanied by drenching rains that wrecked both the British and American camps. Not a tent was left standing, the powder was ruined, horses were drowned, and the army demoral-

[34] In the Wade Orderly Book, August 11, 1778, Sullivan's exhortation is recorded as follows:

"the Commander in Chief of the Army on Rhode Island having Issued Orders for the Army to move on toward Newport tomorrow Morning at Six oClock—takes this Opportunity to Return his Most Cordial Thanks to the Brave Officers Vollentiers & Soldiers who have with so Much alacrety Repaird to this Place to Give him assistance in Extirpating the British Tyrants from this Country the Zeal and Spirit which they have Discovered are to him the Most Pleasing Presages of Victory and he is happy to find Himself Now at the Head of an Army far Superior in Numbers to that of the Enemy actuated By a Sacred Regard for the Libertyes of their Country and fired With just Resentment against those Barbarians who Delug'd with inocent Blood and Spread Disolation on Every Part of the Continent where they have been Suffer'd to March, the Prospect Before us is Now Exceeding Promising, the Several Corps have Every thing to animate and Press them on to Victory—the try'd Bravery of the Continental Officers and Soldiers and the Idea they Must have of the Dependance of their Valiour Both By the Army and their Country Stimulates them to Support the Carrator they have so Justly Acquir'd.— Volentiers who have so Cherfully Come to assist in the Enterprize have Every Inducement to Exart themselves to Support their Reputation they have acquird'd By flying so freely to the Relief of their Distressed Country—the State troops which the Gen'l has So long since had the Honnour to Com'd he has the Strongest Reason to Beleave will Not Suffer themselves to be out Viy'd in acts of Bravery By any troops in the Army, the Malitia Composed of Repputable freemen and Citizens of America who have so Bravely faught and Conquer'd this Last Year Must Now feal Every Inducement to Spirit them on to Conquest and Glory—the Charector of the Several Corps which compose the Army Expectation of the Country, the Safty of Our Land, the Protection of Our Property and in short Every thing which Annimates Men to fight and Conquer Call aloud upon to Act the Part of freemen & becoming the Charector of Americans—The Gen'l on his Part assures his Brave Army that he will with the Utmost Chearfulness Share with them in Every Danger and fatigue and is Ready to Venture his Life in Every Instance where the Good of his Country Calls for it—To them and his Country he Stands Ready to Pledge or to Sacrifice if Necessary his Life,—and from his Officers and Men which he has the Honour to Com'd he Expects to find the Same Sentiments and Disposition and fir'd with the same sentiments, and Engaged in so Just a Cause we Must Conquer we Must win the Laurals that awaite us and Return in triumph to the Arms of a Greatful Country."

ized. At sea the two fleets, maneuvering still before decisive engagement, were completely dispersed. The French *Langue-doc*, 84 guns, was demasted and lost her rudder, some of Howe's ships were driven all the way to the coast of Virginia, and when the storm was done a few inconclusive single ship encounters were broken off as Howe returned to New York and the French turned back toward Newport.[35]

Years later the storm remained the outstanding event in veteran memories of the Newport campaign. When Lafayette passed through New England in his triumphal tour of 1824, he paused for a reception in Ipswich, immediately recognized Colonel Wade, and the two old soldiers embraced. "O my dear Colonel!" exclaimed the Marquis; "you remember Rhode Is-land, and the night of August 12, 1778, when you and I la-mented the misunderstanding of d'Estaing and General Sulli-van?" "Indeed I do," Wade returned, "and never can forget it. It was a dreadful storm, and the soldiers had no shelter; my duty required me to be out to watch the enemy, and you insisted on walking the rounds with me all night, although I urged you to go to your tent." Lafayette's memories were clear: "I was too anxious to sleep and I thought it my duty to conciliate the American officers, as the French admiral seemed to insist too much upon punctilio to the injury of our common operations. We did not mind the rain, altho we were drenched through and through." "No indeed," returned Wade. "Had d'Estaing as-sisted us, I always thought we should have compelled Gen. Pigot to surrender; we missed a fine opportunity. . . ."[36]

General Sullivan was not dismayed. In his general orders of August 13, he advised that "it is with the Most servisable Pain that the Gen'l Sees the Difficulties his Brave troops Officers and Soldiers are Exposed to By the Violence of the Weather and Sin-cerely wishes that anything in his Power Could Contribute to their Relieve, he however flatters himself that they will have a Soldierly Patience a Misfortune which in War Must frequently

[35] Ward, *op.cit.*, II, p. 591; Montross, *op.cit.*, pp. 294-295.
[36] This frequently reprinted exchange was described by a reporter for the *Newburyport Union*. This version of the newspaper story is from notes taken by Daniel Treadwell Wade in 1881.

Happen, and hopes that in a few Days they will be well Rewarded for all their Tryals and Hardships—after a Compleat Conquest over Enemies & Look Back and Victory Must afford us the Greatest Satisfaction and Compel the World to admire the Patience and firmness of the Conqueror, as well as applaud their Bravery. . . ."[37]

The general spent three days wringing out his army, and on August 15 undertook the movement that the storm had interrupted. With a delicacy acquired from his difficulties with the French a week earlier, he kept his army on the eastern side of the island, leaving the western side open to French occupation when and if his allies returned. He concentrated his 10,000 men about two miles from the defenses on the British right—his decision was brave, in a way, for with similar dispositions he had been outflanked and captured on Long Island, and after he was exchanged he commanded the right wing on Washington's army on the Brandywine, where his flank was again turned and the army routed. Siege approaches were begun, and cannonading was heavy from both sides. Apparently the forces remained slightly out of each others' range, for casualties were negligible. Joseph Hodgkins, in the lines, found time to write to Sarah on August 18: ". . . Last Satuday we marched & took Post within two milles of the Enemys Lines whare we still Remain we are Prepairing Battres which will Be oppened on them Prety soon the Enemy Keep a Constant Canonade on our fatigue Partys But they Due But Little Dammage as to the french fleet I hardly know what to write doubtles you heard of there going out sum time ago they have not Returnd yet But it is sayd to Day that they have Ben heard off & that they have taken 21 sail of Transports & are now off Block island I Due not say this is a fact But hope it tis But I hope they will Return soon and if they Du I think we shall soon Du our work hear. . . ."[38]

The French fleet limped into Newport on August 20, battered but without a single ship lost. D'Estaing, though, announced to the American staff that his captains had decided that the safety of the fleet depended on immediate withdrawal to Boston

---

[37] Wade Orderly Book, August 13, 1778.
[38] Joseph to Sarah Hodgkins, Rhode Island, August 18, 1778.

to refit; the French would take no further part in the campaign. No amount of expostulation on the part of the Americans moved their allies—even Lafayette's pleas failed to move his country-man who commanded the naval units. D'Estaing's position was difficult: he was a soldier, elevated to command in the navy by noble rank rather than by training, and on naval matters he was dependent on the advice of his staff. The fleet weighed anchor at midnight on August 21 and left the roads three days later.[39]

General Sullivan met the crisis with another general order; he hoped that "the Event will Prove America able to Procure that with her own arms which her Allies Refus'd to asist her in obtaining; it is with Grief and astonishment the Gen'l finds that a Number of the Volunteers are about to Leave the Island at this time and to Give to America a Lasting Proof of their Want of firmnes and Bravery. . . ."[40] Two days later, when it ap-peared that the good will of the French might be all that could be salvaged from the campaign, he tried to take the sting from his earlier comments: ". . . it having been Supposed By Some Persons that By the order of the 24th instant the Commander in Chief Men't to Insinuate that the Departure of the french fleet was owing to a fixt Determination Not to asist in the Present Enterprize, as the Gen'l would Not wish to give the Least Couler for ungenerous & Illiberal Minds to Make Such unfair Enterpretations, he thinks it Necessary to Say, as he Could Not Posibly be acquainted with the orders of the french Admiral, he Could Not Determin weither the Removal of the fleet was absolutely Necessary or Not, and therefore did Not Mean to Censure an act which the Admiral Might Do un-der absolute Necessity—he however hopes that the Speedy Return of the fleet will Show their attention and Regard to the Alliance form'd Between us and ad to the obligations which the Americans are always under to the french Nation. How Ever Mortifying the Departure of the fleet was to us at Such time of Expectation we ought Not too Suddenly to Sensure the Movement of; or an act of any kind to forget the Aid and

[39] Ward, *op.cit.*, II, p. 591; Montross, *op.cit.*, pp. 295-296.
[40] Wade Orderly Book, August 24, 1778.

Protection which has Been afforded us By the french to Serve the Present Contest. . . ."[41]

"I give up the Rh. Isld. Expedition," wrote President Stiles when news of the French action reached New Haven.[42] In Sullivan's army thousands of militiamen reached the same conclusion and acted on it: nearly 5,000 took what came to be known as french leave within the week.[43] No amount of oratory by the commanding general could halt the desertions—very soon, in fact, the problem for the Continentals and state troops remaining was how they could effect their own retreat with dignity and order. Invading an island with overwhelming force and naval support was one thing, but evacuating it under close pursuit was something else entirely. As General Greene put it, "To evacuate the Island is death; to stay may be ruin."[44]

By August 28 the American army was estimated at 5,400 men, fewer than the British defenders whose strong positions they had hoped to storm. Escape was the only alternative that remained, though as a last gesture Sullivan sent Lafayette galloping the seventy miles to Boston to beg the return of the French fleet.[45] General orders for the 28th commanded a secret withdrawal during the night to the fortifications on the northern end of the island that the Americans had occupied after their landing on August 8. Pursuit was anticipated so troops of the Continental Line were left outside the new positions to delay the British on both the east and the west roads. In addition to this rear guard, a picket of state troops commanded by Colonel Nathaniel Wade was posted between the army and the rear guard between the roads on which the British would follow.[46]

Choice of Wade for this important assignment was in part evidence of the confidence felt in his courage by his superiors, but it also indicates the incapacity of his subordinates. According to his orderly book the picket consisted of 3 subalterns, 3 corporals,

[41] *Ibid.*, August 26, 1778.
[42] Dexter, *op.cit.*, II, p. 298.
[43] Thomas C. Amory, *The Military Services and Public Life of Major-General John Sullivan* (Boston, 1868), p. 85.
[44] G. W. Greene, *Life of General Nathanael Greene*, II (Boston, 1867), p. 99.
[45] Sullivan's report to Congress, in Stone, *op.cit.*, p. 94.
[46] *Ibid.*, pp. 88-89.

and 81 privates—clearly a company-sized unit, with the colonel in the role of captain. Wade played his role well. He assembled his men before dawn, checked their equipment, and marched out from the new lines at Butts Hill on the northern tip of the island to a point about three miles south of the main lines. Sensitive to the deficiencies of New England militiamen, he found shelter for his men in a field surrounded by stone walls, bordering on a cross road connecting the two main routes open to a British advance.

With dawn, the battle unfolded as Sullivan had planned it. The British hurried out in pursuit of the attackers who had disappeared during the night, hoping to trap them in the process of crossing back to the mainland. The action began when troops on the East Road made contact with the American rear guard, and when these dropped back, according to schedule, some British units swung off to the left along the road where Wade's picket waited. Crossing without proper flankers or scouts, they were surprised by point-blank fire from the picket appearing suddenly at the wall bordering the road. Wade's men had time to reload and get off a second volley before the demoralized redcoats fell back to reform.[47]

During the general engagement that followed, the brigades of the Continental Line formed the principal shield protecting Sullivan's position. When the picket, its mission accomplished, withdrew to the main lines, Glover's brigade reinforced the rear guard on the East Road, and in sharp fighting forced the attackers back. Tests of the American right wing found Varnum's brigade, supported by Colonel Christopher Greene's all-Negro regiment from Rhode Island, fully able to prevent further British advance. American cannon fire from Butts Hill was particularly effective and after two hours of the attack the British settled back to a line on hills three miles south of the American positions. Statistically, Sullivan took honors for the day; his men suffered 211 casualties, as compared with 300 for the British.[48]

A modicum of glory was thus snatched from the collapse of

[47] Arnold, *op.cit.*, II, p. 426.
[48] Ward, *op.cit.*, II, p. 592.

the campaign, more than enough to take the sting from the expedition's failure. The next day the British sat idle, for General Pigot had no stomach for another attack on Sullivan's full force. On the evening of August 30 General Glover shifted to his amphibious role; while a show of activity was maintained in the front lines, he commanded the boats that picked the army off the island. By morning the Americans were scot-free, bag and baggage. "The event," reported General Sullivan to Congress, "proved how timely my retreat . . . as one hundred sail of the enemy's ships arrived in the harbor on the morning after. . . ."[49] Congress responded with handsome praise, resolving that the "retreat made by General Sullivan . . . was prudent, timely and well conducted, and the Congress highly approve of the same."[50] This was one defeat that the legislators preferred not to investigate, so Congress closed the incident by resolving that "Count d'Estaing hath behaved as a brave and wise officer . . . and the officers and men under his command have rendered every benefit to these states. . . ."[51] A dutiful satellite to one of the world's great powers could scarcely say less in its effort to preserve so crucial a friendship.

Unhappily, Captain Joseph Hodgkins' comments on the Rhode Island fiasco have not survived. "I would just give you a short account of our Retreet," he began, in a letter to Sarah of September 4, but at this point the letter is torn and the rest of his report is missing. The captain had been with Glover's brigade in the battle of the 29th and, along with the rest of the Continental Line, had been among the last troops to get off the island.[52] Sarah Hodgkins, alert with all New England women to the dangers faced by the army trapped on the island, already had news of his escape. "I was very uneasy about you," she wrote on September 3, but "Doct Manning is come home & he Says he Saw you Sence you come off you was well which was a greate Satisfaction to me to hear . . . I want to See you very much but

[49] Stone, *op.cit.*, p. 93.
[50] William P. Upham, *Memoir of General John Glover of Marblehead* (Salem, 1863), pp. 54-55.
[51] Ward, *op.cit.*, II, p. 593.
[52] Joseph to Sarah Hodgkins, Providence, September 4, 1778.

durst not hardly think of that but I hope too betwene this & cold weather if we are alive. . . ."[53]

"I want to see you Very much," Hodgkins replied on September 10, "& I wish your circumstances was such as you could Leave home so as to Come and see me for I have no Prospect of get Leave at Present. . . ."[54] A month later he was somewhat more hopeful: "I Received yours by Col Wade this morning which gave me the grates satisfaction . . . I hope to Come home soon . . . Tell Brother I whant to get home to Husking But fear he will get don Before I shall get home."[55] Colonel Wade, who played postman for this exchange, got home more quickly—an old habit of his—but he earned his short leave by the diligence of his service in the succeeding months. Once cold weather reduced the threat of further British movements, Hodgkins could leave his veteran company to run itself, and the absence of letters suggests that he was in Ipswich through a good part of the late fall, winter, and spring. Wade on the other hand had to fight a constant battle to keep his raw troops healthy, decent, and disciplined. According to surviving returns from his regiment, he was home on furlough from September 29 to October 13, but after that he was on continuous duty with his men at East Greenwich, Rhode Island, until the regiment completed its tour at the end of December.[56]

From the moment his men reached their permanent post at East Greenwich the local citizens raised constant complaint against plunder of their fields and poultry houses by the troops. The colonel, "Determined to Put a Stop to such an Evill and Unsoldier-like Practice," ordered officers to flog miscreants the moment they were caught, without benefit of court martial.[57] Army stores were even more attractive—one of Wade's men was given fifty lashes for breaking into the commissary rum.[58]

[53] Sarah to Joseph Hodgkins, September 3, 1778.
[54] Joseph to Sarah Hodgkins, Providence, September 10, 1778.
[55] *Ibid.*, October 13, 1778.
[56] Photostats of returns from the Middle Essex Regiment, taken from Massachusetts records during the 1920's by Herbert T. Wade.
[57] "Orderly Book of Capt. Simeon Brown, Colonel Wade's Regiment, Rhode Island Campaign, 1778," *Essex Institute Historical Collections*, LVIII (July 1922), p. 254.
[58] Wade Orderly Book, October 3, 1778.

The colonel's problems were compounded by the fact that his officers were as indifferent to discipline as were the men; his orders of September 22 were repeated constantly with only slight variation in the words: "The Col is Very Sorry to See Such Neglect in the officers in Not attending the Parade for Exercise in Season . . . He Requests them to exert themselves. . . ."[59] Wade, though, forgot and forgave when the time came to dismiss his state troops on December 31. His final order, recorded by one of his captains, expressed "his Sincere thanks to both the Officers & soldiers of the Reg't which he has had the hon'r to Comand for their Universal good conduct and Military Behaviour in their Several Stations . . . he thanks the Officers for their Care in Keeping up that good order amongst the troops . . . he Likewise thanks the Soldiers for the Soldier Like Behaviour in Showing their Readiness and willingness to Do their Duty as Soldiers and that their General Conduct has been such as has gained a Universal Applause of the People wherever the Regt has Ever been Stationed in all which have done themselves Hon'r Done Honour to their officers to the State which they belong. . . ."[60]

Captain Joseph Hodgkins was in camp a few miles to the north at Providence, the winter headquarters for Glover's Continentals.[61] Drill, for the veterans, was not a matter of painful parade and banishment to awkward squads; a sergeant's diary reveals the sophistication of their maneuvers. On September 28, the brigade turned out for a sham battle through the streets of Providence:

"The brigade was divided, in order to perform a sham fight. The right wing went down in front street; the left down the back street. There were two field pieces with each party. The left marched down the back street, turned and came up the front street as far as Genl Glover's quarters, where they met the right. They began the engagement with field pieces which were

---

[59] *Ibid.*, September 22, 1778.

[60] Brown Orderly Book, December 29, 1778.

[61] Hodgkins was well housed at Providence; he and several other officers rented the home of a Captain Frazer, who was at sea during this period. "Captain Lanman's Letter to His Wife," in "Memoir of Gen. John Sullivan," *New England Historical and Genealogical Register*, VII (1853), p. 138.

discharged several times on both parties; after which they fell in the rear, & then the musketry began, which was fired by platoons in great order. The left wing retreated over the bridge. The right pursued them very close till they got to the bridge, where the artillery of both parties was brought in the front. They disputed the bridge some time with the field pieces, but the left wing gained the bridge and the right wing retreated as far as where the engagement began. By this time it had grown quite dark; the general officers came to a parley, and the firing ceased on both sides. Both parties passed to the right-about, & marched to the camp again in the same order as before mentioned. All this was performed with the greatest order and activity possible."[62]

When disciplinary problems found their way into general orders or diaries, they were likely to be serious—old soldiers who decided to steal a chicken or tap the company rum could accomplish their mission without being caught. However, on December 5, the sergeant quoted above said casually, "This afternoon Ebenr Williams was to be shot but the weather would not admit of turning out. . . ."[63] Williams had been convicted of promoting a mutiny, a crime increasing in frequency among soldiers of the Continental Line.

Joseph Hodgkins undoubtedly deplored mutiny but on the other hand he made no reference in his letters of the fall to "this glorious cause." There is some evidence that he turned to speculation after his escape from Rhode Island. He signed a petition dated October 3 and addressed to Governor George Clinton of New York, asking permission to transport four barrels of flour out of the state.[64] Nine days later, in a cryptic postscript to a letter home, he asked Sarah to "Let Mr Sweet Know that it will Be much to his Disadvantage to stay at home any Longer if he has not set out Before you get this."[65] Perhaps these two surviving scraps from the record are unrelated; the

---

[62] "Journal of Ebenezer Wild," *Proceedings, Massachusetts Historical Society*, Second Series, VI (1890-1891), p. 118.

[63] *Ibid.*, p. 119.

[64] Hugh Hastings, ed., *Public Papers of George Clinton, First Governor of New York*, IV (Albany, 1900), pp. 133-134.

[65] Joseph to Sarah Hodgkins, Providence, October 12, 1778.

captain had not before interrupted military zeal with business enterprise. He changed, though, in the course of the Rhode Island campaign and, changing, began to calculate the cost of patriotism. "I am on the main Guard," he wrote from Providence on September 10, "& have had many thoughts in my head to night But it would Be folly in me to commit all my thoughts to writing."[66] In a few more weeks he was sorting out his thoughts: "you say in your Letter that you are afraid that I shall stay in the Cause of Liberty Till I shall mak my self a slave att my Day I have two much Reason to fear that will Be the Case But if it should I have no body to Blame But the Continent in general Who will Ever Be guilty of Ruening thousands unless they Due something more for them then what they Ever have Don yet and now as I have spent so much time in the sarvice & now to ask a Discharge when to apperence the war is most to an end would Debar me from Expecting any further Compensation. . . ."[67]

Pensions, land grants, even half-pay for life were in the air; the problem was to hang on until a greatful Republic acknowledged its debts. For Hodgkins, though, the memory of the Rhode Island affair must have rankled more and more. Major General John Hancock had come out with the one-month men from Massachusetts and entertained lavishly while his army disappeared.[68] Nathaniel Wade had walked with generals, earned mention in reports of the engagement, and returned to Ipswich a hero. The Continentals, who had led the advance and who had guarded the retreat with blood, waited in camp at Providence for orders to the next campaign.

The war, meanwhile, had shifted to unfamiliar theaters—the British took Savannah in December 1778 and raided into South Carolina during the following spring.[69] Reports from these distant places must have added to the doubts in Hodgkins' mind as he wondered where his next march might carry him. Further, he surveyed his uncertain future from a disastrous present. While he served out the winter around Providence, the Conti-

[66] *Ibid.*, September 10, 1778.   [67] *Ibid.*, October 13, 1778.
[68] Stone, *op.cit.*, II, p. xviii.
[69] Ward, *op.cit.*, II, pp. 679-687.

nental paper in which he was paid lost most of its value. When he left Rhode Island on August 30, 1778, four and a half dollars, Continental, would buy one silver dollar. By the following April the ratio was twelve to one and in June it was fifteen to one.[70]

Joseph Hodgkins quit the war in June 1779. He left no report of his reasons for the decision—the record shows only that he offered his resignation in May and appeared for the last time on an army payroll on June 20. He had pondered his action for long months after the Newport affair and, being a sensible man, he was probably reluctant to sacrifice the benefits that his resignation cost. But Sarah's plea for his return would have gained force with his inability to support a family on soldier's pay, just as the collapse of the well-planned Rhode Island campaign must have shaken his faith in the prospect of early victory.

He went no more to the wars. Never an occasional soldier, he had completed four years, two months, and one day of continuous service since the morning he turned out for the Lexington alarm. He was more than four years older.

[70] Dexter, *op.cit.*, II, pp. 298, 328, 346. Davis R. Dewey estimates that the general rate of depreciation during this period was even greater than the above figures, based on purchases made by President Stiles, suggest. Davis Rich Dewey, *Financial History of the United States* (New York, 1918), pp. 39-41.

CHAPTER VIII

True Men

THE WAR raged on for more than two years after the return of Nathaniel Wade and Joseph Hodgkins to Ipswich, but battles in places so distant as Savannah, Charleston, Briar Creek, Camden, King's Mountain, Cowpens, Guilford, Ninety-Six, Eutaw Springs, or Yorktown must have been considered by the citizens of the town as engagements in some alien land. The British abandoned Newport in October 1779 as an incident in their increasingly ambitious southern operations and, except for occasional raids, New England was not again in danger. Hodgkins returned to his shoemaker's last and Wade settled to dignified occupancy of the various local offices that he was to hold for the rest of his life. He was appointed Muster Master for Essex County, with the rank and pay of colonel, on November 27, 1779,[1] and the following year he solidified his standing in the community by becoming a Master Mason, taking his third degree in Unity Lodge, No. 3, on July 13, 1780.[2]

The thirty-year-old colonel served three months more in the field before the Revolution ended. However inconstant the militia might prove in the execution of a sustained operation, as at Newport, it still turned out for each new requisition. Englishmen shrank from more than hit-and-run raids on the New England coast, for the record from Concord to Bennington showed that when the militia began to swarm in local defense, it might swallow up any attacking force. The state troops usually responded loyally too when the nation asked for help. Washington rarely got as many troops as he requested but his requests for reinforcement seldom went unanswered.

[1] *Massachusetts Archives*, CLXXVI, p. 561.
[2] Wade's diploma for the third degree, signed by William McLean, Master, Thomas Dodge, Senior Warden, and Thomas Burnham, Secretary, is preserved in the Wade Papers.

The commander-in-chief, through the closing years of the war, kept his northern army disposed in an arc stretching from northern New Jersey through White Plains to Connecticut. Clinton remained at New York with a sizeable force, and the two armies were constantly testing each other with occasional forays mounted in hope of cheap victories. After 1777 Washington's line was anchored on the rising fortress at West Point far up the Hudson. Generally, he kept his veterans in the field south of the Point, and left the steady strengthening of the forts to levies of militiamen who rotated through the post. Militia service at West Point seems in retrospect to have been thinly disguised forced labor; the bulk of the men who served there spent their terms on fatigue duty rather than on drill and guard.

Nathaniel Wade led a brigade of Massachusetts men out for three months of this duty in the summer of 1780.[3] His Essex County regiment joined units from Hampshire, Worcester, and Suffolk Counties, and Wade proved to be the senior colonel when the force gathered at Great Barrington in late July. Finding men for such an expedition was not too difficult, for Massachusetts had faced up to the facts of the inflation by providing extraordinary bounties to state troops in her service. In addition to Continental pay, according to resolves of October 1779, a colonel in state service would receive 45 pounds per month, a captain 30 pounds, and a private 16 pounds.[4]

The Massachusetts contingent arrived at West Point on August 4, 1780,[5] and within a day, artisans of the unit were busy at their labors. Two days later Major General Benedict Arnold took formal command of the Post.[6] Wade had little contact with his superior, for Arnold made his headquarters across the river at the Beverly Robinson House, leaving to Colonel John Lamb of the New York Continental Line the

---

[3] For a detailed account of this service, see Herbert T. Wade, "The Massachusetts Brigade on the Hudson, 1780. Nathaniel Wade at West Point," *Essex Institute Historical Collections*, XC (1954), pp. 84-99, 167-190.

[4] *Acts and Resolves of the Province of Massachusetts*, XXI, p. 235.

[5] Wade Orderly Book, August 3, 5, 1780.

[6] *Ibid.*, August 6, 1780.

immediate command of the garrison.[7] General Arnold was not much impressed with his subordinates; he wrote to Washington on August 8 that "The officers in general from the State of Massachusetts Bay, have never been in the service before, and are extremely ignorant of their duty, which throws everything into confusion; and, in case of an attack on the post, from their inexperience I believe little dependence can be placed on them. The troops are good and well armed."[8] Apparently Colonel Wade, in contrast to his fellows, was more highly regarded by Arnold's staff. His appointment as deputy adjutant general for the Post and the Department was proposed while he served at West Point, and Lieutenant Colonel Richard Varick, Arnold's secretary, commented on his quality. Varick, although he opposed the appointment of a militia officer to the post, observed that Wade "is a man of the most superior talents as well as appearance of any of these Gentry."[9]

Colonel Wade had little time for thought of problems at headquarters across the river. He led the largest force in his experience—1,565 of all ranks, according to a return of September 5[10]—and his orderly book reveals that such numbers compounded the ordinary difficulties of maintaining a militia unit at reasonable efficiency. His first brush with Arnold's dark design —indeed his only hint, before the fact, of the threat of treacherous command—came on Sunday, September 17, when he crossed with other officers of the garrison to an early dinner with the general at Robinson's House.[11] While the company was still at the table, General Arnold received and read the letters forwarded from the British ship, *Vulture*, that set in motion his fateful assignation with Major John André. The tension that gripped the table in the argument following Arnold's casual explanation of the correspondence probably escaped the colonel, but he retained

[7] Carl Van Doren, *Secret History of the American Revolution* (New York, 1951), pp. 287, 291.

[8] Library of Congress, *Calendar of the Correspondence of George Washington . . . With the Officers*, II (Washington, 1915), p. 1442.

[9] Herbert T. Wade, *loc.cit.*, p. 171.

[10] A return of the regiment for this day is preserved with the Wade Papers.

[11] Van Doren, *op.cit.*, pp. 315-316.

in later years a vivid recollection of an incident that occurred as he returned to his boat:

"On taking leave of his host after dinner, one of the General's Aides de Camp, a Major whose name Col. Wade used to give, but which has escaped . . . memory, rose from the table and walked to the shore of the river where he was to take his boat for the fort, in close company with him. On arriving near the shore, the Major suddenly changed the subject of conversation and said in an impressive voice, 'Col. Wade, there is something going on here that I do not understand and cannot find out. I say this to put you on your guard at the Fort. I fear there is something brewing about us, and all I can say is look out for!' With these words he suddenly returned upon his path, evidently to avoid all inquiry or explanation. Col. Wade was wholly unable at the time to guess from what quarter the threatened mischief might be expected. But after Arnold's defection it became evident that the Major had had his suspicions excited by the secret communications which were carried on, or by the privacy with which Arnold wrote, and the care with which he kept certain papers hidden from all about him. He therefore took this method to rouse the vigilance of a principal officer of the garrison, without going so far as to involve himself by making charges against his General, who, after all might be entirely innocent. Col. Wade always thought it highly honorable to the Major's acuteness and fidelity . . . The warning so impressed Col. Wade, that had suspicious orders been received he might have saved the Fort and the garrison."[12]

The plot, of course, collapsed short of fruition. General Arnold took Major André off the *Vulture* on the night of September 21 and, unable to return him, brought him into the American lines on the morning of the 22nd. The unfortunate

[12] This story was first published more than a hundred years after the fact, in the *Ipswich Antiquarian Papers*, II (May 1881), No. 19. The author, though, had good credentials. He was Professor Daniel Treadwell, late Rumford Professor and Lecturer on the Application of the Sciences to the Useful Arts at Harvard College. Professor Treadwell grew up in Nathaniel Wade's home, Wade having been appointed his guardian in 1803. For a review of the aging professor's memory of the aging soldier's stories, see William Abbatt, *The Crisis of the Revolution* (New York, 1899), p. 44.

major was captured in civilian clothes with incriminating documents during his attempt to escape overland on September 23. Two days followed, before news of André's capture reached Arnold at Robinson's House, minutes before he received General Washington at breakfast on the morning of September 25. The story of Arnold's flight down the river to the *Vulture* is well-known.[13]

Washington, late for breakfast, crossed to the garrison at West Point, expecting to find Arnold there. It was probably noon before he had full possession of the facts, and even then he delayed action through the afternoon while Colonel Alexander Hamilton went in vain pursuit of the traitor. His immediate problem was the extent of Arnold's design; none of the refugee's aides could be trusted and the area had to be secured with men whose loyalty was beyond doubt. Colonel John Lamb, the senior officer at West Point, crossed back to Robinson's with him and then was sent down the river to take command at Stony Point and Verplanck's Point—if the British were moving north, the first blow would fall at King's Ferry, which connected these posts. It was early evening before the local troops were alerted. Lafayette, who rode with Washington that day, reached many years later into his generous memory to describe his chief's reaction to the fact that Wade was the senior, after Lamb, at the Point: "On Being told that it was Colonel Wade, he Said, 'Col. Wade is a true man, I am satisfied!' "[14] The words may not have been spoken but the order that followed was issued in their spirit. Written about 7 p.m., in the hand of Alexander Hamilton, and signed by Washington, the document reads:

"To Col. Wade, at West Point
　　Head Quarters, Robinson's House, 25' Sept, 1780

Sir:

General Arnold is gone to the enemy. I have just now received a line from him, enclosing one to Mrs. Arnold, dated on board the Vulture. From this circumstance, and Col. Lamb being detached on some business, the command of the garrison,

[13] Van Doren, *op.cit.*, pp. 344-354.
[14] See footnote 36, p. 158.

for the present, devolves on you. I request, that you will be as vigilant as possible; and, as the enemy may have it in contemplation to attempt some enterprise, even tonight, against these posts, I wish you to make immediately after the receipt of this, the best disposition you can of your force, so as to have a proportion of men in each work, on the west side of the river. You will see me or hear from me further tomorrow.

I am, Sir,

your mo obet Serv't

Go: Washington"[15]

Men whispered all through the night at West Point, and on down the Hudson. Wade's whole garrison was aroused to wait out the dark[16] and their mood must have been like that of the soldier in Greene's force at Tappan, ordered north for the emergency: ". . . the dark moment . . . in which the defection was announced in whispers. It was midnight, horses were saddling, officers going from tent to tent ordering their men, in suppressed voices, to turn out and parade. No drum beat; the troops formed in silence and darkness. I may well say in consternation, for who in such an hour, and called together in such a manner, and in total ignorance of the cause, but must have felt and feared the near approach of some tremendous shock."[17]

Daylight dissolved the tension of the night and as the hours passed it became clear that no British move was impending. Washington's only order to Wade on the 26th dealt with provisioning the fort[18] and by the next day life in the garrison seems to have returned to normal. Wade convened a court martial that day, in which "Mrs. Warren was tryed for Repeatedly abusing Cap't. Lieut. Archbald." The Lady was acquitted.[19] On September 28 Colonel Wade surrendered his command to General William Irvine, and settled back to his duties with the Massachusetts Brigade.[20]

[15] The letter is framed and displayed today in the home of Francis C. Wade, 5 Woods Lane, Ipswich.
[16] Wade Orderly Book, after orders, dated 2 a.m., September 26, 1780.
[17] Van Doren, *op.cit.*, pp. 352-353. [18] The letter is in the Wade Papers.
[19] Wade Orderly Book, September 27, 1780.
[20] *Ibid.*, September 28, 1780.

After these two and a half anxious days, the Ipswich colonel found the remainder of his service something of an anticlimax. He must have chafed under the strictures of General Irvine, who wrote that he found the place "in a most miserable condition in every respect. About 1800 militia had been at the Post, but were chiefly detached on various pretences. Those who remained had not a single place assigned them, nor had a single order what to do."[21] Irvine expressed the regular general's contempt for a militia post in the usual vocabulary of the times. The American militia baffles to this day the most sympathetic reporter: its men have to be admired, if they are admired, not because they were good or bad soldiers, but rather because they were soldiers at all. New England farmers swarmed, apparently, to every call and if they were inconstant, even incompetent, they were still on hand for every victory, just as they were first to leave the field in every retreat. Before the war was done, Massachusetts recorded 69,907 enlistments, a startling figure composed of double, triple, and quadruple listing of men like Colonel Nathaniel Wade, who came four times to war.[22] The system was untidy, inefficient, and triumphant, a vital factor in the victory of 1783.

Veteran officers can be forgiven for their exasperation. Militiamen always seemed to be coming and going. They might be on hand to wait out a crucial night and might serve the better if the night held no terrors, but they were never around long enough to exchange their separate fears for discipline. Wade's men, for instance, were on their way home a few days after Arnold's defection, for their time was up in early October.[23] The colonel, credited with his final three months and seventeen days of Revolutionary service, took home the order he received from Washington on the night of September 25. The letter ("Col. Wade . . . General Arnold is gone to the enemy. . . .") was his passport to an old soldier's rewards; any patriot would have been proud to have such a testament to his fidelity.

[21] Quoted in Charles J. Stille, *Anthony Wayne and the Pennsylvania Line* (Philadelphia, 1883), p. 234.
[22] Montross, *op.cit.*, p. 455.
[23] Herbert T. Wade, *loc.cit.*, p. 190.

The virtues of an armed, if untrained, citizenry were demonstrated in one final excursion to the field by the Middle Essex regiment. In the winter of 1786-1787, when civil processes in Western Massachusetts were threatened by the several disorders described in history as Shays' Rebellion, Nathaniel Wade mustered his neighbors for a march to the Connecticut River Valley where insurgent forces had taken up arms in vigorous criticism of state officers and institutions.[24] Wade left no record of his opinion as to the justice of western complaint against expensive and inefficient courts, high taxes, scarce money, and the costs of government in general. He simply served when he was called. He reported to General Benjamin Lincoln on January 10, 1787, and assembled his men at Woburn, northwest of Boston, during the following week. The first entries in his Orderly Book suggest that his men were on the march by January 19, and were with the force that guaranteed the operation of the courts at Worcester on January 23. The regiment was with Lincoln when he moved to support General Shepard at Springfield, and participated in the action that scattered Luke Day's men at West Springfield. Doctor Elipha Whitney, surgeon of the regiment, said of this skirmish that the insurgents "Ran like foxes, leaving their guns behind. Some of them arrived at the Meeting House, where the main body paraded with all speed, and betook themselves to the brush with confusion. Our Light Horse followed them, picking up of them about forty or fifty, which were brought to Headquarters, and upon taking the Oath, were discharged. . . ."[25]

The climax of the campaign came on the night of February 3-4, when General Lincoln marched his men thirty miles through a snowstorm from Hadley to Petersham for the surprise attack that destroyed organized resistance by the rebellious bands. Colonel Wade in later years described this march as the most difficult in his experience, exceeding in hardship any of his

[24] A full account of Wade's part in this expedition is available in Herbert T. Wade, "The Essex Regiment in Shays's Rebellion—1787," *Essex Institute Historical Collections*, XC (1954), pp. 317-349.

[25] Whitney to Manasseh Cutler, *Life, Journals and Correspondence of Rev. Manasseh Cutler*, I (Cincinnati, 1888), p. 197.

wartime adventures. He had a vivid memory of the morning
that followed:

"On arriving at Petersham . . . we suddenly came in sight of
the rebels, collected in several masses upon the hill in front of
us. We had come upon them by surprise, and were very soon
so near as to command their position by our field pieces. When
this state of things became apparent to the officer who commanded the artillery he became anxious to bring his guns in
play. The officer was a Colonel, a brave and excellent soldier of
Revolutionary proof, but of singular personal appearance, being
very short and so fat as to render his seat in the saddle somewhat infirm. He bore the temptation for some time, measuring
the distance with his eye; but at last he could stand it no longer.
Putting spurs to his horse he rode rapidly to the head of the
column where I was at the moment talking with the General.
Checking his horse with a jerk which nearly cost him his seat,
he made a hasty salute, and burst out with full force of his deep
voice: 'For God's sake, Gen. Lincoln, let me unlimber and give
um one pouze!' 'Don't be in haste,' said the General; 'the
Sheriff must read the Riot Act first; if they do not disperse at
that, I pledge you my word that you shall have a shot at
them.' "[26]

Instead of a battle, though, the morning ended in a rush by
the insurgents to surrender—throughout the campaign, in fact,
the simple presence of militia columns seemed adequate to restore order. The Essex men moved on through Amherst, Ches-
terfield, and Partridgefield to Pittsfield, where they served
out their final days. The last page of Wade's last Orderly
Book records General Lincoln's thanks to his month-and-a-half
soldiers: "The Gen'l wishes the troops an agreable march a
happy sight of their families & friends & that hereafter they
may be free from internal broils & foreign invasions."[27]

Reports of this "internal broil" have been accepted by generations of Americans as conclusive proof that orderly government
could not be maintained under the Articles of Confederation.

[26] Daniel Treadwell, "Colonel Nathaniel Wade," *Ipswich Antiquarian
Papers*, II (May 1881), no. 19.
[27] Wade Orderly Book, February 22, 1787.

For the record, though, it should be observed that law was restored in western Massachusetts by a band of militiamen and
not by the Constitution of the United States. Loyal state troops
put down the insurgents with remarkable ease and minimum
bloodshed; Colonel Wade was on active duty for only a month
and twenty-two days. For such a term and such a task the militia
proved quite dependable.

After the campaign in the Connecticut River Valley,
Nathaniel Wade restricted his military life to the ceremonies
of fall training days for the militia at Ipswich.[28] His town,
meanwhile, honored him with increasingly important offices.
He had been appointed town clerk in 1784 and on October 30,
1789, he was selected as an escort for President Washington
when the latter passed through Ipswich on his tour through
the eastern states. Colonel Wade and Colonel John Heard led
the President to Homan's Inn and shared with him what contemporary accounts referred to as a "cold collation."[29] In 1792
Wade assumed what was probably an inherited duty when he
was appointed to a committee assigned to develop a compre-
hensive educational policy for the town schools, and later he
served for eight years on the town's four-man board of educa-
tion.[30] In 1795 he was elected to the first of twenty-one con-

[28] A contemporary newspaper account of a muster day in October 1788
reveals one of the more spirited exercises the Colonel directed: "On Wednesday
last, Col. Wade's Regiment was reviewed at Ipswich by the Hon. Major
General Titcomb. After the review, a well planned representation of the
storming of a fort was exhibited with much spirit and propriety. The fort
was situated on a hill near the meeting-house and defended by a party of
infantry and Capt. Brown's horse. The assailants came up in two columns
from different quarters when the fort was summoned, the commander of which
refused to surrender. The battle then began. Each body of the assailants
was opposed by a party or horse; the former were repulsed when three
cheers resounded from the fort; they however returned to the attack, displayed upon the hill, surrounded the fort and carried the work in an instant.
The performance gave great pleasure to many military characters, who were
spectators. After this was finished, the line was formed and the troops went
through the firing with regularity and precision, which could not have been
expected. The men were well dressed, well armed, and paid the strictest
attention to command, which in a great measure made up for their want of
experience and gained them the approbation of their fellow citizens. *The
Salem Mercury*, October 21, 1788, quoted by T. F. Waters, *Ipswich in the
Massachusetts Bay Colony*, II (Salem, 1917), p. 383.

[29] *Ibid.*, pp. 370-371.

[30] The Ipswich grammar school was founded in 1636, and in 1756 the

secutive years' membership in the Massachusetts General Court. Over the years his offices multiplied: he was a town fire ward, justice of the peace, county treasurer, and he planned the town jail.[31] He accepted appointment in his seventy-first year as one of the two Ipswich delegates to the Massachusetts Constitutional Convention of 1820.

The record reveals little of his personal life. He suffered the customary tragedies of eighteenth-century life—his first wife, Mary Foster Wade, died at twenty-nine on Christmas Day in 1785; she survived the death of their infant son by less than a month. After three years as a widower Wade married twenty-six-year-old Hannah Treadwell on October 29, 1788, and their union lasted twenty-eight years, to her death on May 4, 1814.[32] Only one letter in Wade's hand survives from these long years, a detailed account of his being routed from his bed by a major fire in Boston on December 16, 1801.[33] There is no evidence that the colonel took up again his carpenter's tools; he probably lived on the fees from the several offices that he usually held. He was also a man of some property, having gotten full title to his father's estate when his mother died in 1791.[34] A ward who grew up in his home described him as a "very taciturn man, rarely speaking of the events of the war, and especially silent as to his own brave and honorable share in it."[35] Wade gained a secure place in local histories, not so much through the town's memory of his record but rather from his encounter with La-

institution was reorganized and put under the control of four "Feoffees." This pattern of control was made permanent by the General Court in 1787. Three generations of Wades had been school directors before Nathaniel served his term from 1817 to his resignation in 1825. Apparently the office was one reserved for the village elders; he was sixty-seven years old when he took the job. Abraham Hammatt, "The Ipswich Grammar School," *New England Historical and Genealogical Register*, VI (1852), p. 162.

[31] Thomas Franklin Waters, "An Episode of the War of 1812," *Massachusetts Historical Society Collections*, XLVIII (1915), p. 499.

[32] William A. Robbins, "Thomas Treadwell of Ipswich, Massachusetts, and Some of His Descendants," *New England Historical and Genealogical Register*, LX (1906), p. 196.

[33] Nathaniel to Hannah Wade, December 17, 1801.

[34] Ipswich Deeds, 153:61.

[35] Daniel Treadwell, "Colonel Nathaniel Wade," *Ipswich Antiquarian Papers*, II (May, 1881), no. 19.

fayette in 1824. The substance of their exchange, already re-ported here, is worth repeating in its full context.

When the old French hero approached New England on his tour through the United States, the citizens of Ipswich made elab-orate plans to honor him when he passed through their town. The reception committee included Wade and one of his sons, Colonel Joseph Hodgkins, and numerous other survivors of the Revo-lutionary War. A flagstaff was erected at Windmill Hill to mark the approaches to the town, the stone bridge was topped with a decorated arch for the occasion, and the Ipswich Horse Troop waited to escort General Lafayette to the ceremonies. Unfortunately rain and muddy roads so delayed the visitor that the outside reception was spoiled, but eventually he arrived in time for a banquet at Treadwell's Tavern. *The Newburyport Union's* account of the events there is memorable.[36]

"The General was near the head of the table. When in the act of taking his second glass of wine, Col. Wade was introduced to him by one of the Haverhill committee. The cordial embrace of these two veteran companions in arms was affecting beyond description. The occasion was patriotic and triumphant; the recollections of youthful and heroic achievements in which they had both been engaged, were vivid and animating; their meet-ing was but momentary, their parting was soon to be eternal. Under the circumstances so proud, so tender, with bosoms swell-ing with patriotic exultation and now melting into the most affec-tionate expressions of kindness, these Revolutionary chiefs held the following dialogue, during which their hands were never separated:

"Gen. LaF. O my dear Colonel! you remember Rhode Is-land, and the night of Aug 12, 1778, when you and I lamented the misunderstanding of D'Estaing and Gen. Sullivan?

"Col. W. Indeed I do; and never can forget it. It was a dread-ful storm, and the soldiers had no shelter; my duty required me to be out to watch the enemy, and you insisted upon walking the

[36] Daniel Treadwell left in the Wade papers a clipping of the *Union's* account, but after identifying the paper, he failed to note the date. See also Waters, *op.cit.*, pp. 436-439.

rounds with me all night, although I urged you to go to your tent.

"Gen. LaF. I was too anxious to sleep and I thought it my duty to conciliate the American officers, as the French admiral seemed to insist too much upon punctilio to the injury of our common operations. We did not mind the rain, altho we were drenched through and through.

"Col. W. No, indeed. Had D'Estaing assisted us, I always thought we should have compelled Gen. Pigot to surrender; we missed a fine opportunity. But, my dear General, do you remember West Point?

"Gen. LaF. O my dear friend, I do! and when Gen. Washington first heard of the defection of Arnold, he asked, 'Who has the immediate command?' On being told that it was you, he said: 'Col. Wade is a true man, I am satisfied!' Gen Green and myself immediately repaired to the garrison. Do you not recollect seeing me riding rapidly in from the north-east corner when we took the Division up to King's Ferry?

"Here the feelings of the two Heroes became too strong for utterance; they hung upon each other."

Following the banquet, Wade, Hodgkins, and other members of the committee escorted Lafayette to Newburyport, where he spent the night.

Joseph Hodgkins survived too, and enjoyed in the town a degree of the prestige that Wade attained in the postwar decades. The order of rank established by the vote of the Ipswich minute men, however, remained fixed down through the years; Hodgkins played lieutenant to his captain for the rest of his life. Their relative status had probably been fixed at birth, for Wade seems to have been gentry and Hodgkins was not. After the war the captain eventually succeeded to the command of the Middle Essex Militia regiment—the date at which he became a colonel is not recorded, but he occupied the post in the early 1790's.[37]

---

[37] The earliest surviving references to "Colonel" Joseph Hodgkins are on the gravestones of two of his daughters. Mary, who died at twelve in 1794, and Sarah (the "Salle" of his wartime letters) who died at 22 in 1795, were each identified as daughters of Colonel Hodgkins on their markers. "Ipswich Inscriptions," *The Essex Antiquarian*, XIII (January 1909), p. 21.

He was elected to the Massachusetts General Court in 1810, and was returned until 1816, his seventy-third year. During the same years he served, according to his tombstone in the High Street Cemetery at Ipswich, "in some of the most important town offices." Some of his offices wanted dignity. In 1797, for instance, Hodgkins and his family became keepers of the County House, then located on what is the modern County Street. His only remaining marriageable daughter was desolate; nineteen-year-old Martha, the child born while Hodgkins marched from Saratoga to Valley Forge, poured out her heart to her current suitor, one Mark Haskell, of Portsmouth: ". . . as providence will have it that we must remove to a remote part of the town—and methinks you will ask What I mean—why really we are going to keep the county house. I believe it will be as Supprising to you as it is Sudden and disagreable to me but I must try to be content I hope all is For the best—So now Mark if you dont take care when you come this way again you will be put into the county house and we Shall put you in the dungeon along with crazy mary. . . ."[38]

In politics Hodgkins was an outspoken Federalist, as were most of the voters in his town.[39] During the crisis of 1798, for

[38] Martha Hodgkins, Ipswich, to Mark Haskell, Portsmouth, January 19, 1797. Letters in the possession of Alfred M. Wade, Princeton, New Jersey.
[39] Published records of Massachusetts politics indicate that Wade and Hodgkins, for all their dignity at home, were not noticed by the state in which they held office. Neither old colonel attended the Hartford Convention, according to the lists in Timothy Dwight, *History of the Hartford Convention with a Review of the Policy of the United States Government Which Led to the War of 1812* (Boston, 1833), p. 383. By 1814 the more important members of the original Essex Junto had moved on to Boston. The index to the Pickering Papers makes no mention of them. "Historical Index to the Pickering Papers," *Massachusetts Historical Society Collections*, 6 Series, VIII (Boston, 1896). Relevant sections of the papers and biographies of Theophilus Parsons, George Cabot, and Josiah Quincy do not refer to them, and the *Boston Gazette*, through issues in 1814, does not indicate their service on any of the named committees of the General Court that year.
For Ipswich politics, the *Boston Gazette*, April 8, 1813, reports that both in 1812 and 1813 the town was strongly Federalist: the 1812 vote was, for Strong (Federalist), 359; Gerry, 179; and the 1813 vote, Strong, 390, Varnum, 131. In both elections, the returns in the Essex North District, of which Ipswich was part, were heavily for Strong: 2½ to one in 1812, and 3½ to one in 1813. In the election of 1813, the Essex North District also sent two Federalist Senators to the General Court. Unfortunately, the names and votes of men returned to the lower house were not reported.

instance, when relations with France were broken and war seemed imminent, Hodgkins called on his fellows to stand forth in their true colors. According to a contemporary account, "Colonel Hodgkins, thinking that the time was now come when the characters of men should be known, especially in the military line, informed his corps of officers that he should wear his cockade and regimental uniform on Sabbath days and all other public occasions and recommending it to others to do the same, which proposition was immediately complied with."[40] The cockade, a rosette of black ribbon with an eagle in the center, was displayed on the hats of men who supported President John Adams's administration. Years later, he put on his uniform again during the second war with England, accepting a commission in a company of veterans called the Sea Fencibles, enrolled from able-bodied men older than forty-five.[41] Hodgkins was seventy.

The old soldier refused to admit his age for years to come; he continued to work his fields and ply his trade—he had, in fact, just married his third wife, Lydia Treadwell, an aging widow of some property. The marriage that had sustained him during the Revolutionary War had lasted for thirty-one years, to Sarah Hodgkins' death on March 13, 1803. Hodgkins lived to bury ten of his eleven children by his first two wives; only his firstborn, Joanna, survived him. He came to depend in his last years on the advice and aid of his son-in-law, Nathaniel Wade, Jr, who had united the two soldiers' families by his marriage to Hodgkins' daughter, Hannah, in 1801. The last letter that survives from Hodgkins' hand, dated February 16, 1820, describes the dissolution of this marriage in death: "We have been calld to Bearry our Daughter hannah Wade which is a grate Loss to us and much more So to her Dear Children for She was a kinde and attentive Mother. She has Left Seven Children the oldest is about 15 years the younest is little over one. . . ."[42]

Essex County, it should be remembered, was a particularly notorious victim of the "Gerrymander." By this device, Gerry had arranged a slight plurality of the Essex South District in 1812, as had other candidates of his party.

[40] *The Salem Gazette*, August 14, 1798, quoted by Waters, *op.cit.*, p. 376.

[41] *Ibid.*, pp. 419-420.

[42] The letter, unsigned and apparently unsent, began "Dear Sister." It is badly torn and faded, but it is clearly in Hodgkins' hand.

Repeated tragedy seems not to have shaken his confidence in the justice of the God he served nor robbed him of the optimism with which he projected new undertakings. He shouldered a substantial load of debt in 1813, when he bought out the heirs who shared with his third wife an interest in the estate of her father—the house he thus acquired has been restored in recent years and stands now as the museum of the Ipswich Historical Society. A kinsman described him during these years as "a very tall man, with strongly marked Roman nose and thin hair, which was gathered into a queue. To his last days, he would have his pewter plate, which was kept with the platters on a high shelf in the kitchen."[43] When he moved into his last home, according to the memory of an apprentice boy who was there to help, "The venerable old geneleman was never idle. When not in the field he was in the shop, putting things in repair or making new. Every inch a man, every inch a patriot. Honest, body and soul, all the way through. My master (Samuel Wade) married his step-daughter, Lydia Treadwell, and I was, therefore, a good deal in his company. I knew his habits of life; how he hated a lazy man or boy, or anything that looked like fraud or dishonesty. . . .

"The first Pension Law passed by Congress was for the survivors of the War of the Revolution. All who would make oath that they actually needed the pension to make them comfortable could have it. An agent visited the town, and advertised for all the Revolutionary survivors to meet him, and prove that they were soldiers, and subscribe to the oath. James Odell, Esq., of Salem, was the agent for Ipswich . . . He and Col. Hodgkins were well acquainted and met like old friends. The

---

[43] Built in 1638, Hodgkins' last home is recognized today as an outstanding specimen of seventeenth-century architecture. Hodgkins bought the place, variously referred to as the "Saltonstall" or "Major John Whipple" house, from the estate of Deacon John Crocker, who died in 1812 or 1813. The heirs, except for Lydia, Hodgkins' third wife, released the estate to Hodgkins on May 19, 1813. Thomas Franklin Waters, *The John Whipple House in Ipswich, Mass., and the People Who Have Owned and Lived in It* (Salem, 1915), p. 40.

Nathaniel Wade's home, built in 1726, still stands within a block of the present location of the Hodgkins house (moved when it was recently restored), and is still in use as a private residence.

Col. stated that he did not know as he needed the pension to make him comfortable, as he was still able to carry on his land, and see to things generally. Mr. Odell said, 'You can have it, if you will ask for it.' 'Well,' said the Col. 'I will take it one year,' and he did. But when the year came round, the dear old veteran, who spent his best days in the army, and when the war ended had scarce enough to pay his way home, and was surely entitled to a pension, just because he could by hard toil live without it, would only receive it for that one year. He lived the rest of his days on his own honest, hard earnings. Surely this was unselfish love for his country."[44]

Court records of the 1820's confirm this account of Hodgkins' action, but they also show that he regretted it, and spent the last nine years of his life trying to recover his pension. By the United States Act of 1818, officers and men who had served as much as nine months in the Continental army or navy were granted twenty dollars per month on proof of their service and their need. Hodgkins had been generous in his endorsement of Nathaniel Wade's application for a grant for which he was eligible by his service during the Long Island and New York campaigns. "I know," swore Hodgkins on September 18, 1819, that Wade "served & continued thirteen months in said service and was honorably discharged and I further say that his real & personal Estate is but little & will not with the best management afford one fourth part of his support that he is about Seventy years of Age and unable to gain a maintainance by his labors. . . ."[45]

Colonel Wade got his pension but Colonel Hodgkins, on resigning his at the age of seventy-seven, was never able to recover it. He went repeatedly to court to prove his need, but it was only in his eighty-sixth year that he was able to demonstrate his poverty to the magistrates' satisfaction.[46] According

[44] Uriah Spofford's "Reminiscences of Ipswich" were published in the *Ipswich Chronicle* in the early 1880's. This transcript is taken from notes that were made by Daniel Treadwell Wade in his preparation of a biography of his ancestors during the same period.

[45] Wade's Revolutionary Claim Papers, under Act of 18 March 1818. Copy in the Wade Papers.

[46] Essex Court of Common Pleas, Book 246, Leaf 185.

to affidavits offered between March and June 1829, he had sold off real estate to pay debts of $1,210, the bulk of his obligation to the Crocker heirs. His remaining properties—83 acres of unproductive land, a yoke of oxen, two cows, six sheep, a shovel, a hoe, and a fork, and furniture—were valued by the court at $807. His debts totaled $770.32, mostly in small sums due servants, the village blacksmith, saddler, and cooper, even to Thomas Knowlton, the barber, who had shaved the Colonel without pay since August 1820. Hodgkins was clearly eligible for a pension but proof of the fact did him little good because he died on September 25, 1829.

He carried happier memories of these last years to his grave. Both he and Nathaniel Wade journeyed to Boston for the celebration of June 17, 1825, the fiftieth anniversary of the Battle of Bunker Hill. The state paid three dollars each to the 180 survivors of the battle who signed the payroll there, and allowed one dollar for each twenty miles of travel. According to family tradition, Hodgkins, at eighty-two, scorned a carriage for the trip, mounted a horse, and traveled to Boston alone for the celebration. Neither old soldier left Ipswich again. Nathaniel Wade, comforted by the affection of two sons and a daughter, died in the house where he was born, on October 26, 1826, in his seventy-seventh year. Joseph Hodgkins clung to life in his stubborn, proud way to his death at eighty-six in 1829.

Each of the officers, in Washington's phrase, was a "true man," and a worthy citizen of the Republic he had helped to secure; their strength, and ten thousand times their strength, guaranteed the independence of the United States of America. Both Hodgkins and Wade thought this a glorious cause.

The Hodgkins Letters

May 7, 1775 to January 1, 1779

THE HODGKINS letters, reprinted in the following pages, were the primary sources for this study; these and the Wade Orderly Books make up the bulk of the papers held by Mr. Francis C. Wade of Ipswich. The authors turned to standard recent authorities for their general account of the Revolution, a narrative employed here to sustain the fragmented personal stories of the Ipswich men. They were particularly dependent on the works of Christopher Ward, John R. Alden, Lynn Montross, and John C. Miller, but mention should also be made of the great documentary narratives of the nineteenth century—particularly those of Richard Frothingham, Henry P. Johnston, and William S. Stryker—to which all recent military historians are heavily indebted. Footnote references indicate the extent to which the book was made possible by the genealogists, antiquarians, editors, and archivists who have preserved in such voluminous detail the records of New England in the Revolution.

It was the Hodgkins letters, though, that invited the present writer to this account of the private lives and public services of two obscure but possibly representative soldiers from the middle and lower levels of Washington's army. The letters in their entirety are so charming that their full text is offered here, despite the substantial repetition involved. The ellipses indicate torn, faded, or otherwise indecipherable passages in the generally well-preserved manuscript letters. Sarah Hodgkins' letters are interspersed with Joseph's, in the proper chronological order, but they are also listed in the index for the convenience of any reader who wishes to read them as a separate group. Also, each of Sarah's letters is dated at Ipswich, while all of Joseph's are dated from the field.

Cambridge May ye 7 1775

Loven Wife I Tak this oppertunity to Rite a Line to in form you that I am in good health at Presant for whitch I Desire to be thankfull I am also Very glad to hear that you & the Children are well By your Letter whitch I Received this morning at Warter Town I also Received the things that you sent me I have knothing New to Write the Company is well I whant to know wether you have got a paster for the Cows for I cannot tell when I shall com home I Received Martha Kinsman Letter and am glad to hear that she is well tell Martha Magger Wade is Verry Well Brother Perkins sends his Love to you and all his friends But it is now allmost Dinner Time and I must Conclude By subscribeing myself your Loving Husband till Death Joseph Hodgkins

Cambridge June ye 8 1775

Loven wife I take this oppertunity to inform you that I am in good health & we got into Cambridge on tusday about two oclock & whear very Bissy all that afternoon a Pitching our tents upon the Common whare the Company Lives much more Better then thay Could in Barricks the officers have a Verry Plesant Chamber for there quarters so we have our Choice wether to lodg in the Chamber or tents Capt Wade & I Lodged in the tents last knight and we where much Pleased with our Lodgen I must conclude I whant to see you all Thomas is well Liks Verry well   Joseph Hodgkins

NB I should Be glad if you Could git some cloth at Mr Pickards for thomas a Pair of trowssis if you send a Candell stick I should Be glad Brother Perkins is well and is got his cote Cut Verry small

June ye 13 1775

Loving wife I take this oppertunity to wright a few Lines to you to Let you know that I am well and I hope these lines will find you in as good health as they leave me I want to see you all But I due not Expect to come home verry soon we Live Verry well But are obliged to Expend Considerable of Cash I have Received the things you sent By Mr. Tradwell & am Verry glad of them I should Be glad if you could see Doctr Calf & git some Cloth for a shirt for the weather is hot & shirts Durttey verry fast as for News we have not much they say that General gagees Reinforcement is got in to Boston But what Number we know not nor Dont Care much But its now allmost four oclock and Capt Wade & Insign Perkins are gone to take a walk this after noon with there friends & I am obliged to Perrade the Cumpany at four oclock so I must Conclude By subscribing my self your Loving Husband till Death Joseph Hodgkins

I was glad to hear that you whas well Pray Write as offen as you can

June 14 I Received the shirt By Coson Hodgkins Last Knight this morning we are going upon gard Down to Madame Inmons Where our sentnls stand in Plan site of the Ragelars I have sent a shirt & Pair Stockins By Jabez Tradwell Pray send them again as soon as you Can

Cambridge June ye 15 1775
Loveing wife these Lines come with my kind Regards to you hoping thay will find you in as good health as thay Leave me I Recived your Letter By Mr Jewett and whas Very glad to hear that you & my Children whar well I whant to see you & them But I Desire to be content & hope you will make yourself as Content as you Can in your Presant Condistion I have nothing against your going over to Farther's if you Chuse it I whas Verry glad to hear that Joseph is a good Boy I whant to see the Littel Roog I Due Entend to come home to see you as soon as I Can I must Conclude it is almost Dark give my Duty to all Parance & Lov to friends our Company is all well tel Brother John that Thomas is well & John So no more at Presant I Remain
your Loving Husband till Death
Joseph Hodgkins

Cambridge June ye 18 1775
Dear wife I take this opportunity to inform you that I am well att Present I would Just inform you that we had a verry

hot ingagement yester Day But God Preserved all of us for whitch mercey I Desire Ever to be thankful we have Bin alarmed to Day But Came to no Engagement it is all most knight now and we are going to Entrenching to night therefore I cannot Be Pertickler Dont Be Discoredgd I hope that we shall Be Carred thrue all our Deffittes and have abundant occasion to Prase the Lord to gether so no more at Prsant But Remain your Loving Husband till Death

Joseph Hodgkins

NB Remember me to all in quirring friends Brother Perkins is not very well But I hope it is Nothing But Being worried he Desires to Be Remembrd to all in quiring friends

Cambridge June ye 20 1775

Dear wife I take this oppertunity to inform you that I am well but Verry Much Worred with our Last Satterday Curmege & yesterdays moving Down to Winter Hill where we now are & Live in Expectation of further Engagements with the Enemy But I desire to be content with the alotments of gods Providence and hope in his mercy for Salvation & Deliverance from all these Eavels witch we feel & fear I must Be short I what to see you Pray Write as offen as you can I have wrote several Letters But have Received But one from you I must conclud so nomore at Presant But Remain your Loving Husband Joseph Hodkins

NB I sent a shirt & a pair stockins By Jabez Tradwell Last Weak I should Be glad of them soon I sent a suguer Box By Naty Dodge I wish you could fill it with suguar & send it as soon as you can I have sent a shirt By Mr Dannis I Belive it whants a little mending I should Be glad of Sum Coffee

Cambridge June 21 1775

Loving wife these lines Comes with my kind Regard to you hoping thay will find you in as good health as they Leave me I would inform you that I have Received the things you sent But if I Due not mistake you Did not Write to me But I am Very much obbliged to you for what you sent me & whas glad to hear that you where well I whant to see you all Give my

[169]

Duty to all my Parance and Love to all inquiring friends if you see Brother John you may tel him that his two sons are Verry well Nath'l Rust is Verry Poorley I do not know But that he will be sick Brother Perkins is Better and Desires to Be Remembered to all his friends I have heard that Capt Perkins is got home & I shall try hard to get home if nothing should turn up to hinder so no more at Present But Remain your Loving Husband till Death   Joseph Hodgkins

Ipswich June ye 21 1775

Loving Husband I take this oppertunity to write a Line or two to let you know that I am well I received the Letters you Sent me with great joy to hear that you were yet alive and well I desire to Bless God for his preserving goodness to you and hope he will be with you stil and protect and defend you amidst all danger and in his one time return you home our Children are well farther & mother are well and Send their Love to you and Brother I must inform you that Capt Perkins arived yesterday I must Conclude for it grows Late So no more at present

I remain your loving wife till Death   Sarah Hogekins
give my love to Brother I long to see you both

Cambridge June ye 23 1775

Loving wife I take this oppertunity to write a Line or two to you to Let you know that I am well and I hope these Lines will find you in as good health as they leave me I would just inform you that we came from the hill this morning and Expect to stay in Town two Days unless there should Be an alarm I Received the things & Letter you sent me and am Verry glad to hear that you & my Dear Children whare well you sent me word that Capt Perkins is got home and I whas glad to hear of it I hope he is got some Corn for me and you must give my Regards to him and tell him that he must asist in giting the Corn home to you for I Do not think that I shall get home verry soon I have not time to write Perticklers of ye Engagement But we whare Exposed to a very hot fire of Cannon & small armes about two ours But we whare Presarved I had one Ball went under my arme and cut a large hole in my Coate & a Buck shot went throue my coate & Jacket But neither of them Did me any harme Nat is sick and is coming home But he must go to his mothers I due not Expect you to take care of him if he is sick so no more at Presant But Remain your Loving Husband till Death Joseph Hodgkins

Brother Perkins is not Verry well he Complane of Rummettick Pain in his hipes

Loving wife   Cambridge July 3 1775
Mondy Morning about Eight oClock I now set Down to write a line to you to inform you that my Cold is a Lettel Better But my stumick is very sore yet But I have got some Drops to Take whitch I am in hopes will healp me soon I hope you are all well I whant to see you I have nothing Remarkebel to rite Except that geaneral Washington & Leas got into Cambridge yesterday and to Day thay are to take a vew of ye Army & that will be atended with a grate deal of grandor there is at this time one & twenty Drummers & as many feffors a Beting and Playing Round the Prayde But I must conclude By subscribing myself your Loving Husband Till Death

Joseph Hodgkins

NB I have sent you one shirte & two pr stockins & Brother Perkins has sent two shirts & thay are all Tied up in you Piller Case By Mr. Person Due try & git Thom's Britches & send them as soon as you can

Cambridge July ye 5 1775
Loving I take this oppertunity to write a line or two to let you know that I have got something Better of my cold and am in hopes that I shall get well pretty soon I hope you are well I whant to see you all We have no News to write we Live Daly in Expectation of further atacks By the Enemy But I hope that they will not Be suffered to Prevale aganst us I have Bought four yards of Cloth for a shirt & I have sent it a Dirty shirte

[171]

By Brother Heard so I must Conclude from your Loving
Husband till Death   Joseph Hodgkins
the Price of ye Cloth £ 1-5 - O P yd

~~~~~~

Cambridge July ye 8 1775
Loving wife I take this oppertunity to write a line or two to
let you know that I am Cumfortible But my Cof is trubbelsom
yet But I hope it is gitting Better Thomas is sumthing unwell
to Day But I hope he will not Be sick several of our Company
is sick and sumothers Ealing But I hope that god will Presarve
us and Continnue halth whare it is injoyed and Restore it to
those that whant it I whant to sea you all But I Due not know
when I shall I have nothing strange to write we have had
several alarms Latley one this morning aBout half after two
oclock whitch whas occashoned By a party of our men at Rockbury whitch went Down to there garde house at the nek and
Drove of the garde & Burnt the house and sume other Bildings
there whas Considerable of firing But we left no men at tol
thay Lost Sume But we no not how many I Received the things
you sent me By Mr. Lord I should Be glad of the Rest of my
things as soon as you can send them I am afrade that I shall
whare you out By sending you so much work But I cannot git
any thing Don hare so I must Bage your Patience and Conclude
By subscribing myself your Loving Husband till Death
                                    Joseph Hodgkins

~~~~~~

Sept 8 in Camp att Prospect Hill 1775
Loving wife I take this opportunity to Rite a line or two to let
you know that I am in Comfortable Health & I hope thease
Lines will find you in health I want to hear from you to know
how Salle Dose I feel uneasy about her But I hope she is upon
the mending hand I have know news to Rite to you only that
the Enemy have not fired a gun nor sent a Bum at our People
since I have Ben hear Except a few small armes at our People
Who went Down on Chalstown Common after sum hoses this
whas a wensday But at night about 10 oClock the Rifel men

[172]

tuck three hoses With out Receiving any harm But I must Conclude from your Loving Husband till Death

Joseph Hodgkins

in Camp Prospect Hill Sept ye 19 1775

Loving wife I take this oppertunity to write a few lines to inform you that I am well at Present for whitch I Desire to be thankfull I Received your Letters By Mr Appleton & Mr Low & Rejoice to hear that you are well & that Salle is Better for I have Been very uneasy about her ever since I have Ben hear I hope she will Continue Mending till she gets well I whant to see you & our Children But I Desire to be Contented while I am Absent from you & I hop you will make yourself as contented as you can whilst I am hear I should Be Very glad to have you Come hear to see me But I know your sircumstances will not Admit of it at Present But I must be shorte for it is allmost night & I am going upon gard to night But as to that Rum I Due not know how we shall gitt it I think Mr Kendall Whas Very unkind in not taking it according to his Promis for I saw him at his own house that Day I Came hear & he told me he would take it Give my Duty to all my Parance & Love to all my friends Got no more at Presant But I Remain your Kind Companion till Death   Joseph Hodgkins

PS You sent me word that Capt Perkins whas marrid & I Gis By your hints that you mist the Piggs as well I should Be glad of my shirts as soon as you have opportunity to send them if AnyBody should Be Coming hear that you could send me a Pillow I should Be glad I gust Lik to forgot to tell you I Received the Paper By Mr Appelton I am obliged to you But he greast it so I could not write on it it seams as if the Dogs whas in the Luck But I will Write to you not with standing

In Camp at Prospect Hill Sept ye 20 1775

My Dear I will Try to make amens for Past Neglegence so I now sit Down to Write a line or two to you & I hope these Lines will find you in as good health as thay Leave me at Present Bilsed be god for all his mercys to us ward it seams to be Prety health in our Brighade But Wickedness Prevales Verry much to the astonishment of any that Behold them I have not Time to Be Pertickler now about maters I must be shorte I hope you will Rite to me as offen as you Can I whant to see you all I have sent for my Rum By Sam'll Beall & I should be glad that you would get that of Capt Kendalls & send By him & if you Can send me that small Rug that will save me Bying a blancet for Thomas I sopose that you may send anything By Beall so I Conclude By subscribing my self your Loving Husband till Death   Joseph Hodgkins

PS I would just inform you that the Enemy have fired a grate many Cannon & Bums this weak But I dont know as they have Done any Dameg Give my Duty to all Parence & Love to friends Brother Perkins is well I Rote the Above Letter Last Night and I Expected that Capt Dodge would sent Mr Beall home this Day But as he Dose not some Body Eals will soon go I shall rite again

In Camp at Prospect Hill Sept ye 25 1775
Loving wife I tak this oppertunity to Let you Know that I am in good health att Presant Blesed Be god for so grate a mercy I am sorry that I have the occasion to inform you that Capt Wade Continues Very Poorly & Brother Perkins is got the Rumetis in his neck & shoulders so that he is not fitt for Duty But I hope he is somthing Better toDay I have kno News to rite to you only the Enemy have sent a good many Bums at us Latly But thay have Dun no Damege with them But I conclude at Presant By subscribing myself as Before your kind Companion till Death   Joseph Hodgins

NB I wish you would go to Mr Averalls and git me a yallow Ball I whant to hear how you all Due I hope you will write to me as offen as you Can give my love to all inquiring friends

In Camp att Prospect Hill Sept 27 1775
Loving wife these lines come with my most kindly Regards to you hoping thay will find you in as good health as thay Leave

[174]

me att Presant I received your Letter of ye 25 Instant & I Rejoice to hear that you are in a Comfortable State of health I
am glad to hear that Sallie is Better I whant to see her Due tell
her that farder is well I whant to see you all But I Du not Expect
to att Presant But I hope that god will take Care of us and Carry us through all the Difiltis we have to meet with in the way of
our Duty whilst we are Absant and in his good time Return us
home and give us a Bundant occation of Rejoice to geather in
his goodness But I must be short for it is Late in the Eaving
I Received the things you sent me safe & I am much obliged to
you for your care in sind them I wish I whas able to sattisfy
you for your troble But I am not unles writing will Du it for
as to Money we have none and I Dont know when we shall
have any so I must Conclude att Presant By Subscribing as
Before   Joseph Hodgkins

I would inform you that your Oncel Ephm Smith & Cuson
Saml Smith his wife Coson Willington & his wife whas here
yesterDay and thay Desire to Be Remembrd to you Ant Suse
sent Brother & I a Cheese Joseph Smith has Ben Very sick But
he is a good Deal Better Capt Wade & Cosson Thomas
Hodgkins got out for Ipswich this afternoon Both of them
Very Poorley if you have oppertunity I should Be glad if you
would goo & see Capt Wade we have not a man hear But what
is fit for Duty Except Brother & I Believe he will be By tomorrow for his neck is somthing Limber toDay & he Can Eate two
mins however give my Complements to Capt Kendall and tel
him I should be very Prowd to wate on him at our tents

In Camp Prospect Hill Sept 29 1775
My Dear I know set Down to Write a line or two to you & I
hope these Lines will find you in as good health as thay Leave
me att this Time I am as well as ever I whas in my life as for
any thing that I know & I wish I whas more sencebal of the
goodness of god towards me for his mercys are many & grate
to us all But I must be short I hope you are all well I whant
to see you Very much Due Write to me as offen as you Can I
am glad to hear that Salle holds Better I hope to hear she is
well soon I have sent some things By Mr Wade you ned not

send the Britches again I must conclude at Presant By subscribing myself your kind Companion till Death   Joseph Hodgkins

[undated]

Loving wife I take this oppertunity to write a line or two to
you to Let you know that I am in Cumfartable Health at
Presant for whitch I Desire to be thankful I hope you are well
I whant to hear from you to know how Salle Dose Du Rite as
offen as you can and Let me know how you all Due I hear that
sister Chapmans Child is Dead I simpethise with them in their
troble and hope it will Be santified to us all It is Very sickly in
the Cuntry Towns round about hear several of our aquantance
at Wharter Town Died the weak Past we have no News to Rite
the Enemy are Very Peasable at Presant I must Conclude By
subscribing myself your Loving Husband till Death

Joseph Hodgkins

NB I whould Just inform you that I Envited Liet Tradwell &
Sect Harte to com and see you along with sister Perkins give
my Duty to all Parence Love to all friends

Ipswich October ye 1 1775

Loveing Husband these Lines come with my kind Love to you
hopeing they will find you in good health as I am at present
Salla Seems to be got fine and well for which mercy I desire to
be thankful God has been pleased to deal more favorablely with
us in respect to her than he has with many others in this town who
have had their Children taken from them by Death I hope we
Shall not forget his goodness towards us in this and many other
instances it is a good deal sickly both with grone folk and Children there is three funerals to night old Mr Hovey & William
Apletons youngest child & one of Mr Noyes Children the Children are crying So I must Leave of for the present Monday
night I now Set down to write a line or two more to you to inform you that we are all well now but how Long we Shall have
that to Say I know not for Several of our neighbors are very
sick Mr ezekiel Dodge is very bad with a fever I am very much
afraid he will never go abroad again & old Mr Graves is very
Sick I must Jest tell you that I have been to See Capt Wade

[176]

today & he thinks he is a little better he Seems to be very poorly but I am in hopes he will get it over without being any wors I rejoice to hear that you are So well as you inform me you are doo continue to write to me as often as you can for it is a great satisfaction to hear from you Since I cant See you but I must conclude for am allways in a hurry I remain your Loveing wife till Death   Sarah Hodgkins

PS give my Love to Brother Perkins and tell him his little Son is very Sick please to excuse my writing for it very bad I had a very poor pen
we have Sent brother a new pair of mittens by esek I have also sent thomas mittens

                        In Camp att Prospect Hill Octor 2 1775
Loving wife I take this oppertunity to write a line or two to you hoping these few lines will find you in as good health as they leave me at this time I whant to hear from you Very much Due Write to me as soon as you Can Convenantly I have Ben hear four weaks to night & I have sent you a grate many leters & I have Received But three from you But I must Excuse you as I goo along for I am sencible that you have had a grate Deal to hinder you But I must Pray you to imbrace every oppertunity that you may have of sending to me But I must be short as I have Just com of the maine garde and as I groo sleepy I would Just Let you know that I feall Concerned about you on account of your having no money I hope I shall have some to send you in a few Days I would have you send to Capt Charles Smith for som Beaff If you should see him ask him about some Satt day I have no News to write to you Excepting that the Regulars Desarts more or les Every night I must Conclude for this time for I can hardly see give my Duty to father & mother Love to all enquiring friends so no more att Presant But I Remain your most afectanate Companion till Death   Joseph Hodgkins

PS I whant to have you Explain a little upon your not Being admitted to a sarting feast Give my Love to Martha

                    In Camp Prospect Hill Octor ye 6 1775
My Dear having a few minets Leashur I sit Down to inform
you that I am in good health at this time & I hope these Lines
will find you the same I whant to see you & my Little family
I hope they are all well I hear that it is very sickly at town and a
Dieing Time I have heard of the Death of Mr Dodge & Mr
Graves a loud call to us all to Be also Ready for a thousand
unseen Dangers awate us But I must be short as for News we
have not much one Regular came to our People last night at
Plowed hill this Morning the Enemy at Rockbury neck fired
near a hundred Canon at our People But what Dameg thay Did
we have not heard But I hope not much There seams to be
Barraks Providing for all the Brigade Except our Regiment
I am afrade we shall have to live in the Tents for sum time
yet But I hope we shall not suffer Brother & I Can Lodge very
well But the Company are not so well Provided for for Beding
as we Be We are About Receiving our months Pay so long
looked for I hope I shall be Able to sind you some very soon
if not to Day I sent By John Hodgkins yesterday two shirts
one for Thomas & I should Be glad if you could send me two
striped shirts for the weather growes Cool we hear that Brothers
child is very sick But I do not know as he can com home at
Presant for our People are all most Bewitcht about getting home
But I must conclude for this Time By subscribing myself your
Most affectionate Companion Till Death Joseph Hodgkins
Since I rote my letter I have received some money therefore I
send you Eleven Dollers By Mr John Harris

                    Ipswich October ye 9 1775
I take this oppertunity to inform you that we are all well and I
hope these Lines will find you the Same I received you Letter
of the 6 instant & likewise the money you Sent me and I am
much abliged to you for it I rejoice to hear you are So well as
I hear you are from time to time I feel Quite concened about
you all these cool nights on account of your haveing no Better
habetations to live in but I hope the Same that has preserved
hitherto will stil be with you and preserve you from Cole and
Storms & all the evels & Dangers to which you may exposed &

in his own time return you home in Safty for which time I
desire to waite patiantly I must be Short it is with a good deal
of deficulty that I write to you So often as I doo it is greate
plesure to me to write to you & receive Letters from you Since
we have no other way of conversing together doo give my love
to Brother & tell him I wish I had better news to Send him
concerning his Child he remains much as he has been Seven days
past he is a very [*rest of letter torn, but the words remaining, on
the left third of the page include*: "Seems to be very . . . afraid
the poor little . . . able to graple through . . . if he could come
home . . . So I conclude myself . . . till Death . . . PS father &
mother . . . and Brother I must . . . Wade rid by here. . . ."]

In Camp att Prospect Hill Octor ye 16 1775
My Dear I tak this oppertunity to Write a line or two to you
& I hope these lines will find you in as good health as thay leave
me att this time I Received the things you sent By Capt Perkins
& I am Very much obliged to you for them I fear I shall weary
you in sending to have so much Done for me But I must tel
you we live whare we have no woman to Due anything for us
so you must give som Alowance for so Duing But I hope I
shall Be able som time or other to mak you amens for all your
trobble I whant to see you Very much But when I shall I cannot
tell I know that you have a grate Deal of Care upon you & I
wish I could take Part of that Burden from you I must be short
for it is somthing late in the Evening I must Excuse myself
for not Writing for these some Day Past for I have Ben very
Besey at work I have made Brother Perkins a pr shoes & I have
three Pair more spook for & if you would get som Body to spin
me some good shothread I will thank you & Love you I heard
that you where well a day or two ago By som of our men & I
hope you will write to me as offen as you can for I tak grate
satisfaction in Receiving Letters from you & in writing to you
Tuesday Morning I would just tel you that I am a going to
Plowd hill for twenty-four ours & I somthing Expect Brother
Perkins will sett out for home in a Day or two if you should see
Capt Wade give my Love to him & til him not to Come hear
Before he gets Prety well for we have Cool nights I must Con-

clude for this time By subscribing myself your Most affectionate
& Loving Companion till Death   Joseph Hodgkins

I shall heave a shirt or two to send By Capt Perkins to Day
Give my Duty to all my Parance & Love to all my friends There
is a little Box of Chasnuts half for sister Perkins & half for you
since I Rote my Little Brother took my turn of Duty Because
he Expects to Com home tomorrow and so I shall Due his turn
when it comes if you have not got our Pertatoes Dug Due get
frather Hodgkins to Dig them if he can so fair well

In Camp att Prospect Hill Octor ye 20 1775
My Dear having just Come of the Picket gard & Being all alone
this Eauining I set Dowen to Write a line or two to you to let
you know that I am well though Prity much Worred with
Being out a most all last night in the storme But throgh the
goodness of god I am Comfortable & I hope these lines will
find you and my Children the same I whant to see you very
much But as Providance has ordered it so that we are absent
from Each other I Desire to be Content & hope you will make
your self as Comfortable as you can and I hope god will Cary
us through all the Defaltys that we are to meat with in the way
of our Duty things at the Preasant seam to whare a very glomey
aspect But what is before us god only knows But I hope he that
has Carred us through many Defcaltys will still be with us and in
his own time Deliver us from all our Enemys and give us an
opportunity of meeting & harts to Prase his name to geather
so I must Conclude for I am a sleepey Give my Duty to all
Parance and Love to all friends so no more att this time But I
Remain your Most afetanate Companion Till Death
                                        Joseph Hodgkins
if you Could send me a little more Course shou thread you will
oblige me Very much Give my Regards to Brother Perkins and
tel him I Bought the Rabbet by taking his Turn of Duty Last
night
Saterday night I Rote my Letter Last night But not having an
oppertunity to send it to Day I thought I would Rite a line or
two more to let you know that I am Very well though we have
had a very socking time of it But our tents Doe Very well only

it smocked very Bad in the storme I hear that wood is very
scarse I would have you Bye some while the Carting lasts I am
Concerned about farther Hodgkins for I Due not know how he
will mak out to get wood But I hope Brother John will not see
him suffer tel Brother John his Boys is well I hope if Capt
Wade should get well enouf to come hear with Brother Perkins
I shall mak out to get a furlow home

In Camp Prospect Hill Octor ye 23 1775
My Dear these Lines Comes with my Kind Regards to you
hoping thay will find you & our Children in as good health as
thay Leave me at this Time Blesed Be god his goodness to
us in Presarving us all in health & for many other mercys witch
we are Dayly the Pertakers of I must Be short for I have
nothing new to Write I hope I shall be able to get a furlow as
soon as Capt Wade gets Able to Come hear But I cannot tell
how long that will be first But I hope it will not be a grate wile
But I would not have you be uneasy about me I am charming
well & Live Very well only something lonely since Brother left
me I must conclude att this time By subscribing myself your
kind companion till Death Joseph Hodgkins
I sent you a loaf of our Bread By Mr Dutch that you may know
what fine Bread we have

In Camp Prospect Hill Octr ye 25 1775
Loving wife having a fue Minnet Leashur I now set Down to
Write a line or two to inform you that I am well att Presant &
I hope these lines will find you the same I whant to see you
Very much Due Write to me as offen as you can for Letters
from you are a grate Rearite But however not to Enlarge I am
in hast I would Just inform you that the Quarter Master has
just Brought into our tent a fine Peas of Beaf and we have got
it Down a Roosting for supper and I hop that while we are
making our selves merry we shall not forget our Absent wives
and friends But for fear you should think that we should be
unseasonable in our Devoytion I would Let you Know that I
whas on guard all Last night & I Entend to goo too Bead in
season to night I must Conclude for the Beaf is almost Rosted

so no more at Preasent But Remain your Most Kind Companion till Death   Joseph Hodgkins

Thursday Morning I would Just inform you that I am fine an well this morning My supper sot Very well on my stummack I Cannot say Nothing more About come home till I see Brother Perkins hear & I Expect that will be toDay

In Camp att Prospect Hill Octor ye 29 1775

My Dear I whas in hopes not to have trobled you with any more Leatters till I had seen you But as it Remains a matter of unsarttenty when I shall come home I tak this oppertunity to inform you that I am in good health at Presant & I hope these Lines will find you as well as thay Leave me at this time I Received the things you sent me By Brother & I Rejoyce to hear that you and all my friends are well as he informs me Excepting his Child witch he says he Don think it is alive now But how ever that may be I hope god will fit it and all Concernd for his holy will and Pleasure I must be short for it is all most meating time I would not have you be uneasy about me for as soon as Capt Wade Comes hear I shall try for a furlow so I must Conclude at this Time By subscribing my self your Loving husband Till Death Joseph Hodgkins

I Believe you think I am a jocking when I sent for shoe threed But I have made four Pair of shoes & have a number more to make and if you could send me some thread I will Pay you the Cash for it & thank ye into Bargin for I Cannot get any hear Give my Duty to my Parance & Love to all my frinds

Prospect Hill Novmr ye 7 1775

Loving Wife I take this opportunity to Write a line or two to you to let you know that I am In good health & I hope these Lines will find you and my Children as well as they Leave me at this time I have nothing new to write we have had a socking time of it in the late storm our houses are Very good in fair weather But in a storm they are Very Bad for the Rane Runs Douen Chimbely so that we Cannot keep any fire But how Ever our Barraks are a Bulding & we hope By the first Day of

January to get into them so I would not have you Be uneasy about us for I hope we Shall Be Provided for some how or other But I must Be shorte for this time I whas in hopes when I wrote the last Letter I should Been att home By this time But I Cannot Come home till Capt Wade Come hear and when that will be I cannot tel for some People that Come hear say that he is well others say he is Poorley so you can tell when I shall Come home as well as I So I must Conclude at Presant By subscribing myself your Most Afectionate Companion till Death   Joseph Hodgkins

PS I received yours of the 28 instant and I Rogoice to hear you are all well Give my Duty to all my Parance & Love to all my frinds

I due not think harde of you for not writeing no offener But am glad that you can write so offen to me as you Due I should wrote Before nowe But I have had no opportunity for some time Before now

In Camp Prospect Hill Novmr ye 17 1775

My Dear I now sit Down to inform you that I got at Camp a lettle after sunset well & I hope these lines will find you as well as thay Leave me this morning I would just inform you that it is the general orders that all the officers & men Continue as thay whare till the Last Day of December so I am somthing Disapointed about Coming home I would have you tell Brother Chapman to let you have aBout two hundred wate of Beaf if he Dose not ask more then the Market Price I would not have you be uneasy about me I hope I shall Be carred through all the hardships we Exposed to I must Be short Due send me word how Joanna Dos as soon as you can I have Received another months pay this morning & I shall inclose Eight Dollers in this Letter so no more at Presant By Remain your Loving Husband till Death   Joseph Hodgkins

In Camp at Prospect Hill Novr ye 19 1775

My Dear these Lines Comes with my kind Regard to you hoping thay will find you in as good health as thay Leave me

at this time I whant to hear from Joanna I am a good Deal
Concerned about her But I hope she is not Bad I have sent the
Cloth for Thomas Coate Back again By Capt Dodge for Mr
Ross is at home & he has took the Measure and is to mak it at
home & I will let Thomas Come home if Poseble I would inform you that the first Leut Pay is advansed to Better than
forty Pounds pr Month old tennor and had I known it sooner
I should given in to stay But now it is tue Late But I soppose
you are not sorry so I must conclude at this time By subcribing
myself your most afectnate companion till Death

Joseph Hodgkins

PS Several of our Company are enlisted & More are talking
about it men inlist much faster than I thought for witch I am
Very glad

Ipswich Novemb ye 19 1775

My Dear these lines come with my Love to you hoping they
will find you well as I am at this time I received your Letter of
the 17 instant I thank you for the present you Sent me I am
something disapoined about your coming home as you talked of I
beg you would not alter your mind about Staying all winter for
if you doo it will be Such a disapointment that I cant pute up
with it I would inform you that Joanna is a good deal better
Salla was taken not well that day after you went away and has
been very poorly ever Since but I hope She will be better in a
few days Jose Seems to be got pretty well again I hope that all
the . . . aflictions we meet with will be Sanctified to us for our
good So I must conclude by Subscribing myself your kind
Companion till Death   Sarah Hodgkins

In Camp at Prospect Hill Novm 25 1775

My Dear I take this oppertunity to Write a line or two to you to
Let you know that I am well & I hope these lines will find you as
well as they Leave me at this time I have not had any oppertunity to sind to you Lately so you must not think hard of me for it
is not for whant of a good will my Dear I whant to hear from you
Very much Due send to me as offen as you Can I would just

inform you that Last Wensday night our People went to Cabble Hill & intrenched there & have Ben Very Bisey since a finshing there work & have got Down there several Cannon in order to give the ship a worming that lays up above Chalstown all this has Ben Done & our Enemy hath not fired a gon at our People whitch I think is Very Extrodenery But how Ever there seams to be a grate Probablity of a Movement Very soon But whare I can not tell But I hope we shall Be on our garde But our army is Very thin now But in good spirits and I hope we shall Be asisted By him houe is able with a small number to Put thousands to flite So I must conclude at this time By subscribing My self your Most afectnate Companion till Death Joseph Hodgkins

Novemr 28 Tuesday Morning My Dear I wrote the above Letter Last Sataday But had no oppertunity to send it I would inform you that through the goodness of god I am as well as Ever I whas in my life & I hope these lines will find you the same I Received your Letter Last night & I Rejoyce to hear you & our Children are all well again I whant to see you But I Due not Expect to this som time yet But I am Very well Contented Our men inlist very slow and our Enemy have got a Re-inforsment of five Regiments and if the New army is not Reased in season I hope I & all my townsmen shall have virtue anofe to stay all winter as Volentears Before we Will leave the line with out men for our all is at stake and if we Due not Ex-arte our selves in this gloris Cause our all is gon and we made slaves of for Ever But I Pray god that it never may Be so I wish you well & subscribe as Before   Joseph Hodgkins

Ipswich Novembr ye 28 1775

Loving Husband I take this oppertunity to inform you that we are all in a Comfortable State of Health once more through the goodness of God & I hope these Lines will find you posest of the Same invaluable Blessing I received your Letter jest now by the hand of Capt Wade & I am very glad to hear that you are well it is thanksgiveing day night to night and it Seems to be very lonesome and dull I did not know any better way to de-

verte myself than by writing to You I have no news to write but
I remain your Loving wife till Death   Sarah Hodgkins

In Camp at Prospect Hill Novmr ye 30 1775
My Dear I take this oppertunity to write a line or two to you
& I hope these lines will find you as well as they leave me at
Presant I whant to see you Very much Due write as offen as
you can to me I am in grate hast Mr Farley is a wating so I
must be short I Due not know But I shall stay all winter and if
I should I hope to see you Prity soon But Due not be Trobbled
My Dear for I hope I am in the way of my Duty so I must
Conclude By subscribing my self your Most Kind Companion
till Death   Joseph Hodgkins
PS I sent some things home By Mr Fitts I wish you would send
me my Velvet Britches and a little sho thread By Mr Fitts the
Britches I can get them mended hear

In Camp att Prospect Hill Decemr ye 3 1775
My Dear I take this oppertunity to write a line or two to you &
I hope these Lines will find you in as good health as thay leave
me at this time I am Very well for whitch I Desire to be thankfull But I am something worred with Duty By Reason of so
many officers Being absent But I hope we shall Be Carred
through all the Deffilties we are to meat with in the way of our
Duty I have no news to write to you Part of the famos Prise
has arived at Cambridge from Cap ann men inlist very slow
hear I hope Capt Wade will meet with Better suckcess then
what we Do hear I Expect him Down in a Day or two I whant
to see you Very much My Dear Due write to me as offen as you
can for I Due not hear from you But seldom I must conclude
at this time By subscribing my self your most afectnate Companion till Death Joseph Hodgkins
PS Give my Duty to all my Parence and Love to all my friends
if you see Cap Wade tel him I hope he will com hear soon

Ipswich Decembr ye 10 1775
Mr Hodgkins it is with pleasure I now Set down to write aline
or two to inform you that we are all in a Comfortable State of

Health & I hope these lines will find you the Same I received your Letter by Daniel Duch & also the Cheas you Sent me I am much abligd to you for it I want to have you come home & See us I look for you almost every day but I dont alow myself to depend on any thing for I find there is nothing to be depended upon but troble & disapointments I must Jest inform you that I have Sent you a Shirt and pair of Briches by Mr Norton in his horse cart there is Some Shoe thread in the Shirt I have sent a pair of stokins for Thomas by nathanl Tredwell doo write to me as often as you can give my love to brother you have not Sent me word latly whether he is dead or alive but I must conclude by Subscribing myself your most afectionate Companion till Death   Sarah Hodgkins
PS please to excuse what is a mes

In Camp Prospect Hill Decemr ye 31 1775
My Dear I would inform you that I got hear safe about six oclock & am in good health and I hope these Lines will find you the same I have no News to write only thay say there is a grate Number of ships arived in Boston yesterday whitch occasioned a grate fireing I have Received since I came hear about nineteen Dollars for our Reachons & a months Pay for my self & Nath'l Rust & Thomas the hole is about fifty Dollars and I have sint to you By Brother Perkins one thirty Dollar Bill & two seven Dollar Bills & one five Dollar Bill & Perhaps you may have a Chance to Cheange some for silver with sombody that whants to send to Virginia you may get Brother to go & Pay Mrs Scott for the Coffey twenty six shillings so I must Conclude By Sub-scribing myself your Loving Husband till Death
                                    Joseph Hodgkins
NB Believe Thomas will stay along with me But he Expects Part of his weages & I am willing to give him what is hadsom and wright

In Camp Prospect Hill Jan ye 2 1776
My Dear I tak this opportunity to write a line or two to informe you that I am in good health att Present for witch mercy I de-sire to be thankfull & I hope these lines will find you Persist of

the mercy as for News we have none we have just Ben to supper
on a fine Turky and Capt Wade is gone to Bead and I am all
alone & I feall quite Dul on account of Brothers Being gone
home for I miss him a grate Deal But I must heason for it is
Late I would just inform you that your oncel Ephm Smith has
been hear to Day & informs that all your friends at Sudbury
are well Capt Parker is sick' of a feaver Willeby Neason &
several others of the Regt are also sick our soldiers are Verry
much gone home But the gards are Redust so I hope the Duty
will not be over hard I have not Ben on gard yet since I have Ben
hear I must conclude By subscribing as Before

Joseph Hodgkins

PS I Left a bottom of shothred in my old Coat Pocket whitch
I should be glad of I should Be glad if you would spin some
more & send me for several officers insist on my making them
Boots Give my duty to farther & mother Love to all my friends
I would have you leat father Hodgkins have some money &
Charge the same

In Camp Prospect Hill Jany ye 7 1776
Loving Wife I take this oppertunity to write a line or two to
you to Let you know that I am in good health at Presant
through the goodness of god & I hope these lines will find you
Posest of the same Enistable Blesing I am sorry that I have the
occation to inform you that it is a good Deal sickly among us
we Bured Willeby Nason Last thusday John Sweet is Very sick
in Camp & Josiah Persone of Cape ann in our Company is Just
moved to the ospittle Capt Parker is a little Bitter Mr Harden
is sick in Camp John Holladay Died Last thusday night there
whas five Buried that Day we Bured Mr Nason from the ospittle Capt Willm Wade has Lost one man he was Burred a friday
I must Conclude at Presant By subscribing myself your Loving
Husband till Death Joseph Hodgkins
PS we Live in our tents yet But the men are cheafly gone in to
Barracks Give my Duty to all my Parence & Love to all my
friends to Brother in Pertickler Due sind to me as offen as you
Can I have not heard from you since I left home

In Camp January ye 8 1776

My Dear I now set Down to write a line or two to you to Let you know that I am in good health at Presant and I hope these Lines will find you in as good health as thay Leave me at this time I whant to hear from you very much Due write as soon as you can my Dear I have no News to write Capt Perken Remans Very sick I am in hops John Sweet is a little Better one of Capt Dodges sargt is Very Dangerasly sick it is good Deal sickly among us & a grate many Die Verry sudden But I hope god will apear for us and Remove the Pestelance and the swords from us and give us harts & occation to Rejoyce in his salvation I must Conclude at this time By subscribing my self your Most Kind Companion Till Death Joseph Hodgkins

My Dear I wrote the within Letter Last night after I wrote the letter & got to Bed I heard a number of Cannon upon witch we soon saw a fire & we soon got up the Hill and found that the Houses over to Chalstown whare all in flames & since we hear that a number of Generall Putmans men went over & sot them on fire & Brought of one or two Prisnors & they say thay Brought of one woman

Give my Reggards to all inquiring friends my Dear Due sind me a Little shothread for I must mak a pr or two of Boots

Ipswich Jan ye 8 1776

Loving Husband these Lines come with my kind regards to you hopeing they will find you in as good health as they leave me and the rest of the family at this time I received two Letters from you since left home & was glad to hear you were well I want to hear again dont mis any oppertunity you may have of writing to me Sence that is all the way we have to converse together it is much to my greif that it is so I am a good deal concerned about you on account of the army being so thin for fear the enemy should take the advantage I hear you have lost one of your company & hope it will be sanctified to you all a very melancoly Providence hapened hear last monday night Mr Ringe & Spiler as they were coming in from the eastward Struck upon the Bar & were both Lost I have no other news to write

So I conclude by Subscribing my Self your most afectionate companion till Death   Sarah Hodgkins

PS farther & mother Send their Love to you & mother is much obliged to you for the present you Sent her do give my Love to Capt Wade my pens blots so that I have made a wick of my Letter but I trust you wont expose it so I wish you a good night

In Camp Prospect Hill Jany ye 24 1776

My Dear I tak this oppertunity to inform you that I am in good health & I hope these lines will find you Posest of the same invaluble Blessing I would Just Let you know that I got to the Camp a tusday morning about nine oclock & now I am on the main guard it Being a Place whare there is so much Confution that I cannot write But a few lines But I must Conclude for it is Late so I wush you will & hope I shall have a better oppertunity to write soon so I subscribe myself your afectnate Companion till Death   Joseph Hodgkins

NB give my Regards to Brother Perkins and tell him that I have not had oppertunity to go to Cambridge since I have Been hear But I shall go & see about this paper to morrow Thomas is well

Ipswich Febry ye 1 1776

Loveing Husband these lines come with my most afectionate regards to you hoping they will find you in as good health as they Leave me & rest of the family I received your Letter of the 29 instant Mr Coldwel brought me a gun and Some peas a Sater day night your Letters are Something of a rearity I wish you would write oftener if you can this day was the turn for Mr Danas Lecture he thought the times calld for fasting and acordingly he tirnd it into a day of fasting & prayer and desird our parrish to join with them I have been to meeting all day & heard two as find Sermons as amost ever I heard Mr Frisby preachd in the forenoon and mr Dana in the afternoon next wensday is our ordanation it is apointed a day of fasting I Should be very glad if you could be at home but I dont expec . . . deprivd of it god only knows I must jest you inform that your brotr John

Webber has been here he desires to be rembered to you he Says
he wants very much to See you So no more at present but I
remain your Loving wife till Death Sarah Hodgkins
PS give regards to Capt Wade and tell I have wanted his bed
fellow pretey much these cold nights that we have had Father
and mother Sends their Love to you

In Camp att Prospect Hill Feby 3 1776
My Dear I take this oppertunity to inform you that I am will
att Presant & I hope these lines will find you Posest of the same
Blesings I Received yours of ye 28 of January and I Rejoice to
hear that you & our Children are will and as it gives me grate
satisfacton to Receive Letters from you so you may Depend on
my imbrasing Every opportunnity to write to you I have no
News to write we Live in our tent yet only when we are smoked
out and then we git shealter some whare Else we live Pretty
well and our Duty is not hard we go on guard only once in tin
Day but we spend a grate Part of our time in Exersising the
Regiment I must Conclude give my Duty to my Parence and
Respects all my frinds so no more at Presant But Remain your
loving Husband   Joseph Hodgkins
My Dear I whant a little shothread & I should Be glad to have
you send my shirts as soon as you Can Till Brother he must
write to Mr Hall Before he will send the papper

In Camp att Prospect Hill Feby ye 5 1776
Loveing wife I take this oppertunity to write a line or two to
Let you know that I am well & I hope thase Lines will find
you and our Children Persest of the same Blessings that I Enjoy
I Received yours of the first instant & I Rejoyce to hear that
you whare all well You informed me that Mr Frisby is to or-
daned next Wensday I wish I could Be at home But I cannot
you are Pleased to say that Letters from me are somthing of a
rearaty I wish I could send offender But we have not so many
oppertunitys as we ust to have But you may Depend on my
Chearfulness to Embrace Every oppertunity that Presents for
my Part I take grate Pleasure in writing to you & likewise in
Receiving Letter from you But I must Be short I have no News

to write Capt Wade has Ben something unwell But he is Better
now give my Regards to all Enquiring frinds so no more att
Presant But Remain your Loving Husband till Death Joseph
Hodgkins
PS I gave your Regards to Capt Wade But he Did not wish
that you had his Bed fellow But I wish you had with all my
heart

In Camp at Prospect Hill Feby ye 6 1776
My Dear having an oppertunity this morning to write a line
By Capt Wade I would inform you that I am well & I hope
these lines will find you the same I should Ben Very glad to
Come home to ordanation and upon my making applycation to
Capt he whent to the Colol & when he found that one officer out
of the Company might go home insted of speaking a word for
me he spok two for himself But if you should have the oppertunity to see him Due ask him to supper with you though I
Due not Expect you will see him soon enough So I must Conclude att this Time By subscribing my self your Loving
Husband till Death   Joseph Hodgkins
give my Duty to all Parence & Love to all friends

Ipswich Febry ye 11 1776
Loveing Husband haveing an oppertunity this evening to write
a line or two to you I gladly embrace it to Let you know that
we are well hopeing they will find you posest of the Same
Blessing I received two Letters from you on ordanation day
after meeting which was a greate comfort to me to hear that
were well I received one by the hand of Capt Wade but not till
after Supper I have been glad to have invited to Supper if I had
Seen him Soon enough we had a comfortable ordanation but
there Seems to me to be Something wanting I wanted you at
home & that would have crownd all it is very cold to night I
hope you will be provided for with a Comfortable Lodging I
think a great deal about you both by night & by day but I desire
to commite you to God who has hitherto preserved you & he
is able Still to preserve you at all times O my Dear Let me beg
of you to pute your trust in him att all times who alone is able

to deliver us out of all our trobles will doo it if we trust in him aright but I must conclude I remain your most afectionate companion till Death   Sarah Hodgkins
PS farther & mother Sends their Love to you wensday I wrote the above Letter on Sabbath day night I did not know but Capt Wade would go down the next day but I hear he is not gone yet & I dont know as I shall See him but I hoped. . . .

                      In Camp Prospect Feby ye 12 1776
My Dear these Lines Comes with my most afectniate Regards to you hoping thay will find you and our Children in as good health as thay Leave me at this Time through the goodness of god I enjoy a good state of health But we under go a good Deal of Defielty for whant of a Better house But I Expect to move in a Day or two to our Barrak whare we have got a Prety Room as I must Be shor for the weather is Very Cold & our tent smoks so that it is with Defelty that I can stay in it My Dear as for News we have not much But it is sayed that the Generals are Determaned to do something very soon But What the event will be god only knows But I hope god will. Direct them in there Counsels & order Every thing for his Glory & our good so I must Conclude at this time By subscribing my self your Loveing Husband Till Death Joseph Hodgkins
PS Give my Duty to farther & mother and Love to all frinds tel Brother I sent his Letter to Mr Hall But I have not had oppertunity to go to him since I am Prity much tied at home

                         Ipswich Febry ye 20 1776
My Dear I take this oppertunity to write aline or two to inform you that we are all in a Comfortable State of Health through the goodness of God & I hope these lines will find you posest of the Same Blessing I received yours by Mr Smith & I rejoice to hear that you are well I want to See you very much I think you told me that you intended to See me once a mounth & it is now amonth & I think a very long one Since you left home & I dont hear as you talk of comeing but I must confess I dont think it is for want of a good will that you dont come home it is generaly thoght that there will be Something done amongst

you very Soon but what will be the event of it God only knows
o that we may be prepared for all events I am destressd about
you my Dear but I desire to commit you to God who alone
is able to preserve us through all the deficuly we have to pass
through may he Strenghten your hands & incorage your heart
to carry you through all you may be called in the way of your
duty & that you may be enabled to put your trust in him at all
times but I must conclude att this time by Subscribing myself
your most afectionate Companion till Death
PS Joanna Sends her duty to you   Sarah Hodkins

In Camp att Prospect Hill March ye 12 1776
My Dear I take this oppertunity to write a Line or two to you
to Let you know that I am well & I hope these Lines will find
you Posest of the same Blesing I whant to hear from you Very
Much Due Write as offen as you Can for weather you will have
the oppertunity of sending hear to me much Longer is unserting for the army in general have had orders to Be Ready to
March But What Regements will march is unserting yet But
I would not have you make your self uneasy about it for I hope
we shall Be Carred through all the Defeltys we may meet with
in the way of our Duty so I must Conclude att this time By
subscribing myself your Most afectinate Companion till Death
                                        Joseph Hodgkins

In Camp Prospect Hill March ye 17 1776
My Dear these Lines Comes with my Most afectinate Reguards
to you hoping thay will find you and our Children in as good
Health as thay Leave me at this Time I Received yours By
Brother & I Rejoice to hear you are all in a Comfortable state
of health you wrote me words that you thought strange that I
had not sent you any Letter But I wrote By Mr Dannis & he
Did not get home so soon as I Expected My Dear I shall Embrace Every oppertunity to write to you & I shall Expect you
will Do the same But as for News I Must Refer you to Brother
so I must Conclude att this time By subscribing my self your
Most kind Companion till Death   Joseph Hodgkins

[194]

Give my Duty to farther & Mother & Love to all friends my Regards to Brother Chapman & tell him I whant my Briches Very much for I Due not Know But we shall march soon

In Camp Prospect Hill March ye 18 1776
My Dear I wrote a letter yesterday Morning and soon after I wrote there apeared a grate Movement among the Enemy & we soon found that thay had Left Bunker Hill & Boston and all gone on Board the shiping and our army took Posestion of Bunker Hill & also of Boston But none went to Boston But those that have had the small Pox I am in hast Brother can inform you of matters Better than I Can By writing all I can say is that We must Move some whare Very soon But I would not have you mak yourself uneasy about that for our Enemye seems to Be a flieing Before us which seems to give a spring to our Spirits I must Conclude as Befor By subscribing Joseph Hodgkins

In Camp Prospect March ye 20 1776
Loving wife I take this oppertunity to write a line or two to let you know that I am well through the goodness of god & I hope these lines will find you Posest of the same Blesing I Received your Letter By thomas and I am glad to hear that you are well & as you informed me that you whare full of trouble for fear that I should Be Called away I would not have you Be uneasy about me for I am willing to sarve my Contery in the Best way & mannar that I am Capeble of and as our Enemy are gone from us I Expect we must follow them it is not sarting yet who will stay hear But it is generaly thought that our Regt will March some whare I would not Be understood that I should Chuse to March But as I am ingaged in this glories Cause I am will to go whare I am Called with a Desire to Commit myself & you to the care of him Who is able to Carry on through all the Defiltes that we may be Called to I am sensible that the feteagues of marching will Be grate But I hope if we are Called to it we shall March with Chearfullness

My Dear as for News we have Nothing But what you will have in the Pappers the Regulars have Burnt & Blown up the Cassel

[195]

I must conclude att Presant By subcribing my self your Most afectinate Companion Till Death Joseph Hodgkins

PS I wrot the above letter Last night I would inform you that I well this morning I have sent you three Blak Hanchiefs By Mr Burley & he says that he will Change one for a white one if you are a mind to Part with any of them the Price is 9/6

~~~~~~

In Camp att Prospect Hill March ye 23 1776

Loveing wife I take this oppertunity to write a line or two to you to Let you know that I am in good health at Presant for which I Desire to Be thankful I have nothing new to write to you we Remain hear yet & I cant find out which way we shall goe I Determen to see you Before we March if Posebbly I Can I whant to see you very much I whas in hopes that I should heard from you Before I wrote for I Expect Capt Dodge would Ben hear Before now there has Just now orders Come out for six Regts to be Ready to march on the shortest notes which gives me some Reason to think that our Regemt will not March this some time if att Tall But I would not have you Depend tue much on our staying hear for it is only my Thought of the Matter But I must Conclude att Presant By subcribing my self your Most afectnate Companion Till Death   Joseph Hodgkins

PS I Believe By the aperence of your Last that I shall not have another till this gets home to you But however I have sent you a quire of Paper By Jbas Farley for I am so fond of Letters that I Shall not only Embrase Every opportunity to write my self But will furnish you wherewith to Do the same

Give my Duty to my Parence and Love to all my friends the six Regem'ts that I menched on the other side thay Donot any of them Belong to our Brigade

~~~~~~

In Camp att Prospect March ye 25 1776

My Dear haveing an oppertunity to send to you I would inform you that I well & I hope you and our friends are Posest of the Blesing I Receved yours yesterday By Capt Dodge and the Things you sent me I Rejoice to hear that you are all well I have sent By Capt Tho's Dodge some Durty things which he will Deliver I have Tryed on the stockens you sent and thay

Fit Very well I have nothing New to only I have just heard that the Fleet are a Coming to sale But I Due not know the Truth of it for I have Just Come Down from Cambridge I must Conclude By subscribing as Before Joseph Hodgkins

Whalpool Apl ye 2 1776

Loving wife I take this oppertunity to in form you that I am well & I hope these lines will find you Posest of the same Blessing I would just inform you that I Just got to Cambridge as the Reg't Marched & we marched about ten miles then we Put op and got a good Lodging and I judg that we have marched 15 miles to Day it is Now about three oClock we have got to March six miles to night and to Morrow we shall get to Providence where we Expect to Receive orders whare to go Next it is unsarting whare we shall go we may go to Newport But if the Enemy are not there we Expect to go to Norrege

But I must Conclude for we are about to get a Mouthfull of Vittles and then we Must Be upon the March But I must Conclude By subcribing myself your Most affectnate Companion Till Death   Joseph Hodgkins

PS hope soon to have a more Leashur time to write my Regards to all Friends

Providence April ye 4 1776

Loving wife these Lines Comes with my Most afectnate Regards to you hoping thay will find you in as good health as they leave me at this Time through the goodness of god I must Just Let you know how we got along we got to Providence a Wensday in the after noon But we got Pretty whate for it Rained Verry fast But when we got hear we had good houses Provided for Both men and officers and it is a very Pleasent Town But we Expect to Leave it on Satarday Morning and March for Norrege and we Expect to go from there to New York My Dear I would not have you make your self uneasy about me for Marching Dos not worry me so much as I Expected and I hope Providence will Provide for us and Carry me through all the Trobles we have to meet with in the way of our Duty and while we are Absent from Each other

My Dear I wrote the above Last Night now it is Friday this Fournoon our Regiment & Colol Hitchcocks Regt have Ben under armes to Receive General Washington into Town which whas Done with a great Deal of Pleasuer and Honnor to Both general & officers we shall March to morrow morning for Norrege where we Expect to Rest a fue Days & then I sopose we shall go to Newyork By Wharter My Dear I should Be glad to have you Write if you should have any oppertunity I shall send this By the Post & I Do not know But you may sind to New york By the Post so I must Conclude at Presant By subcribing my self your Most afectnate Companion till Death

Joseph Hodgkins

New London April ye 10 1776

Loveing wife I take this oppertunity to writ a line or two to you to Let you know that I am in good health at Presant for which Mercy I Desire to Be thankfull & I hope these lines will find you and all our Children & Friends Posest of the same Blesing I whant to hear from you Very much But I Due not Expect to hear till we get to New York I would inform you that this is the third Letter I have wrote since I Left home one of the secont instan I sopose you have had I wrote another at Providence of the 5 which you may Posibly get

I would inform you that we got to Norwich on Monday ye 8 instant & a Tusday we Marched to this town & we Expect to Embark for New york to Morrow if we have a wind and when we get there I hope we shall have some Rest for I am a good Deal Tird of Marching though we get Very good Entertainment in general People are Very Kind to us in the Contery But where there is so many Pasing it is Deficelt to get things as we should Chuse But I must Be short for it is Late I have no News to Write only what our fleet as Done & that you Will have in the Print Before you will get this so I Must Conclude at Present My Dear By subscribing my self your Most affectinate Companion till Death Joseph Hodgkins

PS Give my Duty to all my Parence and Love to all inquiring friends

[198]

Thomas is well & sends his Love to all frinds there is not a man in our Company that could out Travel Thomas

Thursday I wrote the above Letter Last Night But as the wind Dos not admit of our sailing to Day I would Let you know that I am in good health to Day I whant to hear from you I hope you are well so I conclude at Presant as Before Joseph Hodgkins

New York April ye 24 1776

Loving wife I Tak this oppertunity to write a few Lines to you to Let you know that I am well & I hope these Lines will find you and our Children & all friends Posest of the same Enestable Blesing of health that I injoy at Presant through the goodness of god & that we whare sensible what a blessing health is & whare able to Emprove it awright But I hope god will Direct our ways and Presarve us from Every Evil Especialy from sin while we are absint from each other and in his good time Return us to our Respective friends and to the Place of our Natevity My Dear I would just inform you how we got along on our way from Newlondon we saled from there on Sundy Morning the 14 and the next Sunday we got hear But we had a very Pleasant Passage though it whas Long we whare in several harbers and we saw several Pleasant Towns New-haven in Pertulare is a Verry fine Place But I think this City York Exceeds all Plases that Ever I saw on many accounts But it is Verry Expensive Living hear and so it has Bin Ever sinc we first Marched I Belive I Pade for Every Meal I eat through the Whole March But I dont Mean to Lay that to hurt if we Do But accomplish the grand Desine we are aming at that will Be Every thing I would Let you know that I am Verry well Contented at Present on Every account Excepting Being absent from home for My Dear the thought of Being absent from you and my family is the gratest troble that I have at Presant But My Dear I would not have you Be Trobled about me I dont write this to troble you only to let you know that I am not without some care and truble about you though almost 360 miles of as for News I hardly know what to write only that there is no ships nor Troops hear of our enemy and it Dos not apear to me that we shall stay hear a grate wile But whare we

[199]

shall go next I now not But there is a Report that we shall go
on Longisland which I wish may Be the Case But I must conclude My Dear I whant to hear from you Verry Much I have
not heard a word from you since I Left home & I cant Expect
to This som time yet so no more at Present But I Remain your
Most afectnate Companion Till Death   Joseph Hodgkins
PS Give My Duty to My Parencs and Love to all my Frinds
Thomas is will sends his Love to you and all his friends I
would inform you that the Post that Carry this Letter is to go
as far as Newbury Port & will call at Capt Dodges as he comes
Back to tak letter for any Body that is around to send so you
may have an oppertunity to send to me I expect to Pay the
Postage for carrying & fetching Due send to me every opper-
tunity you have

this is the fourth Letter I have sent to you one of April ye 2
another of ye 5 another of ye 15 I think

LongIsland May ye 9 1776
Loving wife I take this oppertunity to write a few lines to you
to Let you know that I am in a Comfortable state of health
through the goodness of god though I have had a bad Cold But
I have got Prety Clear of that But I have had two Bad Boyles
on my Right arm one of them is not Brock yet and it is very
Painfull But I hope it will Brake soon I have not wore a Coat
for this six Days Except a grate Coat But I hope thay will Leave
me in good health as People say they are holsome But not Toothsome however I hope these lines will find you and all my Children & friends in a good state of health My Dear I whant to see
you Very much But if I Could hear from you that would Be a
grate satisfaction to me there is several men came hear this weak
that Left Ipswich three weaks after I Did But I have not heard
any thing from you since I left home only Capt Wades mother
sent word in his letter that you whare gone to Sister Chapmans so
I conclude that you whare well I have no News to write we
Came over to this Island the second Day of may & Pitched our
tents But the weather Being Cool & the Tents Being verry Bad
we got a Room to Live in Till the weather grew warmer it whas

the order that no officer should Lodge out of the Camp But
the Tents Being so Very thin the General Consented that we
should for a few Day till there Could Be some Boards got to
Rais the tents and Lay floors in them But I must Be short But
I must just inform you that we Do not Live as we Did Last
Campan Everything is Excesive Dear 9 Shilling now full
money a gallon for Rum & Evrything in Preportion so I must
Conclude at Presant By subscribing my self your Most afectionate
Companion Till Death Joseph Hodgkins
PS Give my Duty to Farther & Mother and Love to all frinds
to Sister Hannah in a Perticuler Thomas is well and sends
his Lov to you & all his friends

In Camp on Long Island May ye 22 1776
My Dear it is with a grate Deal of Pleasure that I now sit Down
to write a few lines to you and these lines Comes with my Most
afectionate Regards to you hoping they will find you & our
Children in as good health as they Leave me at this Time
through the goodness of god I received yours of the 6 Instant
which gave me grate stattisfaction to hear that you & our Children
& friends whare all well and that you had Recived all the Letters that I have sent wharein you were informed that I whas
well I feel Rejoyced to hear that you have had so good Luck
as to get all the Letters that I have wrote Except one of the 9
instent & I hope that you have got that By this time if you
have I informed you in it that I whas Lame in my arm with a
Boyle indead I whas Verry Lame for Eight Days and I whas
not able to whare my Coat for ten Days But I have got quite
well of them now for which mercy as well as al others I Desire
to Be thankful and hope god will still Be with us and suckseed
all our indeavors and Carry us through all the Difculty and
Dangers that we my meat with in this Time of grate Difculty
and in his own time Bring us home to our Dear friends again in
safty and give us harts and occation of Rejoycing to geathur in
his Salvation

you may Expect some News in this Letter But I have None
to write Excepting that there is grate Reason to think that we

shall have our hands full soon for there is I Beleve By General order a Considerable Number of Troops Expected hear very soon our men are on fatague . . . all the Time But they are Very healthy in general Our Company are all well Except one and he is not Bad But I must just inform you of our sittivation on the Island the Farry from York is about amile whid & we are Incamped about a mile & aquarter from the Farry whare there is a Reaver or a Bay Runs in each sid of the Island and meat within a mile & we are incamped Between these Bays and have got a forte Just By our incampment and another on a hill at the Northward of us which are a most Don and there is to Be another Built at the south of us on a nother hill and thys forte will stop this Pasage By Land for it is Expected that the Enemy will land on som of the Estward Part of the Island if thay come for about fifty miles to the east of us it is sayed that seven eights of the People are Torrys & I fear that one half in York are not much Better for it is Enough to mak anyBodys Blood Boyl only to think what Destruction whas made Last Campian in our Province By our army & now to see what Destruction the army are under to keep the inhabentins Quite for our People are not alowed to tread on the ground scarcely they are not alowed to get orsters out of the Cove & one man forbid the soldery catching eales But he got nothing for that But Cryes I Believe But I must Conclude at this Time My Dear I whant to see you Very much But as I cannot Expect to this some time I Desire to commit you and myself & Children to the Care of him Who is Able to Due more and Better for us than we are either able to ask or think and may we Be sencible of god goodness to us heatherto and Be Enabled to Poot our Trust in him for the Future So no more at Presant But I Remain your Most afectionate Companion Till Death   Joseph Hodgkins
PS Give my Duty to all my Parence and Love to all inquiring Friends I whant to hear weather Coson Jamey has got home for I hav not heard a word about him give my Love to Joanna & Salle tell them I whant to see them & my Little son too

My Dear this Letter Comes By the same Post that Brough the other and you will have an oppertunity to write again & as I

Due not know weather I shall see him my self or not Before
he goes I should Be glad if you should Chance to see him as it
is not imposible But what he may Lodg in Ipswich as he goes
as far as Newbury that you would see if he would Bring a
Copple of shirts for my shirts whare out Very Fast & I cant
think of Boying any hear as Linnen is so Excessive Dear But I
would have you ask him what he would have for the Postage
of them & not give more then what is Reaseneble My Letter
is folded Ronge side outwards But you must Excuse that

Ipswich May ye 23 1776

Loveing Husband these lines come with my Love to you
hopeing they will find you and the Company all in good health
as they Leave me & Children at this time through the goodness
of God I received yours of the 9 instant yesterday morning it
is a grate comfort to me to hear from you I am Sorry to hear
you are trobled with boyles they are very troblesome but as you
Say they are counted holsom I hope they will Leave you in a
good state of health I am ready to think they proceed from the
humer you have been trobled with for some time I want to
hear whether you have got well of it or no I want to See you
very much but I durst not think much about it at present but
I hope we Shall See one another again all in good time I desire
to be contented with the alotments of Providence you wrote in
your Letter that you had not heard from me Since you Left
home but it is no neglect of mine for I will asure you I wrote
the first oppertunity I knew of which was I think the 6 of May
I Suppose you have had it before now I must Jest inform that
Capt Perkins got in last friday they are well and have got a
good load of corn farther & mother Sends their Love to you
I See Sister Hannah yesterday She told me to give her Love to
you and tell you they were well Brother Johns folks are well
& Send their love thomas So I must Conclude by Subscribing
myself your Loveing wife till Death Sarah Hodgkins
Joanna Sends her duty to you

Ipswich June ye 2 1776

Loving Husband these Lines come with my most afectionate

regards to you hoping they will find you in good health as they
Leave me at this time through the goodness of God I this day
Received yours of the 22 of may i am rejoiced to hear you are
well I am Sorry to hear that you are amongst a People that are
So unkind as you inform me they are monday night my Dear I
began to write a Letter Last night but it was So Late before I
begun I could not write much I have been very busy all day to
day a making you a Shirte you Sent to me to Send you a couple
& I had but one ready for the Cloth that I intended to make you
Some Bodys of I have not got it Quite done So I was abliged to
take one off of the Cloth I had in the house & I have got it done
& washd and Sister Perkins is now a ironing of it I have been
down to Mr Treadwells to desire them to Let me know when
the man comes & if he will bring them I shall Send you a couple
& by that time the Post comes again I hope to have Some more
ready and if you want them you must Send me word but to drop
that I must Jest tell you that Sally meet with a mishap Last
monday She Scolt her arm prity bad but it Seems to be in a
good way to be well Soon the rest of us are in a comfortable
State of health I want to See you very much Sometimes I am
almost impatient but concidering it is Providence that has parted
us I desire to Submite & be as contented as I can & be Thankfull
that we can hear from one another So often I must inform you
that two of our neighbours has died Since I wrote my Last
Deacon Potter Died Last Saturday and Hannah Fitts the Saturday before a Loud call to us all to be ready for Death oh that we
may be prepared for all events and if it is the will of God that
we are not to meet again in this world may we be prepared to
meet in a better where we Shall not have the greif of parting
any more but I must conclude at this time by Subscribing myself your Loveing wife till Death   Sarah Hodgkins

In Camp on LongIsland June ye 10 1776
My Dear I Take this opportunity to inform you that I am well
& I hope these Lines will find you & my children Posest of the
same Blesing that I Enjoy through the goodness of god & for
which I desire to be thankful My Dear I am Charmen well But

I Longe to see you & my Children But When I shall is unsarting
But I hope god will Presarve us while we are absant from
each other & in his own good time Bring us to the Injoyment
of Each other and give us harts to be thankful for all his mercys
I have nothing New to write to you our People are healthy in
general But Stephen Colman & Will'm Stone are sick of a feavor
& a Capann man in our Company is in very weak state & I am
Very much afrad of him there is non Died in our Regiment since
we Came hear our Duty is Very Constant the men are on
Duty 5 Days in seven But it is Chefily fetigue there is not
much guarding to Due only two subaltons guard and I have on
of them to night which will oblige me to be shorte But I Expect
the Post in a few Days I hope then to hear that you and all my
friends are well and it is Likely I shall have another opportunity
to write to you so I must Conclude att this Time By subscribing
my self your most afectionate Companion Till Death Joseph
Hodgkins

NB My Dear I have nothing to send to you But Love & good
will But I hope I shall have some money soon & if I have
opportunity I shall send some home But it is Verry Expensive
Living hear so that I am obliged to spend all most as much as I
earn Give my Duty to all My Parense & Love to all friends
Capt Wade is well & Desires to Be Remembered to you & all
that InQuire after him

this Litter Comes By Colol Littles Brother Who Came hear
he & Capt Kent of Newbury to see there frinds & if there should
Be any gentlemen in Ipswich that should Come this way I
should Be Very glad to have you send me a Pair of shirts But
I would not have you Be unhapy about it for when I Cant Do
no Longer I can by some hear though Linnen is Extream Dear

In Camp at Brookline Long Island June ye 11 1776
My Dear I wrote my Letter Last night to send By Mr Little
to Day but Luckily he does not goo Before to Morrow Morning
and I have just Received your letter of the 23 of May By the
Hand of Mr Napp and I am grately Rejoyced to hear that you
and my Children and all frinds are all well for there is nothing
in this world that gives me more satisfaction then to hear of your

wellfair your Informed me that Capt Jame has got home well I am Very glad to hear it give my Regards to him & his wife & Tell him he must Come and see us give my Love to Brother Perkins and sister Tell them their Brothers are well Thomas is well and send his Duty to his father & mother Love to you and all his frinds

as I wrote my letter last night I shall sind it and these fue lines enclosed in it so I must Conclude as Befor

Joseph Hodgkins

PS as to that humer that you menetned I got some stuff at york witch semed to give a grate check to it But it seams to Come out a little again But I intend to Trye again soon to kill it

I would have you get as much Corn of Capt Perkins as you think you will whant give my Love to Joanna & Salle tell Salle Dady whants to see her Very much

In Camp at LongIsland June ye 20 1776

My Dear I take this opportunity to write a line or two to you to Let you know that I am well for which mercy I Desire to Be thankful and I hope these Lines will find you Posest of the same Blessings that I enjoy through the goodness of god I Received yours of the 2 Instant Last TueDay which gave me grate satisfaction to hear that you whas well and all our friends that god would Presarve us in health while we are absent and in his one Time Return us to our friends in safty I Received the shirts you sent me My Dear and am Much obliged to you for them I hope I shall Be able to Due as much for you some-time or other But I have not much to send now But Love and good will But I whant to see you Verry much But as you say I Dare not hardly think of it at Presant I Desire to make myself as Contented as I Can though I must Confess the thoughts of Being absent so Long is the gratest Trible that I meet with But I would have you make yourself as Contented as you Can and I hope we shall have the happiness to meat Each other again in gods good time I have nothing New to write to you only the fleet is Expected Every Day general Washington is Calling in the Milisha and I hope we shall Be in Readyness to meat our Enemy and show them yankys Play Come when they will I

think we have got Prety well fortfyed and I think they will
meat with a Wharm Reception for our men are in good Spirits
and seem to be impatient & sick a waiting for them But I must
hasson you informed me that Salle had Cutt her arm tel her
Dady is Verry sorry for it and whants to see her and all the Rest
so I must Conclude at this time By subscribing myself your Most
afectinate Companion Till Death   Joseph Hodgkins
PS Give my Duty to all my Parriens and Love to all frinds
our sick that I menchined in my Last are all Bitter and all the
Rest are well Thomas is well and sends his Love to you and
all his Frinds I shall send you a little money By the Post which
you may give him your Recept for I shall Tak his

Ipswich June ye 22 1776

My dear haveing jest heard of an oppertunity to Send you a
few lines I gladly imbrace it to Let you know that I & my
family are well throgh the goodness of God father has been
very poorly but has got better again I received yours of ye 10 &
11 instant & I am much rejoiced to hear you are well oh that
we may be Senceable of the goodness of God to us and live
answerable thereto it was Last wenesday I received your Lettr
I Sent you a Letter & two Shirtes by Mr Craft the post & I
Shall have Some more for you Soon if I can Send them as to
your Sending me Some mony dont be uneasy about it but I
must be Short I remain your Loveing wife till Death
our freinds here are well   Sarah Hodgkins

Ipswich July ye 3 1776

My Dear these lines come with my most afectionate regards to
you hopeing they will find you in good health as they Leave
me at this time throgh the goodness of God which I desire to
acknowledge we are all in a comfortable State of health but
Jose he Seems to be Something unwell now but I hope he will
be better in a day or two I received your Letter and twenty
three Dollars by the Post on the 1 instant I am very glad to
hear you are well and am also abliged to you for the money I
hope you have not Straitend youself for I was not in Present

[207]

want I sent you a letter of the 22 of June I think I due really want to See you very much but dont understand as I am like to at present So I must be contented to Live a widow for the present but I hope I Shant always live So I desire to be thankfull we can hear from each other So often as we doo I hope we Shall See one another again in good time I think the time you ingaged for is now half out & if you Should live to See that out I hope you will Let Some body else take your Place but I durst not depend apon any thing here & Since we See the uncertainty of all earthly enjoiments Let us make it our greatest concern to Secure to our Selves a better portion for if we once get an interrest in Christ we Shall be sure not Lose it to all Eternity therefore Let us not put off this work of the greatest importance to an uncertain hereafter you informed me in your Letter that the fleet was lookd for every day I hope God will apear for you if you are called to battle as he has done heretofore may we be Prepaired for all events due write all oppertunitys I have got Some more Shirts & apair or two of Stokins if you want doo Speek to the Post when he comes again to bring them to you Brother Heard is a mind to buy your gun you Left it at home & if you have amind to Sell it I Should be glad you would Send me word what you would take for it as Soon as you can Cousin Jemmy Sends his Love to you & Says he would writ to you but he think it would cost you Something but I must Conclude by Subscribing myself your most afectionate companion till Death

Sarah Hodgkins

father & mother remembers their love to you Joanna Sends her duty to you Sally is gone to Scool give my regards to Capt Wade

My Dear   In Camp on LongIsland July ye 17 1776
     I Take this opportunity to write a line or two to you and these Lines Brings you my most afectionate Regards hoping thay will find you and our Children and all friends in good health as they Leave me att this Time through the goodness of god which we ought always to acknowledge although we are in the field Exposed to many hardships and Defiltice yet even in

these Circumstances we Enjoy many Blesings which we Due not Desarve and for which we ought to Be thankful I Received your Letter of ye 22 June the 8 of July and that By the Post Last Sunday and I am Very glad to hear you and all frinds are in good health But Jose you said whas unwell But I hope he is well By this Time I whant to see you and my Children Very much But it is unsarting when I shall But I hope god will Presarve us from the many Eavels & Dangers we are Exposed to and in his good Time Return us al to our friends again in safty you may Expect som News But I hardly know what to write only our Enemys are Coming in almost Every Day and we Expect thay will have 25000 men when thay al git in But I would not have you Be uneasy about us for our numbers fair Exceed theirs for we have 42000 men now and thay are Coming in Every Day two Brigades are Coming from Piledel-phia Consisting of 53 Battalons so I hope with the Blesing of god we shall Be able to keep our ground and let them know that yankeys can fite you Put me in mind of the Time I whas Ingaged for Being half out and also if I Lived to see the Time out not to Ingage again But I think so much of this Presant Campean that I have not spent any time Thinking about another But I will Ventur to say if I Live to see this out I think I shall Be intierly willing to Rest a spell at Least you sent me word that you had som more shirts & stockings But I can Due very well with what I have got at Presant and if I should whant them hear after I will send you word I have Received som more money & I shall send you By the Post 45 Dollars for which you may give a Receipt at your Receiving it and as for my gun you menchoned Brother Heard may have it for 12 Dollars and that is But 2 shillings more then I gave for it Last Whinter and guns have Ben a Rising Ever since I must Con-clude at This Time By Subscribing my self your Loving Husband Till Death   Joseph Hodgkins

PS I have wrote to Brother and I must Refer you to his Letter for som perticlars that happened hear as you are so near I thought it needles to write them twice over. I hope you will Write Every oppertunity that you may have & you may Depent on my Duing the same Give my Duty to all Parence & Love to all Frinds My Regards to Coson Jamnae & Capt Kendall

My Dear I would have you Call on Capt Charly Smith for such things as you whant in the Family and I hear that Capt Moses Harris is got home and there is something Due to me from him which you may see By my Book & I would have you get Brother to Call on him to settle for it likely that he is able now

as to that Torry Plot I sepose you have had the accountes in the Papers Before now so its not Likely that I Can Tell anything more then what you have heard one of them was Tried on winsday Condemed on thusday and Executed on friday & I wish Twenty more whare sarved the same

Thomas is well & sends his Love to you and all his Friends

~~~~~~

In Camp LongIsland July ye 22 1776

My Dear as Nothing But seeing & Conversing with you could give me so much Pleasure as writing too and Receiving Letters From you and as this is the only way that we can have at Presant of conversing Do lit us improve Every oppertunity that we have for it gives me the gratest satisfaction to hear from my frinds Espechialy from one that is so near after my afectnoate Reguards to you I would inform you that I am in a Comfortable state of health at Presant for which I Desire to Be thankful and hope these Lines will find you & our Children of the same Blesing I have nothing New to write to you only our army at South Carlino under general Lee hav had a Battle the Enemy atempting to Land a havey Cannanding for 12 hours whas made upon the fortifications near Charlstown Both Fleet & army have Ben Repulsed with grate Loss By a small Number of Vallent Troops Just arived the Enemy had 172 Killed & wounded among whom whare several officers and two Cappitell ships much Dammeged one friget of 20 guns Intirely Lost Being aBandend & Blown up By the Crue and a Number of other ships Very much hurt and all with a Loss on our side of 10 killed & 22 wounded this account you may Depend on for it came out in general orders Last night and I hope this will

anemate me if Called to it to act in like manner as there is
Nothing Turned up hear since I wrote I must Conclude By
Tiling you I whant to see you and all frinds Very much But I
Desire to Be Contented and hop you will not make your self
uneasey so I Remain your Loveing Husband Till Death

                              Joseph Hodgkins

Give my Duty to Farther & Mother Perkins and Love to al
Friends Sargt Hodgkins & Willm Stone are sick with the Flux
But I hope something Bitter Aaron waite is got most well
Solomon Colmon is Very Low indead

                    In Camp Long Island Augt ye 8 1776
My Dear I tak this oppertunity to write a line or two to Lit
you know that I am in good health & I hope these Lines will
find you Posest of the same Blesing

My Dear I Received yours By the Post Last night in witch you
informed me that my Little son whas Verry Low and not Like
to Live I am afrad that he is not Living now But I must hope
that it will Pleas god to spair his Life But that we may Be Prepaired for all Events I whas afrad I should hear some Bad
News from home But I hop god will Do Better for us then our
fears he is able to Raise him Even from the gates of the grave
But I am sinseble that god will Due what is write and Just and
I hope god will seport you & I under all our Trobles and Carry
us through all the Difiltes we have to meat with in this world
and if we should not Live to see one another again in this world
may we Be Prepaired to meat in a Better whare there will Be no
more Sorrow nor morning the Loss of friends it is with a heavy
hart that I now write to you But it is a grate Comfort to me to
hear that you and the Rest of our Children are well what would
I give to see you I hope god will Presarve us and give us harts
and occasion to Prase his name together so I must conclude By
subcribing as Before your afectionate Companion Till Death

                              Joseph Hodgkins

PS I Expect to write By the Post in a few days By that Time
we may have some News give my Duty to all my Parence &
Love to all Friends Capt Wade & Capt Dodge have Ben Poorly

But are got Pretty well again Sargent Hodgkins has Ben Very
Bad for three weaks But he seams to Be Better now

~~~~~~

                         In Camp LongIsland Augt ye 11th 1776
Loving wife after my Most afectionate Regards to you I would
inform you that I am in good health at Presant through the
goodness of god & I Desire to Be thankfull for so grate a mercy
and hop these fue Lines will find you & our Children Posest of
the same Blessing My Dear I cant healp hoping But I Dont
know whare I have any Room for my hope Respecting my Little
son But god knows how it is and I Desire to hope in his mercy
& Commit him if Living & myself & you to the Cair of kind
Providence hoping he will Do Better for us then our fears &
Carry us through all the Defelties & Trobles we have to meat
with in this world and may these aflecttions Be santified to us
for our good you sayed that you whanted me at home to Bare
Part of your Troble I wish I whas at home with you But insted
of Being with you to Bare Part with you I am obliged to Be
hear & Bare it all alone for you have friends to Comfort you
But I have nobody to speak with hear and can hardly have the
Privilege of thinking my one thoughts I mean By Reason of
having my thoughts taken up with the cares and fatiges of the
Campain whitch at this Time are grate But I must Conclude at
this Time By subscribing myself your Loving Husband Till
Death   Joseph Hodgkins
PS a good many of our People are Poorly not many Bad
Sargt Hodgkins is Very weak and Low I am a good Deal afrad
of him
Give my Duty to all my Parance & Love to all friends the
weather hear is Exceeding Dry & Hoot But I hear that you have
had fine Ranes at New England
I Sent a letter By Capt Parsons 3 Day ago

~~~~~~

                              LongIsland Augt ye 12 1776
My Dear the Posts not going so soon as I expected and I being
at Leashur this afternoon I thought I would write a line or two
more to Let you know that I am well I would also inform you
a little about Publick afairs our People fitted out 5 or six Row

galles and sent them up the River to atack the two men of war that whent up there some Time ago accordingly thay whent up about 9 Days ago and the ships saw them Coming they got under saile in order to fite the galles and the ships fired the first gun and then the galles ingaged them for an hour & half But one of the galles split her Best guns and another Received a shot Between wind & wharter so thay thought Best to Retreat But they hulled the ships several Times But what other Dammedge thay Did we have not heard on our side whare two men killed 10 or 12 wounded and since our Peopple have sunk ships and other things which they Prepaired a Cross the Channel so as to stop the ships from Coming Down or and other going up and there Being Talk of the Enemy mak an a Tack soon it whas thought Best not to send the galles up again at Presant I would also inform you that there is a fleet Now a Coming in som of our officers saw them and Judge there whas about 80 sails the fleet are this moment firing there selute so I sepose some of them have got up to Lord Hows fleet it is thought this Fleet is from the Southern Collines so it seams they will git all the strength they Can Before they mak any atack on us But we are a waiting and Expecting them Every Day I hope god will Prosper us and give us Corredge & Resolution and Cover our heads in the Day of Battle and Crown our army with suikses I must conclude I hope you are well I whant to see you Very much But Cant tel when I shall

I Remain as Before your &c   Joseph Hodgkins

In Camp Longisland Augt ye 25 1776

Loving wife I take this oppurtunity to write a Line or two to you to Lit you Know that I am well at Present for which Mercy I Desire to Be thankful and I hope these Lines will find you & our Children and friends Posest of the same Blesing though I never Expect to hear that my little Son is alive But I want to hear Verry much yet I am afrade But I hope god will Prepair me for all that I am to met with in this world and santify his Varrious Dealing with us for our good for while god is a Chastising us with aflection on the one hand I think it my Duty to

acnoledge his goodness to me on the other in a late instence
which I will Relate in a fue words Last monday about noon
there Came orders for a party to Be sent Down the Island to
Drive the Cattle from the South Side of the Island and to Di-
stroy all the Boats that we find so the Enemy mite not be Bene-
fitted By them & I went with this Party the Party Consisted of
two hundred men Besids officers and a Troop of hors about
sixty to asist us so we marched about three oclock in the afternoon & we marcht 25 miles that night and the nixt morning we
proseded on our Besness and Colected a good number of Cattle
& Distroyed a grate number of Boats and on Wensday the after
noon we marched further Down the Island to a Place Called
Jerusalem there we whas till friday about 12 oClock then an
Express from the general Came with all spead and Brought
us word that the Enemy had Landed and got within 5 miles
of our Lines Judged to Be about six or seven thousand and upon
this we got Ready to march as quick as Posible for the Camp
there we whas about 42 miles from the Camp amongst a people
that 9 Tenths of them whare our Secret Enemy and we whare
Cut of from our lines By our oppen Enemy in this sitivation I
whas not without some happrehentions But our men whare all
in good spirits and about one Oclock we got Ready to March and
we whare Determined to get into Camp or Loose our Lives in
the atempt But through the Blesing of god and the asistance of
the Troops of hors we . . . safe . . . Camp that night about one
oClock . . . Cheafly inhabints of the Island and thay Being
aquanted with all the Roads whar a grate healp to us we made
But one Stop the hole march and that . . . about 8 miles from
the Camp there we got a little Refreshment for the men and
got of again and in about one oure after we Left that Place the
Regelars Light hose whas aLong in Pursute of us But we
marched all the By ways we Could so we not whited them once
the Enemy now are in Camp on a large Plane about 4 or 5
miles from us and we have stronge Partye sent Down Near
them & Lay in the woods against them to watch there motion
thay keeping a moderet fire on Both side But the Distence is
so grate they Due But Little Exequition on either side We
have had several men wounded But none killed So I must Con-

clude at this time By subscribing myself your Most afectionate
Companion   Joseph Hodgkins
PS Cosen Abr'm Hodgkins Died Last friday night his Death
is Lemented Both By officers and men I hope it will Be santified
to us all for our good I have wrate a Letter to his farther which
I shall inclose in this Give my Duty to my Parance & love to all
friends Thomas is well and sends his Love to you all Eben
Staniford has had the fever But he is getting Better

~~~~~~

                                    In Camp Augt ye 28 1776
Loveing wife Having a few moments Leashure I would Just
inform you that I am well through the goodness of god though
very much worred with a Curmish we had yesterday with
Enemy it was as followers our Regemant with a number of
others whas sint Down to our advanst Post about 3 miles from
our Lines in the woods and in the Night the Enemy marched
out two Deferant ways and got amost all Round our Division
which Consisted of ours and Colol Hitchcocks Regts after
hearing a very hot fire for some time we whare ordered to
march for the fire But we found the Enemy whar Endevering
to Cut of our Retreet and in a grate measure Did for we whar
obliged to go through fire & wharter But through the goodness
of god we got cheafly in But we had a Verry heavy fire for two
mies Before we got in But I Cant Be Perticular now we Expect
Every moment to Be in action it seams the Day is Come that
in all Probility on which Depends the Salvation of this Countery
But what will Be the Essue god only knows But it is the Determination to Defend our Lines till the Last Extremity I must
subscribe as Before   Joseph Hodgkins
Lieut Lord Received a bawl through his thigh Por Arkelus
Pulsifer is missing I Cant tell weather he was killed or Taken
or Drowned for we had to Pass over a Creek amost up to my
arms Pits and several whare Drowned there Capt Dodge has
one man mising as to the whole Loss it whas Considerable the
Enemy are within a mile an a half of our Lines

New York Augt ye 31 1776

My Dear

having an oppertunity this morning to write a Line or two more to Lett you know that we Left Longisland Last thursday night the Enemy had got all most Round us and they had much the advantage of the ground thay whare Posted on the hights Very near us and heaving up works aganst us to Bumbard us out of our forts which thay might Easely Don for our forts whare Very much Exposed to them on al sides But I Cannot Be Perticular the Retreat whas as followes we whare ordered to Be under arms with Paks and Every thing in order at 7 oclock thusday night we al thought it whas to go out aganst our Enemy But about nine oclock the orders whare to strike our Tents and Pak al up and march to the ferry as quick as Posible and we made al the Dispatch we Could But I cant tel you how I felt and what will be the Event of these things god only knows I Desire to Commit myself to him and trust in his mercy at all Times for according to my oppinion things Look Very Dark on our side But for our Comfort god Rains and what he sees is Best for us will Be Don

I hope you are well I expect to hear from you soon I am well at Presant through the goodness of god But I have had But one night in Bed since Last Sunday But I must Conclude at Presant By subscribing myself your most afectionate Companion till Death Joseph Hodgkins

I Expected Mr Row would Bin home By this time when I first Rote we have heard nothing from Poor Arkelus I fear he is Dead heavy news to his Poor Mother

~~~~~~

My Dear   New York Sept ye 5 1776

these Lines Comes with my Most afectinoate Reguardes to you hoping they will find you & our Children in as good health as they Leave me at this Time through the goodness of God which has Ben grate towards me I wish I whas more sensible of it and had a harte to Live Answreble for all godsMercy I Received your Letter of ye 22 of August Last Sunday By which I whas informed of Death of my Little Son it is heavy News to me But it is god that has Dun it therefore what can I say I hope it will Pleas god to santifie all these outward aflictions to us for our Best good we are all in a Troubblesom world and we in a pertickler manner which are Expossed not only to these axidents which are Common to all men But to Fire & sword and Many hardships which Before now I whas a stranger to and which are too many to Be Numbered But I must Just Lit you know as Near as I can whare I am we have moved three times since we Left the Island and now we are about 6 or 7 miles above the sity of york near the North River to garde a Landing Place But how Long we shall stay hear is unsarting for the enemy are getting up there ships on Each side of this Island for york is an Island Parted from the main Land By a River about 14 miles from the sity which is caled Kings Bridge it is Verry Diffelt to gard Both sides of this Island against a Numer- as Enemy and a large fleet of ships as Ever whas in america it is Expected they will Land from Longisland over hear at a Place Called hellgate this Place is not far from us only across the Island there is a grate Number of our People there and I hope thay will Be able to anoy the Enemy But as for hindering there Landing I Do not Expect they Can and when thay Come we must Either Beet them or they us and if it should Be the former hapy for us But if the Latter the Concequiances will Be shocking to all But Let us not Be Discorredged for if god is for us we ned not fear what man Can Do unto us you may think that I write tu Discorredging But only Considder aminuet we have Ben all this Summer Digging & Billding of foorts to Cover our heads and now we have Ben obliged to Leave them and now we are hear and not one shovell full of Durte to Cover us But in all Probability we must met them in the oppen field and Risk our Lives and Countery on one single Battle I Dont mean that we have no works there is a grate many forts & Battres But the Enemy tak Care not to Come near them Till thay get good foot hold so as to approch them in a Regular Mannar and secuer a good Retreet I Dont write this to Discorrege you or to Encrees you Trobble But only to Let you know as near as I Can of our Circumstances for my Part I am not Discoredged But hope through god we shall Do Vallently As to our Leaving

Longisland I Dont know what most People think of it But if the wind had not hinderd the shipps from Coming up we must Been all mad Prisoners But Lucky for us the wind held to the Norred for some Days But our Retreet whas so sudden and unexpected that we Lost a grate many of our things my Best shirt & a pr Britches & stockins & hanckiefs whas at the wash womans and I had not time to get them and so they are lost & my setoote I lost in the Curmish Down the island But I Dont mean to Lay these things to hart

But I must Just inform you that Willm Goodhue is Dead I shall not have opportunity to write to his farther he whas taken seek about the Time the Regulars Landed on the Island he whas moved to york so I never saw him But onc after he whas moved and that whas Last Sunday I Did not think he whas Dangres But he Died the nix Day Due let his farther know it as soon as you can he whas Very much Like Sargt Hodgkins only had more feavor two of the strongest men in our Company Cut of sudden heavy News to there friends I must conclude at this time By Subscribing myself your most afectionate Companion till Death   Joseph Hodgkins

PS Give my Duty to all my Parence and Love to al friends Tell Brother my not writing to him this time whas not for whan of good will But for whant of time & I hope it wont hinder him from writing

~~~~~~

fryday Morning
having a fue minets Leashure this Morning I thought I would write a line or two more to Let you know some things that slipt my mind Before as to our Loss on the Island as Near as can Be Computed is about 600 men missing and it is said that the Enemys Loss whas about the same Number we had two generals Taken and the Enemy had one killed sarting and it is Reported that thay have two mising But as to our one Regt we Lost But three men and as to Arkelus Pulsifer and one more it is unsarting weather they are killed or taken But I fear they whare killed we had a young man in our Company that had a ball went through his Rist & it was so Brok that he had his hand

Cut of since I had my sleave Buttin shot out of my sleave and the skin a little grased But through mercy Received no other hurt as to Mrs Fetchwells sons I have not sen them neither Do I know what Regts they are in if I Did it is likely I Could find them if thay are in Colo Hutchinson Regt thay are about 5 miles from us

My Dear I Whant to see you Very much But When I shall I Cannot tell But I hope I shall Be Presarved from all the Evils & Dangers that we are surounded with & Returned home in safty in gods good time

Give my Love to my two children and tell them to Be good galls and that Dady whants to see them

it is more healthy among us then it whas we have none sick in our Company we have had Plenty of Rain hear for this three weaks I am Very glad to hear that you have so growing a season Likewise that you have Plenty of West India goods I wish we had we are obliged to give 4 shilling Lawfull Money a quart for Rum I Cant get it for that if the army whas Clean from New York it would Be no matter how soon it whas sunk for of all Places it is the worst

But I must Conclude as Before By subscribing myself

Joseph Hodgkins

I shall send inclosed in this Sargt Hodgkins with which I would have you send it onkel and till him that upon our Leaving the Island so sudding that all his Clothes whas Lost

I have this moment heard that Eben Staniford is Very Bad with the Fever he had Ben sick and had got abroad Last Sunday I saw him he told me that he whas fine and harty Capt Wade is Wrote to Mr Goodhue so you nead not Put yourself out of the way about Letting him know of the Death of his son

Ipswich Sept ye 16 1776

My Dear

these Lines come with my most afectionate regards to you hoping they will find you in good health as they Leave me at this time through the goodness of God I received your Letters by the Post this morning & those by Mr Row Last thursday I was grately rejoiced to hear you were well for I was destrest

about you I desire to be thankful that you have got off of Long
Island I think God has apeared for you in a very wonderfull manner in Several instances of which you informed me in your Letters
oh that we might be Suitabley afected with all Gods dealings
towards us & be sencible of our oblygations to him and devote
our selves to his Glory at all times my heart akes for you to
think of the dificultys & fateagues you have to undergo but all
that I can doo for you is to commit you to God who has hitherto
preserved you and beg of him to be with you & preserve you still
dont be discoraged My Dear God is as able to preserve us as
ever and he will doo it if we trust in him aright tho as you say
I think things Look very dark on our side but it has been observed that mans extremity was Gods oppertunity and I think
it Seems to be a time of grate exstremity Now and I hope God
will apear for us & send Salvation and deliverance to us in due
time and if you Should be called to Battle again may he be with
you & cover your heads & Strenthen your hands & encorage
your hearts and give you all that fortitude and resilution that
is left for you and in his own time return you home in Safty &
may we have oppertunity to praise his holy name together again
but if it be Gods will that we are not to meet again in this
world may we be prepared for a better where we Shall have
no more troble nor Sorrow oh Let us make it our gratest
Care & Concern to get an interest in Christ and then we Shall
be happy ether liveing or dieing I want to See you very much
if you was but one hundred miles of I believe if you and I were
well I should come & See you before long but the distance is
So grate I know I cant therefore I must wate Gods time for my
part I am not wholy discoraged many times the darkest time
is jest before day pray dont fail of writing all the oppertunitys
you have Let the Cost be what it will for I want to hear every
day if I could I heard that Mr Noble went throgh town Last
Satturday but he was not So good as to call to See me I was
very Sorry I must Jest inform you that Cousin Ephraim Perkins
coming from the west Indeas about 3 or 4 weaks ago he had
got allmost home & was taken on Board the milford man of
war where he is with all his hands yet for ought we know Mr
Ingerson Daniel Goodhue Ezek Wells & I cant tell who else

was with him Capt Holms comeing from the west Indeas
founderd at Sea but the men are all got home well our friends
here are all well So I must Conclude by Subscribing myself
your tender & afectionate Companion till Death

Sarah Hodgkins

farther & mother Sends their Love to you Brother sends his
Love & Says he would have write but he was so busie he could
not get time aunt goodhue Sends her respects to you Joanna
Sends her duty remember me to all friends

In Camp at Fort Constitution New Jersey Sept ye 30 1776
My Dear I take this oppertunity to write a fue lines to you to
Let you know that I am well and I hop that these Lines will
find you & our Children & friends Posest of the same Blessings
which through the goodness of god I enjoy at this time and
for which I Desire to Be thankful I Received your Letter By the
Post Last Sartady I am very glad to hear that you whare well &
our friends in general oh that we whare sencible what a blessing
health is Espechaly hear whare our Lives & health are more
Pertickerly Exposed then what those of our friends who are
at home are But we have the same god who is Every whare
Prisant and at all Times the same we have had Experiences of
gods goodness to us in Presarveing us in Battle & Carring us
through many Defilties since I wrote my Last of which I shall
give you a short account Viz on Sartaday ye 14 instant we moved
to harlam and inCamped on an Hill about nine miles from york
and about 12 oClock that night we whare alarmed and marched
about one mile and thene took Post and staid Till sun Rise
then we marched home we had not got Brakfast Before there
whas a very heavy Cannonading at the sitty and we whar Told
that the Enemy whas about Landing Down to harlem Point
whare we Expected thay would Land By there motion But while
our Brigade with two more whar wating there they Landed at a
place called Furtal Bay 3 or 4 miles nearer york and there whar
two Brigades thare But they Being Cheafly Milisha it whas
said that Two hundred of the Enemy made them all Run so
thay Landed with out much Resistance and marched toward
york and Took Posesion of the sitty about 4 oClock on Sunday

[221]

Now you must think they whare in high spirits and thought all whas there own so on monday morning thay thought thay would atack us with about six thousand men and Drive us all over Kingsbridge But thay whare much mistaken But however as soon as we heard that thay whare advancing towards us the general sent out 200 Rangers under the Command of Coll Knolton who soon met the Enemy and fired on them and fote them on the Retreet Till thay got Prety near us then the Enemy Halted Back of an hill and Blood a french Horn which whas for a Reinforcement and as soon as thay got itt thay Formed in to two Coloms But our Brigade whas Posted in the Eadge of a thick woods and By some Climing up a Tree could see the Enemys motion and while they whar aforming the general sent a Party to attack them which answred the eand for which they whare sent for our People made the atack and Retreeted towards us to the Place whare we whanted them to Come and then the Enemy Rushed Down the Hill with all speed to a Plain spot of ground then our Brigade marched out of the woods then a very hot Fire Began on Both sides and Lasted for upward of an hour then the Enemy Retreated up the Hill and our People followed them and fote them near an hour Longer till they got under Cover of the ships which whas in the North River then our People Left them the Loos on our side is about 40 Killed and 60 or 70 wounded there Whas none killed in our Regt and But about 20 wounded one of our Corpl whas Badly wounded through his knees But I hope he will Due well the Loss on the Enemy side is not sarting But according to the Best accounts that we have had thay had near 500 killed and near as many wounded they whare seen to carry off several wagon Loads Besides our People Burryed a good many that they Left we whar informed By two Prisonors that thay found that they had not the Milisha to Deal with at this Time they said the surgone swore that they had no milisha to Day this whas the first Time we had any Chance to fite them and I dout not if we should have another oppertunity But we should give them another Dressing at this Place whare we incamped whas within two gon shots of the Place whare the Battle whas for we whare always Capt on the advanced Post next to the Enemy untill now and now we are

on the Jersey hills whare we have Bin Ever since ye 20 of this
month and I hope we shall stay hear the Rest of the Campan as
I have Ben at the Truble of Building a Log House with a ston
Chimny I got it fit to live in 3 days ago Before which time I had
not Lodged on any thing But the ground since we Left Longisland Capt Wade has been sick & Absent from me Ever since
the 13 Day of this month & has this moment got hear and is got
Prety well again During his Absence I have had a grate Deal
of Troble and Care But I have Been fine and harty all this
Campan and I hope god will Continue this grate Blessing and
Presarve us and carry us through all the Defeltices that we may
met with and in his good time Return us home to the Place of
our nativety in safty My Dear I am much obliged to you for
your Kind Regards you Express and Consiarn you Discover
for my wellfair in your Letter I hope your Prayers will Be
Answred Both in Respect of spiritual & Temporal Mercys I
wish I could answer your Letter more Pertickler But I have not
Time nor Room But must Hason I whant to see you very much
But I Cant Till when I shall But I hope tue within 4 months
Give my Duty to farther & Mother Perkins and Love to all
friends I am very sorry to hear the misforting of Capt Epheram
& Capt Holmes But I must Conclude at Presant By subscribing
my self your Most afectionate Companion Till Death

Joseph Hodgkins

Thomas is well and sends his Love to you & al frinds He whas
with us in all the Battle & Behaved like a good solder

Octor ye 1 1776

My Dear as I wrote my Letter yesterday and having Taken
some money since I shall send some home in Closed in this
Letter and you may Let Farther Hodgkins have some if he neads
& you have it to spair I think you said that Mr Noble went
through Town and whas not so good as to Call as I Dont know
But you might have hard thoughts of me for my not writing
By him But I will tell you how it whas I Did not know that
Mr Noble whas going home Till he whas mounted and got of
I then met him in the Rode & Desired him to Call at Deacon
Perkins and see you he Told me he would But as he Did not I

[223]

have not got him to thank I shall send 30 Dollars I Believe that will Be your third So I subscribe as Before

Joseph Hodgkins

Ipswich Octobr ye 19 1776

My Dear haveing an oppertunity this evening to write a few Lines I gladly imbrace it to let you know that I am well through the goodness of God & I hope these Lines will find you posest of the Same Blessing I received your Letters a Satturday morning I was grately rejoiced to hear that you was So well as you inform me that you are & have been ever Since you Left home I think as your day is So your Strength Seems to be & I hope God will Continue this Blessing of health to you dureing your absence you inform me that god has been pleased to preserve you through another Battle which I think lays us under fresh obligations to devote our selves to his Service & Glory & of that we may be truly Senceble of it I understand you have gone through a grate deal of dificultys & hardships since you wrote before it greives me to think what you have to undergo but I hope it will be for our good by what you write I think you are not in so Dificult a Situation as when you wrote before I am glad to hear you are So well off as to have a log house to live in and I Should be glad if you could have more of the Comfortable nesecaries of Life than you have but I hope you will be carried through all you are to meet with in the way of your duty & in Gods good time be returned home in Safty I want very much to See you I hope if we Live to See this Campaign out we shall have the happiness of liveing together again I dont know what you think about Staying again but I think it cant be inconsistant with your duty to come home to your family it will troble me very much if you Should ingage again I dont know but you may think I am too free in expressing my mind & that it would have been time enough when I was asked but I was afraid I Should not have that oppertunity So I hope will excuse my freedom I must jest tell you I have been abroad today up to uncle Smiths Cosin Lucy sends her kind regards to you I had Like to forgot to thank you for the money you Sent me I think If I can get my thirds these times I shall come well off I Sent you a pair stokins for Thomas by cousin Perkins I woud Sent a shirt but he could not Bring it I did not know of his coming Sone enough to write if you want Shirts or Stokins due Send me word when Mr Craft comes again & I will get him to bring them if I can Mr Craft was So good as to call & See me as he went through town it grows Late So I must conclude at this time by subscribing myself your most afectionate Companion till Death

Sarah Hodgkins

Farther & mother Sends their Love to you & Sister Chapman likewise your Fathers family are well & desire to be remembered to you Joanna & Sally Send their duty to you give my regards to Capt Wade

---

In Camp at Phillipse Manner Novm ye 15 1776

Loving wife Haveing an opportunity to write to you I gladly Imbrace it as nothing Except Being Presant with you gives me more Pleasure then writing too & Receiving Letters from you & as we hav no other way of Conversing to geather at Presant I Chearfully imbrace Every opportunity & Doubt not But you will Due the same these may informe you that I am in good health at Presant & I hope these fue Lines will find you & our Children & all frinds Posest of the same Blessing we have Ben Much Harriet about for this Month Past & now we Expect to move soon But Cant Tell whare as the Enemy Some time ago Drue Back from us & moved to the North River at a Place Called Dobbs Ferry But what there Desine is we Cant Tell But yestirday they moved from that & it is thought they will atack fort Washington But we are Just informed that 10000 of them are imbarked on Board the Transports But whare Bound we have not heard I think it is likely they are Bound to the Easterd

having Just Looked over your Last Letter I think I have not answered you to one or two Perticklers Relletive to my ingaging again But I Doubt not But you will forgive my neglect when you Consider the Sittuation we whare in at the time I wrote Last and as to ingaging again I have no thoughts of ingaging again in the Capacity that I now Sistane and as for any thing Better I Shall not Seek after it neither Due I Desire it as there is officers Enough that are fond of the Sarvis & Perhap more Caperble of Sarving the Cause than I am . . . therefore I hope I Shall have the Pleasure of facing you & all frinds in a fue weaks more if nothing Extrodinary happens I think you hopt that I would Excuse your freedom in Expressing your Desire of have me Com home My Dear you are Verry Excusable for I am Senseble that my Being Absent must of nesesity Create a great Deal of Troble for you and if you will Belive me My Being Absent from my famely is I think the gratest Troble I have met with Sence I have Ben Absent therefrom I hope Shortly to have the Happeness of See you & all frinds thin I hope these Trobles in Som measure will Be Don away But may we not account these Trobles much Considering what god has Don for us in our absents & is Still Doing Every Day Espechaly in Presarving our Lives & Health whare they have Ben So much Exposed as ours hav Ben hear so that we may Be Senceble of god's goodness to us and Be Enabled to Live answerable for al his mercys

as for any other Perticklers there is gentilmen agoing home that Can give you a better acount then what I can write So I must Conclude at this Time By Subscribing my self your most afectionate

Companion Till Death

Joseph Hodgkins

PS Give my Duty to all my Parrance and Love to all frinds Tell Brother Perkins I would hav Wrote to him But there whas So many gintelmen going hom that they Could give him a better Detail of afairs then what I could write Capt Wades Reguards to Mr Hodgkins

if you have any opportunity to write after this I whant to know weather you have Sold my gun Due Tell Capt Staniford that we heard a fue Day ago that Eben had got Better whas Likely to Due will also Tell Mrs Pulsifer that Arkelas whas will on Long island about 2 months ago he whas taken there & whas wounded in his Cheek But then he whas got most well

Tell Joseph Wises wife that he is along with Eben Staniford he has Ben Sick But is Recovered

these four Dollars in Gold are for Joseph Wises wife

Pixskille Decemr ye 3 1776

Loving wife I Received yours By the Post Last Wensday which gave me grate Pleasure to hear that you & all friends whare well & hope these will find you Posest of the same Blesing it being through the goodness of god what I ingoy at Presant & for wich I Desire to Be thankful I would Just inform you that we marched from Phillips Manner Last fryday morning and we Expect to Pass over the North River to Day & then Proseed to Bromwock which is our headquarters at Presant the Enemy seem to Bend there strength that way as if they whare a mind to winter in Philadelphia But I hope they will Be Disapinted our People go over the ferry called Kings Ferry and then to Bromswick is 70 or 80 miles this march whas Very unexpected to us all & the traveling verry Bad But I hope we shall Due well My Dear I am in haste for the Brigade is now marching I whant to see you Very much and hope I shall in good time I Did Expect to Ben home By ye 20 of January if it had not Ben for this movement But now I Expect it will Be Longer But I Conclude By subscribing myself your most afectionate Companion till Death

Joseph Hodgkins

PS This Letter I send By Colol Littles son give my duty to all Parance & Love to all friends Thomas is well & sends his Love to you & all his friends Tell Joanna & Salle to Be good gals & that Dady whants to see them

Buckingham in Pansalvania Decemr 20 1776

Loveing Wife these Lines Comes with my most afectionate Regard to you hoping they will find you & all friends in as good Health as they leave me at this time through the goodness of god tho we are Very Much fatagued with a long march we have Ben on the march ever since ye 29 of Last month and we are now within 10 or 12 miles of general Washingtons Army we Expect to Be there to night But how long we shall stay there I Cant tell neither Can I tell you much about the Enemy only they are on one side of Dilleway River and our army on the other about 20 miles from Philadelphia we Pased over Dellewar River Last Sunday 40 or 50 miles above head Quarters on account of the Enemys Trying to intersept our Crosing But I Cant give you But a very Poor account of our march for whant of time Doutles you will want to hear how genl Lee whas Taken I will Tell you that general Lee whas invited By a gentleman to Put up with him that night & weather that man or another informed the Enemy I Cant say But some Body Did so about sixty of the Lite hors Came ye nex morning & surounded the house the general whas som way of so they Did But Little good ye genl whas five miles from whare the army in Campd that night.

We have Marched since we came from Phillips Manner aBout 200 miles the gratest Part of the way whas Dangrus By Reason of the Enemy Being near & not only so But the Contry is full of them Cursed Creaters Called Torys My Dear I hope I shall Live to get home But I Due not know when for the Pasing is Dificlt at this season of the year But I Expect to Lay my head to the Eastward in aBout fortanate we have had Extraordnary Pleasant weather But now it is a snow storm But I must conclude at this time By subscribing myself your most afectionate Companion Till Death   Joseph Hodgkins
PS Give my Duty to all my Parance & Love to all friends I Left Thomas at Peekskill so I Expect he will Be at home Before I shall Jonathan Wells is with us he Desires that if you see his wife to let her know that he is well & Expects to get home By the last of January

Loving Wife   New Jersey in Crossix Decemr ye 31 1776
    these Lines Comes with my Most afectionate Regards to you Hoping they will find you & our Children & all frinds in as good health as they Leave me at this Time through the goodness of God which has Ben grate towards me in many Instances Espechaly since I Left Peekskill I Cannot Express the hardships & fetague we have under gone on our March from Place to Place

But I desire to Be thankful that I am alive & well & in good spirits at Presant I hope god will still Presarve us & Carry us through all Defcltyes & Dangers we have to meet with in the way of our Duty & give us an oppertunity of meeting together again in this world & give us harts to Prase His name for all his Mercys

I must Just give you a Brocken account of the Proseeding of our army for this fue Days Past on Sunday ye 22 of Decm we marched to Bristol & in Camped in the woods near the Town & on Christmas night we marched with about 2000 Men to a ferry about 7 miles from Camp in order to Pass over to the Jersey side of the River to atack a Party of the Enemy that Lay at a Place Called Mount Holly But the Ise Prevented our Crosing that night But the Troops that Lay up about 20 miles up the River against Trintown got across the River & marched Round & Came in upon the Bak of Trentown about Dawning & Began a heavy fire with there field Peases which seprised the Enemy so they sirrendred the hole that whas took 925 Take about 20 kill & wounded Six Brass field Peases a grate quanty of small arms & Blankets this gave the Enemy a grate shock so they soon Retreated from the other Places whare they intended to stay while the River whas frose stron enofe to cross [*rest of letter missing*]

Worcester July ye . . .1777

Loveing wife these Fue Lines Come with My Most afectnate Regards to you hoping they will find you & our Children & friends in as Good health as they leave me at this Time through the goodness of god I must just inform you that I got at Worcester on Sartaday & I am to march from hear toMorrow with the first Devision of the Regt Which I whas in hops I should not have Don But as I had not But one Lieut appointed & he is not able to march so there is nobody Else to Take Care of the men But myself But I must confess I feal Concerned about the small Pox [*rest of letter missing*]

Loving Wife   Camp Near Sarratoga Sept ye 28 1777
these fue Lines Brings you my most afectionate Regards

hoping they will find you & our Children & all friends in as Good health as they Leave me att this Time through the goodness of God I am as well as Ever I whas in my Life & I wish I was sencible what a mercy health is & Be inabled to Live answerblr & improve all those mercys aright I received your letter Last night of ye 18 instant By Mr Burley & I was Grately Reioycet to hear from you thou I am sorry to hear you are Poorly I hope you will Be Better soon My Dear Dont Ponder two much on any Trobles that we may Be Called to go through But may you & I Be innabled to Put our Trust in god who alone is able to Due more & Better than we Can ask or think & I hope we shall Both Be Prepared while Absent & in good time have the happiness to meet and injoy all the Blessing of a free People I Received the shoes you sent me & am much obliged to you for I was all most Bair foot I wish I could make you any Returns But I Cannot Except Love & good will But I hope I shall Be able to send you some money By the Next Post we have not Drawn any since we Left Springfield & it is Very Expencive Living But Soldiers must not Complain we have good Provisions But nessarys are Very Dear & Scars I wish you would send me word how things are at home with you for we hear that things are Exceeding Dear & if you meet with any Difflty in gitting the Nesserys of Life Due send me word for I due not mean to Live in the Sarvis my self & have you suffer at home for I think I suffer Enough for us Both on that account I am in grate hast Excuse My Bad writing & Likewise inditing so I must Conclude for this time By subscribing my self your most afectionate Companion Till Death   Joseph Hodgkins

Monday Morning Sept ye 29
I must Just inform you that I am well this Morning through the goodness of god & hope these will find you Posest of the same Blessing I would inform you that when I was at Springfield I sent fifty Dollars to Worcester to Nathan Heard Desiring him to send it to you By the first good oppertunity I Expected you had Received it Before this time But your not meanching it I fear you have not

I am in want of some things But we are in such an unsettled state that I am at a loss to know what to send for . . . Cool Country & I should Be glad of a pr Mittens & if you can send me a pair good half soles for my Boots I should Be Exceding glad for there is nothing to Be got hear Your sircumstances is such that it makes me Loath to send for two meany things But I hope youel Be able to make me a Pair of Winter Shirts & if we should Be Prospered as we hope I shall Try to come & see you and get them Mr Shaw is got into Camp But I have not seen him yet But I intend to send By him

Give My Duty to my Parence & Love to all inquiring friends To Joanna & Salle tell them to Be good gals So I Subscribe as Before   Joseph Hodgkins
PS I must Refer you to Brothers Letter for some Pertickelars that I have omitted in this

~~~~~~

[*The following letter, written on paper of much more recent origin than that used by Hodgkins, and not in his hand, is labeled "copy," and is filed apart from the other letters in the Wade papers. Presumably the punctuation and paragraphing were inserted by the person who copied it.*]

My Dear,   Saratoga, October 17, 1777

These may inform you that I am well, through the goodness of god and hope these lines will find you and all friends possessed of the same blessing. I must just inform you that this day we have received Gen. Burgone and all his army as Prisners of war, and may we all rejoice and give the glory to whom its due. I have not time to be pertickelar, we are to march immediately to Pike Rill, and then I hope we shall have a little rest.

Brother Perkins has been here today, I expect he will return to Boston with the prisoners. But I shall send this letter by Major John Story, who will set out from here tomorrow and will be likely to get home much sooner than Brother, so I must conclude it this time by subscribing myself your most affectionate companion Till Death.   Joseph Hodgkins

P.S. I received yours by Brother, and was very glad to hear you was comfortable give my Duty to all Parents and love to all friends. I have been sick since I wrote to you but have got Rite well again. I did not leave Camp, but perhaps I was as sick as hundreds that do. But Major Story was a good friend to me, for he helped me to sum necessaries that I could not get

~~~~~~

Loveing Wife   Albany Octor ye 27 1777

these Fue Lines Brings you my most affectionate Regards hoping they will find you & our Children & friends in as good health as they Leave me at this time through the goodness of god I am Prity Well now I have had somthing of the Camp Disorder & Lost most all my flesh But I hope soon to Pick up my Crumes again we have had a Very fartagueing Campain But as we have Don the Bisnes we Came hear for I hope None of us will Complain of a little hardship I wish I Could inform you that I thought our fartague was over for this year But to the Contray I Expect we shall march to Morrow Morning Down the River to wards the Pakskills & I Expect we shall Be ordered towards Philledalpha to Take another winters Camppain in the Jerseys Soldiers must not Complain I hope I shall have the Pleasur of seeing you Between this & Spring But I Dont know how it will Be if Genl Washington is But Able to Take Care of Gel How I hope we shall get into winter Quarters in season But we must Leave the Event with him who knows what is Best for us

I am in hast I have nothing new to write as the Compleet Victory gained over our Enemy in this Part of the world is By this time an old story it will Be Needles for me to say much about it Espechaly as you will have the Pecticklers By them that whare hear on the spot But I think there is a Remarkable hand of Providence in it & we shall Due well to acknowledge it So I must subscribe as Before your Most afectionate Companion Till Death   Joseph Hodgkins

PS Give my Duty to all my Parence & Love to all friends I have no money to send you I know not how you will Live But I have not Received any money since I Left Springfield I Expect Every Day to Receive three months Pay My Dear Due

Get a good stock of syder if you can git any Body to Trust you
for it I have sent two Letters to Coson Tome to have him Come
Due till him he must Come if he Can I send this Letter By Mr
Hidden who with several other of my Company have got fur-
loughs for two months Mr Ireland is Very sick at the New Sity
Joseph Lord is sick in Camp the Rest are stiring about

~~~~~~

[*November 1777. First page of letter missing.*]
Desire to Be Remembered to his friends
Sunday ye 16 the Brigade is Now Crossing Kings farry we shall
Take the Best Rode to Philadelphia hope we shall Be able to
Give some good account of Genl How Before we Return I hear
that it is thanksgiving with you this weak I wish I Could Be with
you But though we are Deprived of the happiness of Being
togeather yet we have grate Cause of thankfullness
We have Drawn some money But I have no oppertunity to send
any to you But hope you will not think hard of me for I feall
Very uneasy

~~~~~~

Valleyforge Camp Jany ye 5 1778
My Dear these fue Lines Bring my most affectionate Regards
to you hoping they will find you & all friends in as good health
as they Leave me at this time through the Goodness of god I
Received yours of the 15 of Decemr on Newyears Day and
that of ye 7 Last Night and I am Rejoyced to hear that you have
Been cumfortabley Carred through all the Defelties that you have
Ben Called too in my absents oh that we ware sencible of the
goodness of god to us ward and ware more Devoted to his
sarvice I wish I could have the sattisfaction of seeing you & our
Children Esphaly my Little Darughters I am sorry to hear that
the Babe is got that Distresing Coff But I hope god will apear
for it & Rebuk its Disorder & Restore it to health again and
give us an oppertunity of Rejoycing in his goodness
My Dear you say that you have not heard from me since the
27 of Octr I Received your Letter of ye 17 Octor By the Post
that minnet I left Albany & Could not Light of him afterwards
to send By him But I wrote about ye 16 Novemr from Kings

farry & sent it By Capt Blasdon But it seams you have not had that But I have sent By Colol Colman a letter & some Cash wich I gudge you have Received By this time & have sent another By a Post since you say in your Letter of the 7 that you Depend on my Coming home if I am alive & well But My Dear I thought when I wrote Last that I should not Try to get home this winter & wrote you some Reasons why I should not But since I have Received your Letters & seeing you have made some Dependance upon my Coming home therefore out of Reguard to you I intend to Try to get a furlough in about a Month But I am not sarting I shall Be sucksesfull in my attemptes therefore I would not have you Depend too much on it for if you should & I should fail of Coming the Disapointment would Be the Grater But I will Tell you the Gratest incoredgement that I have of getting home that is I intend to Pertishion to the Genel for Liberty to go to New England to Tak the small Pox & if this Plan fails me I shall have But Little or no hope I Believe I have as grate a Desire to Come home as you can Posibly have of having me for this winters Camppain Beats all for fatague & hardships that Ever I went through But I have Ben Carred through it thus far & Desire to Be thankfull for it we have got our hutts allmost Don for the men But its Reported that Genl How intends to Come & See our new houses & give us a House warming But if he should I hope we shall have all things Ready to Receive him & treet him in Every Respect according to his Desarts you say you have Named your Child Martha & you Did not know weather I should Like the name But I have nothing to say if it suts you I am content I wish I could have the sattisfaction of seeing it So I must conclude at this time By subscribing myself your most affectionate Companion Till Death   Joseph Hodgkins

My Dear   Pensalvania Valley forge Jany 11 1778
   This may inform you that I am in good helth at Presant & hope these fue Lines will finde you & our Children & friends Posest of the same Blessing I have knothing New to write only

that I am Dull to think of loosing Thomas who was not only my koock But my wash woman & nus in sickness in short he is good for all most Everything But he is Going home & I wish him well with all my hart David is Ben a water in the mess sometime & he is going too so it seams as if we must Brake up house keeping unless we can find some New ones But as my Paper is Very Bad and having wrote so Lately I must Beg to Be Excused so I shall subscribe myself your most afectionate Companion Till death   Joseph Hodgkins

PS Rimember me to all inquiring friends I shall send this By Thomas who can tell you how we Live hear Better than I can write

I want to see you very much But I know nothing more about going home now than what I wrote By the Post

I shall Be Verry glad of some winter shirts if I come home & if I should not come Home I must go naked for I can get nothing hear

Head Qt Feby 22 1778

My Dear having an oppertunity to write to you I gladly imbrace it I would inform that I am in good health at Presant through the goodness of god & I hope these Lines will find you & all friends Posest of the same Blesings I have not Ben able to Proquer a furlough as I Expected when I wrote Last But I hope you Did not Depend a grate Deal upon it as I think I wrote that I was not sarting of getting one when I tryed

I am in grate hast as the Barer is wating I must just inform you that what our soldiers have suffred this Winter is Beyond Expression as one half has Ben Bare foot & all most Naked all winter the other half Very Badly on it for Clothes of all sorts and to ComPleat our misery Very shorte on it for Provision not Long since our Brigade drue But an half Days aLownce of Meat in Eight Day But these Defeltis the men Bore with a Degree of fortitude Becoming soldiers But I must say one word to the people at home who I fear have Lost all Bowles of Compassion if they Ever had any for the Contry Towns have Provided Clothing for there men and Brought them to Camp But

[235]

as there has Ben none from the seeport Towns I fear they have Lost all there Publick Spirit I would Beg of them to Rouse from there stupedity and Put on som humanity and stir themselves Before it is too Late I would not have them think hard of maintaining there soldiers for what the soldiers has sufferd the past year Desarves a Penshon During Life My Dear I hope to get Leave of Absents Before the opening of another Campain I have Drue some money for the men that are at home But I shall not send it as I shall com home as soon as Ever I Can I am in hops to Draw the Rest of there wages Before I Come home so I must Subscribe as Before your most afectionate Companion till Death   Joseph Hodgkins

Sargt Quarles is Very Bad with the feavor Give my Complements to all that inquire after me I hope you will have some shirts for me against I get home for I am all naked

---

Ipswich Februay ye 23 1778

My Dear after my tender regards to you I would inform you that I and my Children are in good health I hope these lines will find you posest of the Same Blessing I now set down to write between hope and fear hopeing you will come home before I get to the Bottom but fearing least you Should not come this winter I heard of an oppertunity Send a letter U I thoght I would not mis of it though you have of writing to me Cousin Perkins told me he Saw you & you was well but he Says he dont think you will come home so he is but one of Jobs comforters I was very glad to hear you was well but my Dear I must tell you a verbal Letter is what I Should hardly have expected from So near a freind at So greate a distance it seems you are tired of writing I am Sorry you count it troble to write to me Since that is all the way we can have of conversing together I hope you will not be tired of receiveing letters it is true you wrote a few days before but when you was nearer you wrote every day Sometimes I was never tired of reading your Letters I Long to See you am looking for you every day if you Should fail of comeing my troble will be grate surely it will be atroble indeed but I must hasten I have a Sorryful peice of news to tell you it is the

Death of Cousin Ephraim Perkins he died on his pasage from the west endies the fifth of January he is much Lamented by all who know him

Feb ye 28

After I had wrote part of my Letter I did not like the oppertunity that presented & I would not send it but now I have heard of another I think I will send it for fear you Should not come home

the time Seems Long I am almost impatiente alooking for you & allmost give over your coming but dont know how to bear that our freinds hear are well in general Sister hannah Sends her Love to you my Babe is got well of her Coff for which & many other mercys I desire to Bless God and commending you & myself & Children to his care and protection & hopeing you will be at home before this gets to ye army I Shall now Subscribe myself your most afectionate Companion till Death

Sarah Hodgkins

Pennsylvania Head Quarters April 17 1778

Loveing Wife these Lines Brings you my most afectionate Reguards hoping they will find you & our Children & all friends in as good health as they Leave me at this time through the goodness of god I am Very well Now But since I wrote Last to you I have Ben a good Deal Trobled with the Rumetisen But through mercy it is Left me & I feal harty But I am Very uneasy in my mind about you for I am sarting that you have Long Looked for me home & I am affrade you will suffer for the Nesarys of Life for I am informed that things are as Dear with you as they are hear & if that is the Case I wish you would Let me know it & if you Due suffer I am Determined to Come home and suffer with you I Believe you think I Dont Care much about you as I Do not send any thing home But my Dear You are allways near my hart & in my thoughts But I am sorry to inform you that I am obliged to spend grate Part of my wages or Ells I should suffer But I should sent som money home Before now if I had not Expected to Come home myself Before this time But I am all most out of Patience awating for things to Be settled so as I can get away on some terms or other which

is my Determination to do as soon as Posibly I Can for the time seams as Long to me I Dare say as it does to you there is a New arrangement of the army which is Likely to take Place sometime this Spring we have Ben Expecting it to Come out Every Day for this month But the Reason it Dos not Come out is unknown to me many officers were Very uneasey about the affair as many officers will Be obliged to Leave the sarvice But for my Part Leaving the sarvice Dos not troble me for it will Be my Choice to Leave it But to Be sent home without any Reason why is not agreable to me and if it should Be the Case I Believe I shall not troble the army much more But when I think how I have spent three years in the war have Ben Exposed to Every hardship Venterd my Life & Limbs Broke my Constitution wore out all my Clothes & has got knothing for it & now not to be thanked for it seams two much for any man to Bare no more of this for the Present My Dear I Received your Letter By Mr Wescot the Post ye 21 of March & the 25 I wrote to you & sent it By a soldier that was gooing through Ipswich But for fear it should Miscarry I would Just menchon that I have had the small Pox & all my men and they are all Prety well that Belong to Ipswich Except Josh Pettengill who has got the feavor I have sent By Mr Wescot the Post one hundred Dollars for which you may give him your Recept & settle for the Postage which will Be one shilling on a pound I have nothing more to write only I must Repeat my earnest Desire of seeing you as soon as I Possibly Can & Beg you to make yourself as Contented as Possible and now Commending you & my self & Children to the care of Kind Providence hoping he will Presarve us while absent & in his good time give us an oppertunity of meeting to geather again which is the Harty Desire of him who is your most afectionate & Loving Companion till Death   Joseph Hodgkins
Give my Duty to my Parence & Love to all friends I Dont no But I must go naked soon without I can get home But I would not have you send anything without I send for it

Ipswich April ye 26 1778

My Dear

 these lines come with my most afectionate regards to you hoping they will find you in good health as they Leave me & the rest of my family at this time through the goodness of God but I am very full of trouble on account of your not comeing home I received your Letter of the 22 of febray by mr Horten he told me you was anoculated for the small pox a day a two before he came away you wrote me word you Should come home as soon as you could but did not set any time when I concluded you would come as Soon as you got well if you lived to get well & I never heard a word from you Since till about ten days ago which you must think gave me great uneasyness fearing how it was with you Nat Treadwell wrote a few lines home which they received about ten Days ago & he was So kind as to Send word that you had had the Small pox & was got well which I was rejoiced to hear and it gave me new corage to Look for you but I have Looked for you till I know not how to Look any longer but I dont know how to give over your not writing to me gives me Some uneasyness for I am sure it is not for want of oppertunitys to Send for I have heard of a number of oficers coming home latly I wrote to you by a post about two months ago & have had no returns Sence I should be glad to know the reason of your not writing to me the first oppertunity you have if it is not too much troble for you

Monday afternoon I am very Low in Spirits allmost despare of your coming home when I began I thoght I would write but a few lines & begun upon a Small piece of paper but it is my old friend & I dont know how to leave off & Some is wrong end upwards & Some wright if it was not that I have Some hope of your coming home yet I believe I Should write a vollum I cant express what I feal but I forbear disapointments are alotted for me So commiting you to the Care of kind providence I once more Subscribe myself your most afectionate Companion till Death   Sarah Hodgkins

PS Brother Perkins & sister Sends their love to you Sister Chapman is got to bed with a fine Son I have got a Sweet Babe

almost Six mounths old but have got no father for it but Sally
Stanwood

Ipswich July ye 27 1778

My Dear these lines come with my most afectionate regards to
you hopeing they will find you in good health as they Leave me
at this time through the goodness of God I received yours by
Mr Weskeat this morning was very glad to hear you was well &
that you had got So far throu your journey well but I should be
glader if you were a going to take the Same journey again as
Soon as you had rested yourself I must Jest inform you that I
am at my Fathers mother was taken last thursday morning with
a terible pain in her Side the pain has Left her but She Seems
to be quit weak & poorly I hope She will get better in a few days
I have been here ever Sence she was taken my Sweet Baby Seems
to be Something unwell but I hope it is nothing more than
Breeding teeth She longs to See her farder She is a Scolding at
me like a dogges tal now you informed me in your Letter that
you had left two of your old Campanions in the late Battle a
Loud Call my Dear may we take Sutable notice of it had you
been there it might have been your Lot but Blessed be God it
is otherwise I think we have reason to hope the enemy will be
defeated this year we have very hot dry weather here we have
had no rain of any value since you Left home I expect to Send
this by a Post that I hear is going to Camp I must conclude at
this time by Subscribing myself your most affectionate Companion till Death   Sarah Hodgkins

Camp att Rhode Island ye 18th of Augt 1778

My Dear I take this oppertunity to write a Line or two to Let
you know that I am well & hope these Lines will find you Posest
of the Blessing I have had no oppertunity of writing to you
since I have joyned the army & Now I Do not know Who I
shall send this By But hearing of a young man going to the Eastward tomorrow I thought I would write a line I would inform
you that we Landed on this Island Last Sunday . . . & Last
Satuday we marched & took Post within two milles of the
Enemys Lines whare we still Remain we are Prepairing Battres

which will Be oppened on them Pretty soon the Enemy Keep a
Constant Canonade on our fatigue Partys But they Due But Little Dammage as to the french fleet I hardly know what to write
Doutles you heard of there going out sum time ago they have
not Returnd yet But it is sayd to Day that they have Ben heard
off & that they have taken 21 sail of Transports & are now off
Block island I Due not say this is a fact But hope it tis But I
hope they will Return soon and if they Du I think we shall
soon Du our work hear & I hope we shall have an oppertunity
of Seeing our friends in Peas But I must Be short as I Expect
to go on Duty to night

I met with the misforting to Loos my hose at Pakeskill and
marched afoot till I got so Laim I could not Travel then I was
obliged to By another which I have got now But I intend to seel
him the first oppertunity for it took all my money to By him
But I hope I shall not Loose any thing By him

I should Be Very glad if you Can Turn my old Coate so that
if I should have an oppertunity I can send for it But I must
subscribe myself your affectionate Companion Till Death

Joseph Hodgkins

PS Give my Duty to all Parence & Love to all inquiring friends
if I had a good oppertunity I should wrote more Pertiklers I
like to forgot to tell you that I received your Letter By Jacob
Hodgkins which I Did soon after I got on this Island and whas
Very glad to hear that you & our Children & friends whas well
I hope you will not miss of writing every oppertunity

Ipswich Sept ye 3 1778

My Dear I take this oppertunity to write aline or two to Let you
know that I and all our Children are well for which mercy as
well as many others I desire to be thankfull I hope these Lines
will find you posest of the Same Blessing

I received your Letter by Capt Goodhue Last thursday morning
was very glad to hear you was well I Beleave you and many
others are disapointed in your expectations but I hope it is all
for the best I am very glad to hear you are well off of the Island
for I was very uneasy about you Doct Manning is come home

& he Says he Saw you Sence you come off you was well which
was a greate sattisfaction to me to hear when I first heard you
was got so nigh as Providence I was in hopes to have heard from
you oftener than I have done pray dont fail of writing all oppertunitys I want to See you very much but durst not hardly think
of that but I hope too betwene this & cold weather if we are alive
and well I received the money you sent me by mr Pickard it
was very exceptable to me I am Sorry for the Loss you met with
in Loosing your horse it Seems to be rather against us I think I
wrote by the post Last week which I trust you have received
before now I am at work upon your old Coat I can hardly Spare
time to write I Shall have it ready to Send next week I hope
if an oppertunity presents if I dont spoil it our friends hear are
well in general father Perkins is not very well I believe he has
worked beyond his strenth he Seems to be quite week & feeble
but I hope he will recrute again he sends his love to you &
mother likewise I must jest tell you my Baby has got two teeth
& She can Stand by things alone I have no news to write so conclude by Subscribing your ever Constant wife till Death

Sarah Hodgkins

PS Brother & Sister Sends their Love to you Brother is over
head & ears in work So that he cant write to you he is agoing
afreiting tomorrow Sister Hannah has been here about aweek
She desires to be remembered to you Joanna & Salla send their
Duty to you if my Leter is not so correct as might be you must
consider from whence it came and excuse all thats amis So Leaving you with the care of kind Providence I Subscribe myself
yours as before

Camp Providence Sept ye 4 1778

My Dear these Lines may inform you that I am in good health
through the goodness of God & hope these Lines will find you
& our Children & Friends Posest of the Same Blessing I would
just give you a short account of our Retreet of the [*rest of page
missing*] hours we continuard on the Island till Sunday night
then the army all got of the Island with all the artilery &
Bagging with out the having the Least notice we incamped on

monday & Tusyday we marched for Providence and we got there Wedsady night whare we are now incamped But I must Be short for the man is waiting I . . .

Thursday Morning 7 oClock Providence Sept ye 10 1778
   after my most kind Love to you our Children & all Frinds these may inform you that I am in good health at Present & hope these Fue Lines will find you Posest of the same Blessing although I wrote yesterday By Mr John Story yet noing that Dr Maning was a going home to Day I thought I would write a line or tou I have no News only I am on the main Guard & have had many thoughts in my head to night But it would Be folly in me to commit all my thoughts to writing But however I want to see you Very Much & I wish your circumstances was such as you could Leave home so as to Come and see me for I have no Prospect of get Leave of absence at Present now wishing you all the happiness your sircumstances will admit of I subscribe myself your affectionate Husband till Death

Joseph Hodgkins

My Dear   Providence Octor 12th 1778
   I wrote a Letter Last Sartaday But the storm Prevented Majr Story from setting out till this Morning and I having felt the Cheange of the weather Putes me in mind of what I Like to want & I haveing no wooling gloves I must just Put you in mind of it and Desire you to Prepair me a pr as soon as you Can Conveniontly But for your Incuregement I will Tell you that I intend to Come home to get them and hope that will in some measure satisfy you for the Present as it is all I Can Bestoe So wishing you our Children and friends Every nessary Comfort I subscribe my self Dear Wife your most Kind Companion till Death   Joseph Hodgkins
PS give my Duty to all my Parents and Love to all friends I wish you would Let Mr Sweet Know that it will Be much to his Disadvantage to stay at home any Longer if he has not set out Before you get this

Providence Octor 13 1778

My Dear

I Received yours By Col Wade this morning which gave me the grates satisfaction to hear that you and our Children whar well Espechally my Little Matty who I was mush Concerned about I Desire to Joyn with you in wishing we may be truly sencible of the goodness of god to us in this Respect as well as many others and acknowledge our Dependence on him at all times who has heatherto Presarved us and Carred us through so meany Defclties I hope these Lines will find you and our Children still in the injoiment of that Inestimatable Blessing of health which through Mercy I injoy at this time But my Candle is almost out so I must Be short I hope to Come home soon and see you so Wishing you good night I subscribe myself Dear wife your Most Kind & affectionate Husband Till Death

Joseph Hodgkins

Tell Brother I whant to get home to Husking But fear he will get don Before I shall get home

PS Give my Duty to my Parents & Love to sister Hannah & all frinds My Complements to Capt Kendall & wife we have Just heard that there is accounts from Genl Washington that twelve Regt of the Enemy from N York are imbarked and sailed to the Estward and it is thought the same are Now off of Newporte But weather they are to Land there or goo further is unsarting I have Leet another Candle so I will write a word or two more you say in your Letter that you are afraid that I shall stay in the Cause of Liberty Till I shall mak my self a slave att my Day I have two much Reason to fear that will Be the Case But if it should I have no body to Blame But the Continent in general Who will Ever Be guilty of Ruening thousands unless they Due something more for them then what they Ever have Don yet and now as I have spent somuch time in the sarvice & Now to ask a Discharge when to apperence the war is most to an end would Debar me from Expecting any further Compensation as I sayd Before set Don By the Loss But I hope to see you in a short time and then we Consider further of these Matters I Wish you would Contrive some way or other that I Can Live without work for you know that soldiers Cannot work

Espechally Continantal Officers who have Lived so high as we have Don Espechally Last Winter But not to Joke about the Matter I hope you will Excuse my rudeness so I subscribe as Before

J Hodgkins

~~~~~~

My Dear   Providence Jany 1st 1779

these may inform you that I am well at this time only a Little Laim in one of my Lags By Reason of Braking the skin a little and gitting cols in it But it is not Bad so I hope it will git well in a fue days I hope these Lines will find you and our Children in Comforteble surcumstances we have had shocking Bad weather since I Left home Which gave me grate uneasonness But through mercy the weather now is Pleasent I have nothing of importance to write I got to Providence Thursday night after I left home By Traveling 32 miles that Day which worred me Verry much

You may tell Mrs Ireland that I Did intend to sent her money But the Pay Mastr says he shall get the Back alowance money Next weak and then he will settle al to geather

I have no news to write so I shall Take the freedom after wishing you a happy new year to subscribe myself Dear Wife your most affectionate companion Till Death

<div style="text-align:right">J Hodgkins</div>